MACIEJ KAWKA

MACEDONIAN DISCOURSES

Text Linguistics and Pragmatics

JAGIELLONIAN UNIVERSITY PRESS

Reviewer
prof. Maksim Karanfilovski, PhD
prof. Snežana Venovska-Antevska, PhD

Cover design
Marta Jaszczuk

Photo on the cover
Maciej Kawka

This publication has been printed thanks to the financial support of the Faculty of Management and Social Communication of the Jagiellonian University.

ISBN 978-83-233-4031-7

JAGIELLONIAN UNIVERSITY PRESS
www.wuj.pl

Jagiellonian University Press
Editorial Offices: Michałowskiego 9/2, 31-126 Krakow
Phone: +48 12 663 23 80, +48 12 663 23 82, Fax: +48 12 663 23 83
Distribution: Phone: +48 12 631 01 97, Fax: +48 12 631 01 98
Cell Phone: + 48 506 006 674, e-mail: sprzedaz@wuj.pl
Bank: PEKAO SA, IBAN PL 80 1240 4722 1111 0000 4856 3325

MACEDONIAN DISCOURSES

Table of contents

B. LANGUAGE IN THE DISCOURSE: MACEDONIAN–POLISH

C. LITERATURE. TEXT IN THE DISCOURSE

Introduction

Macedonia is a multinational (dominated by a population composed of Macedonians and Albanians), multiethnic, multilingual (dominated by the Macedonian and Albanian languages) and multi-religious (dominated by Orthodox Christianity and Islam) country. Macedonians and Albanians, Turks, Roma, Aromanians and other national and ethnic groups live in this country with a population of two million. Macedonian is the official language used by the majority of the population in the state (70%). Albanian (25.17% of the population), along with the Turkish, Serbian and Croatian languages (during the reign of J. Broz Tito – Serbo-Croatian language) as well as other languages are also in use. Orthodox Christianity is the dominant religion (67% of the population); however, there is also a significant number of Muslims, who represent less than one third of the society. The Macedonian language belongs to the group of South-Slavic languages together with Bulgarian, Serbian, Croatian and Slovenian. It is estimated that the Macedonian language in Macedonia, is spoken by 2 million out of 2.5 million people, together with the Macedonian emigration.

In the postwar history of the Macedonian language, the need of legal and grammatical status regulation and the destiny of the literary standard, greatly dependent on political motives, were expressed by the highest legislative bodies that strived towards its establishment. State committees that determined the Macedonian alphabet, and the basis for language development, were created. After World War II, when the Macedonian standard was established under the influence of the not so great, but highly influential elites, non-linguistic factors involved in the codification processes were obviously right. This was not so difficult when it came to that small South Slavic republic, subordinate to Belgrade until 1991.

The creation of the modern Macedonian state was related to three historical events, namely, the Balkan Wars (1912/1913), and the establishment (1943) and the breakup (1991) of the Yugoslav federation. As a result of the Balkan wars, the historical and geographical territory of Macedonia, heretofore belonging to the Turkish state, was divided between three states: Pirin Macedonia was attributed to Bulgaria, Aegean Macedonia to Greece and Vardar Macedonia to Serbia. Due to these events, the population spoke Slavic dialects for everyday use and at the beginning of the struggle for their identity, they had clearly defined feeling for national identity, easily becoming subject to disagreement and claims, generally from Bulgaria, Greece and Serbia. Serbian and Bulgarian aspirations had historical and linguistic backgrounds; the Greek, had historical and religious ones. The Greeks took it as their right to claim that all Orthodox peoples were under the jurisdiction of the Greek Orthodox Church. After 1913, the population of Macedonia, which thus far was within the borders of the Ottoman Empire, was subjected to a process of a national and linguistic Hellenization, Bulgarisation and Serbianisation. In the contemporary Macedonian language, formed in the second half of the 20th century, after the five-century-rule by the Ottoman Empire, Slavic tradition and local culture revived and local activists – authors of textbooks, grammars, and dictionaries – began to write in their own local dialects, making heroic efforts for their language to be ranked on the level of a literary language.

These processes were not neutral when it came to the development of the contemporary Macedonian language. Postwar efforts of Macedonian intellectuals led to success, enabling a basic language codification[1] and publishing of the *Dictionary of the Macedonian Language* with Serbo-Croatian interpretation *Речник на македонскиот јазик: со српскохрватски толкувања*[2], as well as the *Grammar of the Macedonian Literary Language (Граматика на македонскиот литературен јазик).*[3] Year after year, editions in contemporary literature, poetry and prose, started to increase, and in the eyes of Macedonian citizens, a literary standard was born.

---

1 During this time, three state language commissions, who codified the Macedonian language, were established – First 27 November–4 December 1944, Second – 15 February–15 March 1945 and *Third Commission* on 3 May 1945. In the history of Macedonian language, the codification by K.P. Misirkov is discussed in his work, *За македонцките работи*, published in Sofia in 1903.

2 *Речник на македонскиот јазик: со српскохрватски толкувања*, ed. Б. Конески, Скопје 1961.

3 Б. Конески, *Граматика на македонскиот литературен јазик*. Дел I и II, Скопје 1976.

A. PRAGMATICS OF DISCOURSE

I. Basic Tendencies in the Linguistics of Discourse

The notion of discourse in humanities and social sciences, as well as in linguistics, is, among all else, due to necessity, must to include a communication element in its description of the functioning of language. This prompted the beginning of involving a description of statements and texts from general communication perspective in research.[4] When it comes to the discourse of neo-liberalism, more often than not, we come across the use of the term with its popular meaning in informal use by the media and some social sciences, in which case, this discourse refers not only to those ways of speaking, as adopted by neoliberal thinkers or politicians, but also to the concepts and ideas they propagate, and studies of neoliberal discourse, in general, may not include and are not concerned with, the use of language.

The view for common determinants of both types of descriptions – theoretical and empirical – has begun to dominate linguistics at a relatively late date. The traditional differentiation between system (*langue*, competence) and use (parole, performance) represents dynamic network connections between authentic language information and data (computer databases and information corps), and their conditionality in the communication processes – the discourse. "Interdisciplinarity," the empirical orientation and social conditionality of language use, reinforces the processing of discourse interactive character as a set of instructions or strategies used in the communication game in order to achieve, primarily, understanding.

---

4 According to Teun van Dijk, 'The term discourse refers to the language used in public events or, more generally, to the colloquial language (spoken language) and the ways of expression, the manner of statement. We come across such meaning when speaking of the speeches of President Ronald Regan.' See: T.A. van Dijk, *Badania nad dyskursem*, in: *Dyskurs jako struktura i proces*, ed. by T.A. van Dijk, transl. by G. Grochowski, Warszawa 2001, p. 10.

Ambiguity of the term discourse, also posed difficulties in the methodology of linguistic description which arises mainly from the absence of an appropriate method according to which, texts, thanks to special additional indicators, may prescribe or incorporate not only grammatical and semantic information but also cultural, political, and societal tradition. Within this framework, besides the structural methods (linguistic discourse analysis), cognitive discipline and related disciplines such as anthropology, sociology, logic, semiotics (critical discourse analysis), a special place belongs to corpus linguistics as a discipline that can greatly modify the methodology for text analysis and discourse as the basis of linguistic data that integrate these, so far, divided research fields.

Modern communication linguistics is a scientific discipline that studies the functioning of natural languages in the midst of culturally marked, designated social relations. The term discourse, is in the center of linguistics and it is understood and interpreted as such. The emergence of communication linguistics as an autonomous, separate line of investigation, is credited to the English school of functional linguistics from the middle of the XX century, with its eminent researchers and scientists such as: John Austin, Bronisław Malinowski, Dell Hymes, Michael Kirkwood Halliday, John Searle, Peter Frederick Strawson, Basil Bernstein, Herbert Paul Grice, etc. The guidelines they presented, create the foundation of linguistics and communication, and they are embedded within contemporary theories of linguistic communication which is further branched out:

1. The theory of illocution, pragmalinguistics (pragmatics of language), John Austin, John Searle, Peter Frederick Strawson, Herbert Paul Grice.
2. The ethnography of speaking, sociolinguistics Bronisław Malinowski, Dell Hymes, Michael Kirkwood Halliday, Władysław Lubaś, Kazimierz Ożóg.
3. Cultural linguistics, linguo-culturology, ethnolinguistics (basic patterns and cultural contents embedded in linguistic units, reconstruction of forms, relationship between language and culture), Janusz Anusiewicz, Jerzy Bartmiński, Anna Wierzbicka, Jan Ożdżyński.
4. The theory of discourse (manner of language use), Roland Barthes, Michael Foucault, Jacques Derrida, Teun van Dijk, Ruth Wodak, Stephan Jaeger.
5. The theory of text and expression, Maria Renata Mayenowa, Janina Laboha, Teresa Dobrzyńska, Maciej Kawka, Bożena Witosz, Aleksander Wilkoń, Maria Wojtak.
6. A critical discourse analysis, initiation of new interdisciplinary program in order to merge linguistic and societal discourse analysis, Teun van Dijk, Norman Fairclough, Anna Duszak.

In Polish linguistic science, the term discourse in its modern sense first appeared in the book *A Linguistic Theory of Language* by Leon Zawadowski, who, fifty years ago, wrote:

> An expected feature, required by an author in most cases, is the text to communicate in an appropriate manner or to announce a major extra-textual complex in an appropriate and consistent manner. We define the text which is formed with maximum linguistic elements so that it meets the aforementioned requirement, as a discourse. It is a term that has been consistently missing so far, which can also refer to a literary work, as well as an everyday conversation between acquaintances. Hence, discourse, is an alignment of sentences explaining how a certain apparatus works, for example: providing weather forecasts for holidays, describing how a teacher examined a child at school, etc.[5]

Today the term discourse can be found in different, often least expected contexts, not only and primarily linguistic ones. Hence, we can name political, medial, film, literary, educational, parliamentary, environmental, repressive and similar discourses, that have meanings quite distinct from typical linguistic views. This is not just to get away from de Saussure's theory of language, which is considered imminent in itself, but to find an intermediary level between a system and a text, and to establish norms of verbal action, upon which are based the techniques of creation, and development of expression in given communication situations stressed in a given culture.

Each of the humanities cherishes and creates its discursive paradigm with additional supplements to the discourse, encumbering it with new, often unnecessary, empty words that function as terminological and mental labels. Today, language is characterized by a modern discursive paradigm in linguistics, i.e. pragmatic, anthropological, critical paradigm etc., treating it as an open-end system connected to its suitable communicational environment. Discourse slowly mastered the fields of knowledge, and researchers, who were not only unprepared for it, yet, but were aware that they had methodological flaws, expected the very use of the word discourse to improve this methodology, even to recreate it and reshape it.

The linguistic discourse is further bound to its evolution (term and definition) as is with the development of the science of language regarding a research subject, as well as to the needs to introduce new

---

5 L. Zawadowski, *Lingwistyczna teoria języka*, Warszawa 1996, p. 146.

complex (holistic) methods for the description not only of a language, but also of a communication process.

Regarding linguistic research subject matter, the interest in differentiating more complex and larger units of expression – text and discourse – becomes ever bigger, and is leading to the formation of new methodological approaches in the theory of discourse: an analysis of text and discourse, pragmatic and cognitive analysis of speech acts, use of text and discourse in relation to political and social structures and institutions – the so-called critical discourse analysis. The transfer from static descriptions to dynamic communication and cultural processes, is characteristic of modern linguistics.

In defining discourse, we move beyond the two basic ways of communication – speaking and writing. Hence, discourse can refer to the meanings communicated by subject matters or organizations of social space through symbolic codes. Similarly, it is about a new phenomenon of the elimination of writing and speaking from their function as the primary means of communication, and the creation of text and discourse – the code of printed language is represented by a (audio) visual code. Texts obtain monitoring dimension; they are read from computer screens, so the recipient receives a picture of the letter, of the written text. There is a need to determine, explain and define this new phenomenon, for example, the audiovisual discourse. Moreover, the visual dominance – as is the media, particularly the print media, using hypertext – violates the principle of linearity, which causes the need for a constant re-contextualization and the creation of continuous re-readings and interpretations. In this case, this phenomenon can be interpreted as the discourse of reconceptualization.

Modern linguistic research concerning the theory and the analysis of communicational linguistic processes are dominated by two positions:

1. The first emphasizes the problems of the discursive analysis as part of textological pragma-linguistic research.
2. The second is more directed towards the psychological and the cognitive (mental, ideal, cognitive, associative and other conditionality of linguistic communication) matter, although the term discourse, defined in accordance with the accepted criteria and scientific paradigms, is used more often.

These are two sub-disciplines of modern communication linguistics which compete among themselves. The first uses the well-known and firmly founded term with a clear, crystallized methodology – text linguistics and discourse. The second attempts to explain and interpret the notions of linguistic communication in the process of the grammaticalization of speech acts theory. If, however, there were no attempts to include the communication perspective in traditional language descriptions – in these descriptions, for example, predicate-argument syntax was treated in isolation and not as part of the communication act (there could not have been a possibility of attributing the pragmatic function to a predicate-argument structure), then the opposite direction would have been chosen to impose a communication component on a petrified matrix shaped in the meta-operators of interaction, emotion or modality. Thus, there are two tendencies, one that strives to create a discursive grammar ("discoursivation" of grammar) which means the inclusion of communication components in the theory of language in its widest possible scope of description, and second, the opposite tendency, by which a methodological defeat of the former strives toward that which is fundamentally and by definition discursive, that is, the language in use, the acts of speaking, towards an imposition of patterns of formally perfect grammar and at the end – to "grammaticalize" the discourse. Such a methodological impasse arises mainly from old structural descriptions and divisions and it is difficult to think that there may be useful methods with which to "grammaticalize" the discourse – operators of interaction and other formal categories of communication grammar.

II. The Language of National and Cultural Discourses

The essence of creating national and cultural identity is comprised within discourses led on different levels of societal communication. This process of creation or reconstruction of cultural or national identity functions as social public discourse, taking part in all forms of social life and all discursive formations – cultural, political, cognitive, medial, etc.

After the breakup of Yugoslavia, the countries that thus far were under the rule of a totalitarian regime faced bigger political, social and economic changes and turmoil. During this transition period, Macedonia, as well as Serbia and Montenegro, maintained EU candidate status since 2006, while Croatia became a member state in 2013. These Balkan and European changes led to an actualization and a modernization of the language (the code) of national and cultural discourses of the Balkan states (including Macedonia), for the purpose of forming their own identity or reconstruction of their current identity, partially by confronting it with similar discourses of their neighbors, building democratic values and integrating with the European Union.

The following questions relate to this:

Is the Language image of Macedonian and the Balkans created by Europe, or by the Balkan countries themselves?

How long will the Balkans remain a mystery for their European neighbors? The cultural heterogeneity of the region seems to be the most important, but not the only reason for it this state of affairs.

In what language were the language images of Macedonia created, and what language will they be created in – which ones of those were usual and how will this influence Balkan conflicts and misunderstandings?

1. Discourses – Macedonian, Balkan and European Discourses – Definitions and Language Determinations

National myths are transformed in political myths through discursive procedures and thus fulfill a very important role in the creation of the identities of certain Balkan states. Balkan and Macedonian national discourses appear both on a local (regional) and state (national) level as well as on a bilateral level (Macedonian – Bulgarian, Serbian – Croatian, Macedonian – Greek discourse) and, by inclusion of Turkey, Russia and the USA, on a multilateral (European and international) level.

Since the beginning of the 1990s, the question of the cultural and national identities of the Balkan peoples has been discussed many times, and this question is still a popular topic and source of controversy and challenges for many historians, sociologists, anthropologists, political scientists, and linguists. It could be said that the Balkan discourse was started even then, within the framework of that research process, when new notions and solutions, essentially being not only challenges but also contributors to the creation of stereotypes for "Balkanism" and the Balkans, were established.

Even though there are many unknowns regarding criteria used for defining the notion, here, the Balkans are seen as a cultural – historical and political community in which cultural marks are decisive, as to whether a particular country belongs to it or not. These marks encompass: language – included in the Balkan language union, some folklore elements, societal traits; multi-ethnicity – the coexistence of Catholics, Orthodox Christians and Muslims; and history – the submission to the Byzantine Empire in the past, the settling of Slavic peoples and their subjugation under Ottoman rule.

The notions Balkanism, Balkanization, Balkan or homo Balkanicus (*homo balcanicus*) as discursive mechanisms for the ghettoization of the Balkans, were verified and today they function as the basic elements creating a negative image of the Balkans, namely, in the Polish and European discourse concerning the Balkan states. Research of imaginary stereotypes in the Balkan, in context of the Balkan drama concerning post-communism, in the reflection of language slogans and phraseologisms such as the *Balkan cauldron, sick man of Europe, barrel of gunpowder*, etc., can be deduced not only by comparison with the Balkan perspectives – the Balkan states have always been interested in their own selves – but also more objectively, in a wider European context.

2. General Types of Macedonian National and Cultural Discourses

a) Discourse of multilingualism – within which different ideologies are often presented through heterogenic (unrelated) languages, and different ideological codes strive towards overpowering the society – even a political polyphony due to the reproduction of the meanings in the discourse, and through the discourse, creating a dominant ideology. Multi-constituent and polyfunctional relation between language and government leads directly to the emergence of semiosis, which becomes a codifier of convictions and ideas. In the process of societal and cultural projection of a national idea, we come across many concepts that can be differently interpreted and thus is created the discourse of rivalry of meanings, that is comprised in the permanent construction of new meanings and new contexts (lexical, syntactic, stylistic, phraseological and genre related) together with their axiological associations and connotations for the purpose of convincing the recipient of our own arguments, and by repetition (reproduction), disseminate this conviction.

The most evident effect of this rivalry between languages is the elimination of dialects and certain ethnical languages by literary and international languages. However, a defensive reaction, caused in conscious interlocutors, that is comprised of support for multilingualism and multiculturalism, is one of its undesired consequences.

The media are used as weapons and exploited in different discourses – political, medial, literary as well as in discursive analysis of literary works by Macedonian contemporary authors (handbooks, historical, literary and other texts) as an expression and manner of creating the linguistic image of the world. For instance, Luan Starova[6] and his novel *Балканвавилонци* (*Balkanbabylonians*) represent an example of the literary discourse of memory.

b) Convincing – a (rhetorical) discourse of values in its relations towards different questions, this can be researched in different manners. The choice of discourse and its genre imply the ideological (political) standpoint of the code user and his choice of world of values, in which, by using certain rhetorical means, he // she gets to convince himself // herself. From this aspect, an analysis will foremost include the language of the political (parliamentary) discourse, public speeches, exposes, religious texts, sermons, and manifestos of political parties and social non-governmental groups. An analysis will concern the

---

[6] Л. Старова, *Балканвавилонци*, Скопје 2014.

linguistic – lexical and syntactic, textual – means of expression of positive and negative values – hate speech in public communication – public conversation.

c) Cognitive models of a language analysis of Macedonian and Balkan discourses. The most important basis for understanding (conceptualization) of a linguistic image of the world is the lexis understood as a collection, inventory of terms relevant not only from the historical, social and cultural aspect, but also based on associative, often, cultural changes, increase in knowledge and social needs. This collection of terms changes depending on certain historical conditions, cultural changes, and an increase in knowledge and social needs. Some relations and notions, once defined, gain linguistic determinations different from their past ones. Moreover, the connotation of many key words needed for understanding the social processes and historical changes undergoes changes. This also concerns the manners of definition (nomination) and their ontological foundations, which are revealed by means of a structural and etymological analysis and associative research (usually in the form of a survey with determined stimulations), thanks to attested different meanings in sentences. For example, Macedonians – a South Slavic nation which populates the state of Macedonia; and Macedonians – the ancient people, genetically related to the nations that used to populate the conquered countries.

d) Types of discourses in view of certain disputes regarding national, historical, cultural and political identities: Serbian and Croatian identity, Bulgarian and Macedonian identity, Greek and Macedonian identity, Serbian and Kosovar identity, etc.

3. Subject to a Linguistic Analysis of Macedonian and Balkan Discourses

A subject of the analysis of Macedonian and Balkan discourses of national and cultural identities is to prove the kinds of differences existing in the language of discourses relative to the acceptance of the same events, viewpoints, stereotypes and myths depending on the state as well as the role of each state in the creation of the modern linguistic image of the Balkans – relative to the feeling of national identities by certain Balkan states and their comparison, for example, with the Polish national discourse and other European national discourses: Serbian, Croatian, Bosnian, Montenegrin, Macedonian, Bulgarian, and Slovenian.

A discourse analysis comprises:

a) Linguistic and semiotic mechanisms of cultural and national discourses and their types to show how they create or modernize the cultural and national identity of the existing and newly formed (Kosovo) Balkan states, as well as the differences in a perception of the same events, texts, viewpoints, stereotypes and myths depending on the country and to examine each of their roles (discourses: Macedonian, Serbian, Bosnian, Bulgarian, Montenegrin) in the process of building a linguistic image of the Balkans;

b) Cognitive (comprehensive) analysis of the perception by European neighbors and Europe (as a whole), Russia, USA and the countries of the former Yugoslavia, with a special emphasis on Serbia, Macedonia, Bosnia and Herzegovina, Croatia and Albania – largely based on materials from newspapers and other media. What types of linguistic images are created within the discourses, what do they have in common and how do they influence the Balkan conflicts, challenges and misunderstanding;

c) Study of the linguistic image of the world, a semiotic analysis of the discourse (quantitative and qualitative), associative research with a reconstruction of the mental vocabulary for every language and semantically differential scale by Charles Osgood[7];

d) In an ethno-linguistic research of identity, the principal material for finding the so-called national concepts, i.e. notions such as Serbian, Croatian, Macedonian, etc., create the following facts:

- dictionary data (word definitions);
- textual data of current texts borrowed from the given public discourse;
- corporal data placed in the largest textual corpora of the given language (same language) national language corpora – Polish national corpus, Croatian national corpus, Russian national corpus, Internet corpus – WebCorpLive, Corpus Gralis, etc.;
- data obtained as a result of associative research and other survey research;
- data and documents taken from official speeches and addresses of political leaders, international and regional, expressions of influential world and local intellectuals and international settings and institutions shaping public opinion.

---

[7] C. E. Osgood, *Semantic differential technique in the comparative study of cultures*, "American Anthtropologist" 1964, 66(3), p. 171-200, http://dx.doi.org/10.1525/aa.1964.66.3.02a00880 (accessed on: 15 May 2015).

III. On Codification of the Norm of the Contemporary Macedonian Language

In the history of the Polish language, there have never emerged such situations or necessities where linguistic norms were dependent on the findings of a commission or were determined by a group, not solely of representatives of science and literature, but also of political activists, as was the case with the literary Macedonian language taking shape in the second half of the XIX century. Trans-language conditioning of the codification of the Macedonian language was especially evident in the post-World War II Balkan reality.

Linguistic norms have played a principal role in the formation of the literary Polish language; these norms were binding at the ruling royal court (court language) as well as being the language of writers and educated people (Jan Kochanowski, Andrzej Trzecieski and Łukasz Górnicki). With regards to other Slavic languages, whose contemporary literary norms were created during the XIX century – specifically the southern Slavic languages: Serbian and Croatian (the activities of Vuk Karadžić), Bulgarian (the works of Christo Botew, Luben Karawełow and Iwan Wazow) as well as of Macedonian[8] language – some manner of solution was attained by undertaking a process of codification. These procedures dealt with not only letters of the alphabet and writing norms, but also with some rules of grammar as well as planned lexicographical descriptions of vocabulary.

Codification, and somewhat later *standardization*, and also *unification* are universal terms used in relation to the Macedonian language of

---

8 Macedonian belongs to the group of south Slavic languages, together with Bulgarian, Serbian, Croatian, and the Slovenian language. Today, it is the official language of Macedonia, and is used by about 2 million of its inhabitants. It is estimated that the Macedonian language, including dialects, is spoken by about 2 to 2.5 million people including those Macedonians who have emigrated.

the last fifty years.[9] These terms appear with others, including: *the standard Macedonian language* (*стандарден македонски јазик*), *determining linguistic norms* (*нормирање на македонскиот јазк*) and establish a set of official formal measures as well as taking positive or negative decisions regarding more or less regular and typical linguistic phenomena with the aim of imposing upon them mandatory normative powers by passing the appropriate laws or decrees. There are two ratification dates currently recognized in Macedonia: May 3, 1945 – the establishment of alphabet (the alphabet was announced in the "Nova Makedonija" daily newspaper) – and 2 June 1945 – the adoption of spelling rules (this was confirmed in writing on 7 June by the Ministry of Education).

It is universally accepted that the origins of the Macedonian language are linked to writings of texts in Old Church Slavonic language, with translations of the Bible, the works of Thessaloniki brothers, Saints Constantine and Methodius, as well as of their disciples, who translated the Holy Scriptures (X–XI centuries) into the local dialect which they knew from childhood (Macedonian) from the region of Thessaloniki. These creators of Slavic writing thus made a new alphabet, modeled on, as is generally accepted, the Greek alphabet. In this context there is also mention of the XVI century collection of homilies from the Greek preacher from Thessaloniki – Damaskin Studit, which was named after his first name "damaskina." Bishop Grigorij of Prilep translated sermons into a local dialect in Macedonia. From that time until the XIX century and even later, this name was also employed in relation to a collection of translations of texts on mixed subjects and in various publications, even in those which did not contain any of the homilies of Damaskin Studit.

The modern Macedonian language (written), developed in the second half of the XIX century, when after four hundred years of Ottoman rule, the Slavic tradition was reborn, and local writers and cultural activists – authors of textbooks, first grammar books and dictionaries – started to write in their own local dialects, making heroic attempts to raise their dialects up to the level of a general, national language.

However, the first Macedonian folk texts were written in the Greek alphabet. In the opinion of B. Koneski, in some regions of Macedonia (Ohrid) until the middle of the XIX century, the Slavic alphabet was not generally

---

9 Sometimes, in this context, we can speak about two codifications: the codification by Sts. Cyril and Methodius, which was the basis for the first Slavic literary (church) language and general codification of the Macedonian language in the XX century – including the book On Macedonian Matters by K.P. Misirkov and the codification after the World War Treaty (Language Commissions) – thus indicating that it was a kind of a long-term process and not a single event.

known. Dimitar Miladinov himself, a teacher from Struga, didn't learn the Cyrillic alphabet until he was 50 years old – his *Collection of Folk Songs* was originally written in the Greek alphabet, and Dimitar rewrote it in the Cyrillic alphabet just prior to its publication. One could mention the following outstanding writers amongst the precursors of the XIX Macedonian literary language: Dimitar Miladinov, who collected and wrote down folk songs, and Grigor Prličev (Grigor Prlichev), who wrote in the Ohrid dialect. The texts of two other authors, Joakim Krčovski (who wrote in the northeastern dialect – Kratovo) and Kiril Pejčinoviḱ (Kiril Peychinovich) (who wrote in the Tetovo dialect) – linked folk elements and the language used in the Macedonian Orthodox Church. One would have to include the following authors in the group of so-called text book authors (as they were authors of text books and educational books): Partheniy Zografski, Kuzman Shapkarev (who collected folk tales) and Dimitrij Makedonski. Zografski intended to introduce his own regional slang from Galichnik into the literary language. Gjorgji Pulevski, the author of two dictionaries and a Macedonian grammar (*Slognica rečovska*[10]), wrote in his native dialect from the region of Debar, with addition of attributes characteristic of the slang of central Macedonia. Konstantin Miladinov, Rajko Ivanov Zhinzifov, and Grigor Prlichev, represented diverse poetics, and their compositions abounded with powerfully individualized linguistic variants from different origins. Miladinov wrote poetry in a folk language (a dialect from the Struga region), Zhinzifov linked various lexical linguistic elements in his works, including elements of Russian (he spent virtually his entire adult life in Moscow, where he gained an education and worked) as well as Turkish origin. Prlichev initially wrote in Greek, but he was also an advocate of creating one universal Slavic language. In 1868, in Carigrad (currently Istanbul), he published, with this goal in mind, his *Short Slavic Grammar*.[11]

The language of authors of this period was dominated by a variety and individuality regarding the very choice of the language itself, which was often a conglomerate of various origins including attributes from Slavic and non-Slavic languages alike, as well as from diverse stylistic cores. Therefore, in this sphere, it is exceptionally difficult to speak of any, regardless of how insignificant, scholarly linguistic norm, let alone a literary one, although there were pioneering attempts to break

---

10 G. Pulevski, *Slavjansko-naseleniski-makedonska Slognica Rečovska*, Sofia 1880.

11 In 1994 in Ohrid, Dimitar Pandev and Dragi Stefanija published a phototypic edition of the *Short Slavic Grammar* together with a Macedonian translation and a short commentary.

through the heretofore stagnation, imbalanced styles, and diversity of variations typical of multinational settings.

B. Koneski wrote about the linguistic situation in Macedonia before the XIX century, and he proved, that in this period, until the Balkan Wars, there was not a single dominant language in the region: "Нема во Македонија доминантен јазик" (There is no dominant language in Macedonia). A little further on page 23 he states:

> Our written language, until the XIX century, had a limited number of lexemes at its disposal, which resulted from the fact that the language was used principally in the Orthodox Church to express ideas which were of an ecclesiastical-didactic content.[12]

B. Koneski's standpoint confirms the fact that considering the lexical fond of Old Church Slavonic language, Macedonian language was in no way privileged compared to the other Slavic languages. According to W. Mańczak's research, in the group of Slavic languages, there are fewer lexical associations between the Old Church language and the Macedonian and Bulgarian languages, than in Serbo-Croatian and Slovenian languages.[13] In addition – as suggested by T. Lewaszkiewicz –

> Influenced by intensive contacts with the Turkish and the Greek languages, the Macedonian language (as the Bulgarian language) lost many of its words of ancient Slavonic origin. Moreover, Albanian and, to a lesser degree, Aromanian influence, was also very important.[14]

However, researcher could certainly not describe the developmental basis of the Macedonian language as "our written language," most often being an editing of ecclesiastical texts in Greek, Serbian, Bulgarian, or finally in the Macedonian language, without a wide reception, limited by the conditions of the Church, but rather, it was described as the language which was universally spoken by the common people. This may be attested to, by the rich collection of folk tales originating in

---

12 Б. Конески, *Македонскиот XIX век. Јазични и книжевно-историски прилози*, Скопје 1986, p. 22, 23.

13 W. Mańczak, *Język staro-cerkiewno-słowiański – kompromis między dialektem macedońsko-bułgarskim a morawsko-panońskim*, in: *Językoznawstwo, Prace na XIV Międzynarodowy Kongres Slawistów w Ochrydzie 2008*, Warszawa 2007, p. 139–145.

14 T. Lewaszkiewicz, *Prasłowiańskie dziedzictwo leksykalne w języku macedońskim (rekonesans badawczy)*, in: XL Scientific conference at the International Seminar on Macedonian Language, Literature and Culture (Ohrid, 29–30 June 2013), Skopje, p. 172.

Macedonia, but which have not been published in their original form so far. Multi-volume collections of folk texts (Cepenkov, Šapkarev, Verković), including minor clarifications of first editions, were published in the finalized (codified) standard Macedonian language after 1945.[15] Perhaps these publications are important from a folklore perspective, but as far as historical-linguistic research and studies of the Macedonian folk language are concerned, they are of secondary importance.

The XIX century, the turn of the XIX and XX centuries, and almost the entire XX century represent an era when southern Slavic folklore blossomed, thanks to the activities of M. Cepenkov, K. and D. Miladinov, and K. Šapkarev. Today there is no doubt that these authors and gatherers of folklore used a written language, and when they were writing down Macedonian short stories, tales, proverbs, songs, etc., they discovered and immortalized a vocabulary, which until today has remained the lexical basis of the contemporary literary language of Macedonia. These collections of folklore texts from Macedonia were wrought by B. Koneski.

None of the works of H. Polenaković and K. Penušliski, T. Sazdov and other Macedonian researchers exist in photo-type, which renders a scientific editorial study difficult, and in the instance of abbreviations and a cover version, renders a critical study of the text impossible. K. Penušliski points this out when he writes:

> In 1945, Blaže Koneski had already issued the first *Collection of Macedonian Folk Songs* as an exceptionally well done anthology, which has remained unsurpassed until today. His abbreviations and interventions in relation to specific songs resulted in an increase in the esthetic value, however, from a folklore viewpoint, corrections in the texts of folk compositions are impermissible.[16]

---

15 In 1974, a photocopy of the first edition of *За македонцките работи* by K.P. Misirkov (Sofia 1903) with an introduction by B. Koneski and commentary by T. Dimitrovski was published. It was only in 2000, however, that a photo-optic edition of the collected folk songs of the Miladinov brothers was published in Скопје. Earlier, in 1983, collected works, ред. Х. Поленаковиќ, Т. Димитровски, were also published. These included: *Зборник на народни песни*, the original title was: *Бѫлгарски народни пѣсни*. See also the collected works of Кузман Шапкарев, *Сборник от български народни умотворения. Част първа. Простонародна българска поезия или български народни песни*, София, 1891–1894 and S.I. Verković, *Стефан Веркович, Народне Песме Македонски Бугара*, Beograd 1860. None of the Macedonian editions contain a catalog of the previous editions. There are also no critical evaluations.

16 К. Пенушлиски, *Одразот на фолклорната традиција врз македонската уметничка проза*, in: *Битовото и историското во македонската уметничка проза*, Skopje 1986, p. 5.

In accordance with the activities of the admirers and gatherers of folklore, significant activities concerning the Macedonian literary language formation took place during the inter-war period and during World War II itself, and may be attested to by the literary works of such poets as Kočo Racin, Venko Markovski and Kole Nedelkovski as well as of the authors of dramas such as – Risto Krle, Vasil Iljoski, and Anton Panov. The role of Venko Markovski merits special attention in this field, as he already achieved significant renown earlier as a poet; he was also recognized as a literary and linguistic expert and, in addition, he actively participated in philosophical discussions preceding the Macedonian language codification. There was also another poet – the author of a popular poem entitled *Beli mugri* (*White Dawns*) – Kočo Racin, who was a partisan and died at the age of 35, in 1943 in the region of Mount Lopušnik.

Venko Markovski was well known and was one of the few (besides K. Racin, K. Nedelkovski and R. Krle) writers, who wrote in the literary – for the time – Macedonian language, and together, they created the basis for a linguistic norm. In this capacity, Markovski was asked to be a member of the "Commission for Matters Dealing with the Macedonian Language, Alphabet, and Culture." The commission deliberated from 27 November to 4 December 1944. Besides Markovski, the following people were members of the commission: R. Prodanov, Gj. Šoptrajanov, M. Petruševski, V. Iljoski, Gj. Kiselinov, H. Zografski, D. Džambaz, M. Pavlovski, K. Toševski i B. Koneski, J. Kostov.[17]

Since the problem concerning the recognition of various dialects spoken in Macedonia as basis for the literary language was solved quickly, on 27 November it was already determined that the dialects of central Macedonia (in accordance with the propositions of K.P. Misirkov from 1903) would be thus designated. However, polemics regarding the alphabet and spelling went on. At one of the Commission's sessions, Hristo Zografov, a members of the Commission, said:

> The works of Venko Markovski and Kosta Racin constitute a basis significant enough to solve the problem of the Macedonian literary language.

---

[17] Blaže Koneski was born on 19 December 1921 in Nebregovo, near Prilep. He studied Slavistics in Belgrade but graduated in philology in Skopje. After his graduation in 1945, he worked as a lector in the Macedonian National Theatre, in the Agritropot of CC and then in the Ministry of Education. In the name of the Ministry, he was included in a group that was to make the arrangements for establishment of the Faculty of Philology. In 1946 he began working as a lecturer at the Department of Macedonian Language with the newly established Faculty of Philology. In 1957, he was elected a full-time professor; http: // eprints.ugd.edu.mk/3719/1/megun-sem-mak-jaz.pdf (accessed on: 12 February 2015).

> The many volumes of works by Venko Markovski [Markovski in 1944 published poems and collections of poetry entitled *Partizani* (*The Partisans*), *Orlite na Makedonija* (*Macedonian Eagles*), *Robii* (*The Slaves*), *Na istok* (*In the East*), *Niz požarite na Elada* (*In the Fires of Ellada*) – M.K.] as well as the works of Kosta Racin are written in the central dialect and thereby this dialect became, in essence, our literary language.[18]

Another member of the Commission, Gj. Šoptrajanov, voiced a similar opinion:

> We Macedonians, have in the works of Venko Markovski, a literary language which is already wrought. Fortunately for us, this language is of the central Macedonian dialect. This patois, hence, has been worked out and elevated to the level of a literary language.

Only B. Koneski, referring to Serbian scholars, postulated that the literary language should be – as he put it – the "western Macedonian dialect":

> In the scholarly works of Oblak, Miletić, and Belić, the term "a-dialect," or "western-Macedonian a-dialect" is used. I therefore think that this term is more correct. The term "western Macedonian a-dialects" has already been created, and I think that we should use it.

B. Koneski's statement evoked an immediate response from Markovski:

> Those who have submitted reports until now, have proposed that the central dialects would form the basis of the Macedonian literary language. Now somebody wants us to say "a-dialects" or "western a-dialects" (...) but it's not commissions that create a language, but rather writers (...) And that's how it will be for us as well. This language will not be created by philologists, but by writers.

The next day, 28 November an open conflict broke out between Markovski and Koneski concerning the alphabet, when the latter affirmed:

> If we adopt the Serbian Cyrillic alphabet, our language will remain Macedonian (...) This specifically deals with the letters: ћ, ђ, љ, њ (...) And, now,

18 All comments by members of the Language Commission are contained in: С. Ристески, *Стенографски белешки од првата јазична комисија. Факсимил*, Скопје 2000, p. 125.

what are the reasons for accepting these two symbols: ћ, ђ? There are those who would opine that "tj" and "dj" are characteristic of Slavic languages, which developed in a varied manner in different languages, in Russian: ч, ж, in Serbian: ћ, ђ, and in Bulgarian: щ, жд. But in Macedonian, these characteristics can not be taken into consideration. This change in the Macedonian language has been achieved via the Serbian language (...).

Venko Markovski:

But here we're speaking about the central Macedonian dialect. Please don't mix these two subjects, sir.

Blaže Koneski:

Please allow me to finish, and than you may make some comments. I heard you out...

Koneski continued:

The majority of the Macedonian literate population can use Vuk's alphabet. If we do not include these letters, many of them will become illiterate. If we introduce 5–6 new letters, many of the people will become illiterate (...) Common people often write "quickly," without using the letter ъ, and this means that they can't feel it, either. Others, I know a case from Gevgelija, who writes "трагнам" and "барзо" instead of "търгнам" and "бързо" (get off and quick, respectively). This means that their speech includes this ъ and they replace it with the sound closest to it, i.e. they replace it with "a." As I said, I personally consider the vocal r (р) to be absent, because I do not feel it, with lower vibration than the Serbian vocal r (р). Given all the reasons that I presented, I advocate keeping the letters ћ and ђ, in our alphabet and excluding ъ from the written language.

Krume Tošeski voiced his opinion on the subject:

(...) when the Bulgarians see these Serbian letters, they will say – "they are being Serbianized." When the editor of "Bregalniczki Głos" is going to be reminded of these Serbian letters, he will flee (from the subject) as if he were burned. On the other hand, we may have some unpleasantness in the Yugoslav federation. This is why it's better to adopt the Serbian, instead of the Bulgarian, letters (...) We'll thus find a happy medium. Blaže can make a concession, and Venko can make one as well, and thus, we shall arrive at a happy medium.

Reaching an agreement and "finding a happy medium" proved to be more difficult than expected for the members of the Commission. B. Koneski didn't participate in sessions from the third day on. Accordingly, the discussion was carried on in two sub-commissions, which concluded their work on 4 December announcing a Resolution in which it was affirmed that the central dialects would constitute the foundation of the contemporary literary Macedonian language.

The Macedonian alphabet which was adopted had 32 letters:

А, Б, В, Г, Ѓ, Д, Е, Ж, З, Ѕ, И, Ј, К, Ќ,
Л, Љ, М, Н, Њ, О, П, Р, С, Т,
У, Ф, Х, Ц, Ч, Џ, Ш, Ъ.

Amongst the specific propositions contained in the Resolution, those that are especially noteworthy include a differentiation between the Macedonian Л and the Serbian Љ and also the Macedonian Н and the Serbian Њ – "there are also the specific Macedonian half-soft signs n' and l' (for example *Ljuba* is not the Serbian *Љуба*)."

> Ѓ and Ќ are typically Macedonian sounds with an insignificant fricativity and are more explosive, therefore new letters were proposed for these sounds.
> Ѕ is an old Macedonian letter. We may find it in the texts of Saints Cyril and Methodius as well as in newer literature, while the у sound often appears in the living language (*sid, svezda, svonci*).
> Ъ is essential in the Macedonian language, it's an old-Macedonian letter. For example: *ъrbino, ъrt, kъrv, vъrv, kъsmet.*[19]
> The letter Ч is necessary in our alphabet, because this sound may be heard in both foreign and domestic words (...) Similar to the letter j.[20]

The Commission completed its work on 4 December 1944 at 6 p.m., but the codification of the Macedonian language was stalled. On 7 December 1944 the Ministry of Education used a certain ploy and made the decision not to announce the Resolution until it would obtain the approval of two Soviet scholars – S.B. Bernstein and N.S. Deržavin. Today, it is difficult to discern to what degree all of this activity was just for appearances sake or it was really necessary. Nevertheless, one thing is certain, the Resolution was not announced and did not come

---

19 Today, the Macedonian "ъ" in some words: *'рбет, 'рѓа, 'рж* has been replaced by an apostrophe, and in others it has been omitted: *крв, врв, ксмет*.

20 С. Ристески, *Стенографски белешки од првата јазична комисија...*, p. 317.

into force because the invited scholarly guests failed to appear, and therefore, a Second Language Commission was convoked on 15 February, 1945.

The decision to postpone the Resolution was adopted on the XIV session of the ASNOM Presidium on 7 December 1944 as a third item of the agenda *Доклад по резолуцијата на комисија за македонската азбука*, for which the minutes state:

> The Resolution is not to be used by Decision of the Presidium and not to be published so as to prevent wide public discussion, which would only be harmful for our small state today. In order to grant the matter a higher scientific authority, it proposes an interim stay of the Resolution's publication, and to invite from Moscow two world renowned researchers in the field of Slavic philology and the best scholars familiar with the languages of all the Balkan people: Bernshtajn and Deržavin. The proposal was accepted.[21]

Information concerning the course of the proceedings of the Second Commission is contained in two documents (however, there is no stenographic transcript of what happened, as during the sessions of the First Commission) entitled: *Текот на јазичната конференција* (*The Proceedings of the Language Conference*) and the *Резултати на јазичната конференција (како предлог)* (*Results of the Language Conference – A Proposition*). As a result of the Commission's efforts, letters similar to those in the Serbian alphabet were adopted (Serbian Cyrillic) with one addition in the form of the letter S.

According to S. Risteski, the author of a book entitled *Создавањето на современиот македонски литературен јазик*[22] (*The Creation of a Contemporary Macedonian Literary Language*), the Commission's decision evoked dissatisfaction from political and social activists. This resolution also induced the Central Committee of the Communist Party of Yugoslavia to send a telegram to the Central Committee of the Macedonian Communist Party with the following message: "Odmah uputite Malinsku, Konjevskog i Markovskog da definitivno uredimo pitanje makedonske azbuke" ("Send Malinska, Konjevski and Markovski immediately, with the goal of finally sorting out this affair of the Macedonian alphabet"). This author may, based on interviews

---

21 *АСНОМ. Документи од Првото и Второто заседание на АСНОМ*, Скопје 1984, т. I, кн. I, p. 383.

22 С. Ристески, *Создавањето на современиот македонски литературен јазик*, Скопје 1988, p. 185.

with witnesses to these events and various documents, affirm that after returning from Belgrade, Malinska, Koneski, and Markovski instituted the Third Language Commission, and it was this third one, and not the Second Commission, which on May 3, 1945, completed the final codification of the Macedonian alphabet. S. Risteski nevertheless wrote: "I have not found any documents related to the establishment of this commission."[23] He only found certain traces (abbreviations of words) on the reverse side of the last page, supplied to the members of the Commission, in a report entitled *За азбука* (*On the Alphabet*), written by Venko Markovski and at the same time indicating the people who voted for the letter ъ. This was supposed to have indicated that this problem was once again a subject of discussion. Ultimately, the ъ symbol was not accepted, in spite of the fact that five members (Ilija Topalovski-Avram, Dare Dżambaz, Gustav Vlahov, Vlado Maleski and Venko Markovski) of the ten-member Commission had been in favor of accepting it.[24]

V.A. Friedman – the American linguist and expert on problems related to the Balkans – when presenting the disputes concerning the Macedonia alphabet, wrote:

> The object of a most lively discussion were the letters for signifying phonemes (k', g', l, ń, dz, dź, j). The principle: one letter – one sound, resulted in Macedonia's orthography being closer to Serbian, rather than to Bulgarian or Russian orthography. There is a striking lack of a graphic representation for "shva". It was, in principle, eliminated from the literary phonological system and obtained graphic representation only in the first edition of the orthographic rules.[25]

In this manner, "shva", which "was eliminated from the literary phonological system" nevertheless obtained "graphic representation", that is, an apostrophe, which is until today the most controversial element of the Macedonian script.[26]

---

23 Ibidem.

24 Ibidem, p. 15–16.

25 V.A. Friedman, *Charakterystyka socjolingwistyczna współczesnego języka macedońskiego*, „Socjolingwistyka" 1993, XII–XIII, p. 188–189.

26 In an introduction to collected works issued in Ohrid in *300 македонски народни песни*, Охрид 2001 Dragi Stefanija wrote: "Not one of the songs from Ohrid, Struga, or Prespa can't be sung unless one uses our old half-vowels – the great 'yer' universally used in the XIX century which erroneously was ejected from our alphabet in 1945, and replaced with an apostrophe, and that's how we designate this lost letter" (p. 3).

In the last version of the Codification Act from 3 May and 7 June 1945, the adjudications of the previous Commission, which deliberated from 3 November till 27 December 1944 and formulated specific propositions in the sphere of the codification of the language, and normalization of the alphabet and Macedonian spelling, were not taken into consideration. In addition, there was no reference to the literary norms of the then contemporary Macedonian language, as it was being formed in the second half of the XIX century, nor to the interwar period of the XX century (there was no reference to the poetry of K. Racin, V. Markovski, K. Nedelkovski, or the dramas of R. Krle, V. Iljovski, and A. Panov). All of these facts have brought about a situation where currently, more than fifty years after the codification, this problem is still the subject of disputes, discussions and polemics in Macedonian philological science.

In 1966, Aleksandar Spasov, one of the renowned literary critics of that time wrote about the beginnings of contemporary Macedonian literature, saying that

> The years between 1936–1941 were one of the most important periods in Macedonian culture prior to the liberation; it was a period when the basis of contemporary Macedonian literature was being formed (...) The appearance of a large number of writers including K. Racin, V. Markovski, K. Nedelkovski, the majority of whom are almost totally forgotten, but their writings, irrespective of to what degree they may be deprived of any significant literary value, nevertheless are undoubtedly, from a historical point of view, endowed with considerable significance as a manifestation of a tendency to reinforce the Macedonian literary language (...) Racin, Markovski, and Nedelkovski are not individual and isolated phenomena. They are some of the most outstanding representatives of an extensive movement in Macedonia in the years immediately prior to the Second World War, dedicated to the creation and affirmation of, at that time, contemporary Macedonian culture.[27]

Until today, however, original issues – especially those in print or phototypic editions – of the works (prose and poetry) from the interwar period, in particular from the period immediately prior to W.W. II (1936–1941), are inaccessible – they are neither in print, nor have they been printed. There is also a dearth of editions which possess a critical evaluation. The problem of selecting a base edition (publication),

---

27 А. Спасов, *Развојниот пат на Рацина*, in: *Кочо Рацин. Стихови и проза*, Скопје 1966, p. 22–25.

in principle, is not taken into consideration, in spite of the plethora of varieties and variations of texts. The basic method of textology – collation – is not employed. A negligible number of first printings are either found in private collections, or were lost. A popularization may be observed, however, in mass publications of contemporary literature (especially poetry), in the press, radio, and television, of the codified norms and models contained in the *Grammar of the Macedonian Literary Language* by B. Koneski (1976) and in the only three-volume work of its kind, the *Dictionary of the Macedonian Language* (1965), in which definitions of specific words are given principally in the Serbian language, but written in the Latin alphabet. Publications of prose and volumes of poetry which popularize the linguistic norms established by the decree are published in Skopje, in editions which run into many thousands. The creative inspiration, however, for contemporary writers is the living language of the people, which they spoke in their childhood and which their fathers speak until today. There is also the example of one of the greatest Macedonian writers – Zhivko Chingo, whose novels and short stories were written in the stylized language of the region of Ohrid, continuing the narrative tradition initiated by Marko K. Cepenkov.

The problem of Macedonian norms regarding orthography, the alphabet, and writing have come alive in the 1990s. Articles have appeared in the press ("Glas," "Makedonsko Delo"), which postulate a reform of the Macedonian language (change in orthography). Texts criticizing the codification decision were published. The authors of these texts were demanding a change in the manner of writing employed until then or were justifying the illegitimacy of the proposed modifications ("Start"). It should be added here that a language, and especially its alphabet, are factors which are singularly important in the Balkans, and as far as the matter of identity goes, they are in an exceptional manner, a factor of national identity.

Currently, Macedonian philological science (mainly textology) has an urgent need to take a new look at literature and folklore texts as well as to undertake research on a wide scale (linguistic, historic, and above all editorial), on the beginnings of the Macedonian literary language, research based on authentic texts (originals, first printings, photo-type editions and facsimiles). The first attempts at researching original texts have already been made – a photo-type edition of a collection of the folklore texts by the Miladinov brothers has already appeared. Such an editorial enterprise should be undertaken to include all Macedonian texts printed before 1945 – folklore as well literary texts. Only then will studies on the formation of the contemporary

Macedonian language assume their proper dimension, quality, and the desired scholarly effects. This is especially important for folklore texts, which have already been published in large numbers in modernized and codified versions. At the most, additional comments could include some data on the significance of words or clarifying errors. An evaluation, not preceded by textological analysis, of text correctness resulting from editor's subjective decision, should be performed. For instance, the differences between the original and its published version is called transcription.[28]

Only after a complete editorial compilation of texts unpublished till today, followed by their publication, together with already existing variations, which is an indispensable component of textological critical apparatus, could one initiate a scholarly discussion on Macedonian literary history, especially concerning its interwar situation, when the norms of the contemporary Macedonian language were created.

28 Т. Димитровски, *Белешки за транскрипцијата на текстовите во Зборникот на Миладиновци*, in: Д. и К. Миладиновци, *Зборник на народни песни*. Под редакција на Харалампие Поленаковиќ и Тодор Димитровски, Скопје 1983, p. 537–553.

IV. Notions of *Macedonian Man // Macedonian Woman* and *Macedonian Language* in Scientific Discourse

1. The notions *Macedonian Man // Macedonian Woman // Macedonian People*

In text linguistics, expressions are analyzed on three levels, intratextual, intertextual and metatextual level. Internal (intratextual) analysis concerns text structure and cohesion; intertextual – concerns relationships between different texts; metatextual – concerns an analysis of elements in a certain text which concern the same text, not the real or fictitious world the text addresses. Therefore, a form of scientific texts and discourses is mainly analyzed, not so much their content, historical events or their interpretation.

The notion of text competes with the notion of discourse, and the borderline between them is not clearly distinguished. And there is voluminous theoretical literature on this topic.[29] The most important mark differentiating text from discourse is the fact that the text is a finished product (according to Wilhelm von Humboldt – *ergon*), and the discourse is a process (*energeia*)[30]; The text, as an already shaped expression, is

---

29 Only few books containing an overview on this topic are listed here: R. de Beaugrande, W.U. Dressler, *Wstęp do lingwistyki tekstu*, transl. by A. Szwedek, Warszawa 1990; U. Żydek-Bednarczuk, *Wprowadzenie do lingwistycznej analizy tekstu*, Kraków 2005; J. Labocha, *Tekst, wypowiedź, dyskurs w procesie komunikacji językowej*, Kraków 2008; M. Kawka, *Sześć dyskursów o języku*, Skopje 2012.

30 W. von Humboldt, *On Language, On the Diversity of Human Language Construction and its Influence on the Mental Development of the Human Species*, ed. by M. Losonsky, Cambridge 1999, p. 25–64.

not interactive, and the discourse, according to the definition, is active. Scientific discourse on the notions of Macedonia and the Macedonian language, is primarily interactive since it requires a confrontation between different opinions of different authors. This trait is basic, and constitutive for the said speech act (speech genre).

Namely, it is about a more detailed analysis of the scientific discourse concerning the said notions: Macedonia and the Macedonian language and their conceptualization in scientific literature. The term conceptualization implies a process of the creation of a notion based on a general knowledge of the world and a definition of a given word, which arose in the discourse.

a. Macedonians

Macedonians are one of the Slavic peoples who live mainly in Macedonia (formerly a part of Yugoslavia), Greece and Bulgaria and in small number in Albania. Macedonians are mostly Orthodox Christians, although some of them are Muslim. However, for the majority of the population in Europe, the names Macedonia and Macedonian are not associated with the present-day Balkan republic. For them, Macedonia was once a powerful military empire of King Philip II and King Alexander the Great.

The lack of an ability for a differentiation in the common world knowledge, between Macedonia as a military, prosperous empire of Kings Philip II and Alexander the Great, and Macedonia as a republic in Southern Europe, does not only result from ignoring the historic knowledge relying on sociologically and culturally conditioned semantic connotations, but it also depends on, not only Polish but also Macedonian points of view regarding Macedonia, and the Macedonians today.

The linguistic image of the world that is enclosed within the language, differently verbalized, represents an interpretation of reality that can be summed up in the form of complex world views. According to J. Bartmiński, they can be "petrified views" based on the very essence of the language, i.e. grammar, vocabulary, and on clichés (for example sayings, proverbs) but also on presupposed or implicit linguistic forms, stances, views and opinions fixed on the level of societal knowledge, beliefs, myths and rituals.[31] However, two stand points dominate the interpretation of the linguistic world view – the first that deals with the linguistic image as a cognitive structure consolidated (petrified) in

---

31 J. Bartmiński, *Językowe podstawy obrazu świata*, Lublin 2006, p. 12.

a language system, and the second, as a collection of rules and regulations contained in grammar and language structures pointing to the different manners of seeing and understanding the world. The first is prescribed to Renata Grzegorczykowa (R. Gzhegorchikova) and the second to Ryszard Tokarski.

R. Gzhegorchikova claims that

> Language picture of the world would like to be seen as a conceptual structure established (secured) in the system of a language, and thus in its grammatical and lexical properties (within the meaning of words and their connection).[32]

According to R. Tokarski

> (...) human reality can be differently conceptualized in any different language, in the sense that it facilitates and points to some ways, typical for a specific culture, of interpretation of the world.[33]

Based on these assumptions, the author of this conception suggests adopting certain procedures in language profiling on two different levels i.e. cultural and textual profiling. He understands the first as a linguistically relativized conventionalization of a given encyclopedic knowledge. Thus, the image of the world is interpreted in a cultural way, fixed in word units, and lexical fields in categorical grammatical relations. The second profiling is defined as the actualization of the aforementioned semantic structures. Thus, we have a culturally interpreted worldview, fixed by means of a lexis, word formation patterns and formula, phraseologisms, and lexical and grammatical relations. The last is defined as an upgrade of the aforementioned semantic structures functioning as:

> Certain idealizations i.e. overall frameworks (conceptual models) from which a specific part of the overall framework is actualized, in a certain text or specific group. This actualization of part of the model, and the possible reassessment of the model, can be defined as textual profiling.[34]

---

32 R. Grzegorczykowa, *Pojęcie językowego obrazu świata*, in: *Językowy obraz świata*, ed. by J. Bartmiński, Lublin 1999, p. 41.

33 R. Tokarski, *Kulturowe i językowe aspekty profilowania*, in: *Profilowanie w języku i w tekście*, ed. by J. Bartmiński, R. Tokarski, Lublin 1998, p. 40–41.

34 Ibidem.

LIW (linguistic image of the world) methodology allows for the analysis of linguistic and cultural data in the process of cultural and textual profiling to approach the manners of human perception and human adjustment to the world. A concretization itself, develops in two phases: the first is realized in a

> (...) specific speech act, here and now, being a product of (resulting from) a certain expression (...), the second, on the level of social convention, is a mark on which its repetitiveness is applied in different expressions (texts and discourses).[35]

The concept of aspect (type of the starting expression), domains and sub-domains, facets (group of opinions and definitions of objects) has[36] the most important role here.[37]

Concretization as well as facet selection and the subject qualitative characteristics, also determine what can be qualified as profiling. The profiling itself

> (...) is a process and its result is a profile. What we understand by this term is not so much a variant of meanings as is one variant of the idea for an entry object shaped from the selection of facets, whose arrangement is in accordance with the rules of implication and the filling of their content is in accordance with, the established knowledge of the world.[38]

In the reconstruction of the profile of Macedonian, it will be most important to keep in view not only the national stereotypes (different conceptual images, representative of the Southern Slavs) but also the concretization of the speech act (specific historical text) as well as the level of social conventions (repetition of different statements and texts that are mainly colloquial). A conceptualization of this idea or the concept as a structure, which is adopted as a determined and petrified model thanks to the use of the words Macedonians // Macedonian in specific texts, will also be of essence.

In addition to defining terms and concepts or explications of the concept, grammar and specific grammatical categories including person, number, tense, case, etc. are considered to be an important basis

---

35 J. Bartmiński, S. Niebrzegowska, *Profile a podmiotowa interpretacja świata*, in: *Profilowanie w języku...*, p. 214.

36 R. Langacker, *Wykłady z gramatyki kognitywnej*, ed. by H. Kardela, Lublin 1995.

37 A. Wierzbicka, *Semantyka. Jednostki elementarne i uniwersalne*, Lublin 2006.

38 J. Bartmiński, S. Niebrzegowska, *Profile a podmiotowa interpretacja świata...*, p. 217.

of the methodology of discovery and concretization, or the linguistic profiling of the worldview, adopted by many researchers and their supporters. For example, within the image of the Macedonian language in the Macedonian historical narrative (having in mind only the historical scientific articles and works), this word appears only in plural. The use of the singular "Македонец – Macedonian" is rare (the word "Македонка" [Macedonian feminine] correlates only to the image of the ancient Macedonian woman), independently from the period for which it is used. The first fact testifies to the collective understanding of the concept of nationality in historical works. The second – is dominated by gender point of view, in the sense of psycho-societal mechanisms for the categorization of phenomena (ideas and events).

The most important basis is the human knowledge of the world as a collection of words, inventory of notions with historical and socio-cultural relevance, that are not only based on associations usually hidden as subjective ideas in the subconscious. This collection varies depending on certain historical conditions, depending on living conditions and cultural changes, and on an increase of knowledge and social needs. Some relations and concepts are defined repeatedly and gain their own linguistic indicators, which differ from the previous ones; there is a change in connotation of many words crucial for an understanding of these socio-cultural changes. This also applies to the methods for designations and their ontological foundations discovered through an analysis of structurally and etymologically different meanings (pol. Niemiec – deaf man, pol. niemota, dumbness) that are situated in the sentences (I. **The Macedonians** – 3 nation that lives in the state of Macedonia; II. **The Macedonians** – an ancient people related to the peoples who lived within the boundaries of Greece).

b. Ancient Macedonians

Historical studies and different types of encyclopedias are dominated by the view that the ancient Macedonians had their own language that was closely related to the ancient Greek language. Members of the Macedonian elite, who decisively dominated society, were taught to speak Greek because they considered that all Macedonians originated from the Greeks. At the same time, they also looked upon the Greeks with disdain, believing them to have led comfortable lives not comparable with their own, harsh existence. The Greeks returned the feeling. The renowned rhetorician, Demosthenes (384–322 B.C.) described the Macedonian King Philip II's (rule 359–336 B.C.) as follows:

> (...) it is not only that he is no Greek, neither related to the Greeks, nor a barbarian from any place that can be named with honor, but a pestilent knave (hobbledehoy) from Macedonia, whence it was never yet possible to buy a decent slave.[39]

In the first volume of the five-volume *Историја на македонскиот народ* (*History of the Macedonian People*),[40] published by a group of authors from the Institute of History in Skopje, which includes data on prehistory up until 1371, or the beginning of Ottoman rule, the word *Macedonians* is not defined and appears almost exclusively with supplementary qualification. However, it is used in isolation in contexts where expressions referring to ancient Macedonians, not present-day Macedonians or Slavs, are used, for example:

1. The ancient Macedonians (p. 17, 33, 35, 38);
2. Paleolithic people in Macedonia, Neolithic people, p. 2–24; autochthonous Macedonian population;

– or in context referring to names of other tribes, as part of a collection.

3. Tribal groups of Thracians, Illyrians, Hellens, Dardanians, Epirians, Macedonians and others, were defined in the Balkans, Macedonians and Bryges, and Macedonians who lived in their vicinity (p. 9);
4. Standpoints of Macedonian, whose origin and language were similar to those of the north Greek tribes, became dominant because they were a completely independent people related to the Thracian and Illyrian ethnos (p. 35).

In the following parts as well as in the entire first volume, the word "Macedonians" is used to designate the ancient Macedonians, without supplementary qualifications and collections.

The image of ancient Macedonians present in the *History of the Macedonian People* is rather full, although it manifests a slightly legendary character:

> Macedonians were different from their neighbors the Greeks, Thracians, Illyrians and the people from other states because of their customs. Macedonian women – as described by Herodotus – unlike the Greek women, could not take part in celebrations organized by men. In this regard,

---

[39] Demostenes, *Trzecia mowa przeciwko Filipowi*, transl. by R. Turasiewicz, http: // www.wiw.pl/hisloria/starozytnagrecja/095-krolestwomacedonskie.asp (accessed on: 1 October 2014).

[40] *Историја на македонскиот народ*, т. I–V. Редакција: К. Битовски, Н. Вељановски, И. Катарџиев, Б. Панов, А. Стојановски, Скопје 2000. (All quotes are taken from this abridged edition. Further noted as *Историја*).

> Macedonian women deferred from Illyrian women who ate and drank with the men and who latter gathered together in their homes. Moreover, Illyrian women sat while eating unlike Macedonian women, who ate lying down. There was a custom among Macedonians not to wash with warm water. Since ancient times, Macedonians, as a courageous and warlike people, differed from the Greeks. There was a custom amongst them for the warriors who kill an enemy to bear a characteristic birthmark. Macedonians, who couldn't catch game using a net, lost the right to feast with other hunters in the lying position. This is why the myth of Andromeda was widespread in Macedonia.[41]

According to Macedonian authors, all these traits caused the ancient Macedonians not to disappear during the long process of ethnogenesis, and evolve in the middle of the fourth century B.C., into a separate nation.

c. Macedonian Slavs

Beginning with page 285 of the first volume of the *History of the Macedonian People*, there are changes in the situation regarding the field of the linguistic conceptualization of the picture since, according to the text, "the territory of Macedonia (at the end of the VI century) was populated by a large number of Slavic tribes" (p. 286). According to the authors of this historical work, it at this time, when the "symbiosis between the Slavic settlers and the existing autochthonic Macedonian people" occurred. Therefore, not only mutual cultural, religious and economical influences began to pervade, but the Slavic people also began to accept the old name "Macedonians" as well as the name of the land "Macedonia" (p. 291). Unfortunately, the symbiosis lasted from the IV century B.C. (when the "ancient" Macedonians were formed as a separate nation) until the VI // VII AD, when "the territory of Macedonia was populated by a large number of Slavic tribes," a period not described in the work. Historians and scientists researching this period covering almost ten centuries do not agree, which people lived in the territory of Macedonia, at the time when the Slavic people started to settle there.

This question is differently treated in the not voluminous but instructive synthesis, titled *Македонија низ вековите* (*Macedonia through*

41 *Историја...*, Vol. 1, p. 43–44.

the Centuries) by the historian Stojan Kiselinovski, from the Institute of National History who wrote:

> After three Macedonian-Roman Wars, Macedonia became a Roman province. Upon the division of the Roman Empire in the Western and Eastern Roman Empire (395 AD), Macedonia fell under the government of Byzantium. In this long historical period, the population in Macedonia changed its ethnical character, it was gradually "latinised" or fell under Byzantine influence, and lost its former ethnic character. Under Slavic pressure, a large part of the Ancient Macedonians withdrew to today's Thrace (around Edrene) and formed the region known as "Macedonia." At the end of the VI and the beginning of the VII century, Macedonia was massively populated by Slavic tribes including the Dragovits, Velegezits, Berzits, Sagudats, Rimhits and others; they were "slavicized" (by assimilation of the local small numbered pre-Slavic population that remained on the territory of Macedonia, forming the so-called "Sklavins").[42]

For the determination of representatives of this small numbered population, the author uses a new term, "pre-Slavic people." Moreover, today one cannot determine with certainty how or if the ancient and ethnic population that lived in the territory of Macedonia in the past, should be included in the ethnogenesis of the Slavic Macedonians.[43] For example, Byzantium had a heterogenic population – they spoke different languages, were comprised of different ethnic groups and for these elements to integrate, the Latin language was introduced as a state language.

In an analysis of the historical discourse, the ethnonym "Macedonian," here used to determine the people, at the beginning, was not contained in the *History of the Macedonian People* to denote the Macedonian Slavs. On the pages of the *History*, for a long time this term was competing with terms such as "Slavic nation," "Slavs," "Macedonian Slavic Society," "Slavic pagans" in the description of the time of the rule of Tsar Samuel, only to win the battle at the end (end of the X century). As authors write:

> The common use of the names "Macedonia," "Macedonian country," and "Macedonians" tells us that the use of tribal names: Dragovits,

---

[42] С. Киселиновски, *Македонија низ вековите*, Скопје 1998, p. 7–8.

[43] See: L. Moroz-Grzelak, *Obraz przeszłości antycznej w historiografii macedońskiej*, "Slavia Meridionalis" 2005, 5, p. 45–59.

> Sagudats, Smolyans, Strumians and others in the time of Tsar Samuel's rule, was already disappearing, which confirms that the long and complex ethnogenetic process of uniting the Macedonian Slavic tribes into one Macedonian people, named a "simple people" by Jovan Skilica, ended.[44]

In the second volume titled "Macedonia under the Ottoman Rule,"[45] the authors no longer try to define the concepts of "Macedonians" and "Macedonian people" but these terms are almost completely removed from the historical narrative. Instead, synonymous expressions, such as "local population," "Macedonian Christian population," and "villagers" occur, and authors pay more attention to religious divisions, writing more often about Christians and Muslims instead of ethnical groups and people.

In the modern Macedonian scientific discourse regarding the events from the end of the nineteenth and the beginning of the twentieth century (volumes II–V), the meaning of the terms Macedonia and Macedonian stabilizes and becomes separated from the meaning of a Slavic people. According to the renowned historian Ulf Brunnbauer:

> The inclusion of Ancient Macedonians in the Macedonian national narrative was a retreat from the myth about the exclusion of the "Slavic roots," having lost the need for a state now, when it was no longer a part of the Yugoslav Federation. This strive towards autochthon genealogy imposed pushing the nation's roots deep into the past, to the time before the arrival of the Slavic people, who came from somewhere else, definitively after the Greeks. This could also be a reaction to trends in Bulgaria, suppressing the emphasis on Slavic tradition and focusing on the ancient Thracians as ancestors.[46]

According to the author, the "historical sources dating before the nineteenth century rarely, if ever, speak about 'Macedonia' as political entity and about 'Macedonians' in the period when Macedonia was not a political entity (subject)."[47]

---

44 *Историја...*, Vol. 1, p. 385.

45 Ibidem.

46 U. Brunnbauer, *Drevna nacionalnost i vjekovna borba za državnost: historiografski mitowi u Republici Makedoniji (BJRM)*, in: *Historijski mitowi na Balkanu*, Sarajevo 2003, p. 303–304.

47 Ibidem.

d. Neighboring Nations' Point of View

Even today, the remains of this complicated past can be seen in the everyday linguistic picture of the world regarding Macedonians, Macedonia and the standpoints of the other nations – neighbors to the Macedonians and the ethnic minorities living in Macedonia; the existing fixed stereotypes for the nation and the state, are conditioned by a point of view.

For the Greeks, "Macedonia" is an usurpation of the name of an eponymous Greek province and the potential risk of losing it. According to the Greeks, the Macedonian state unjustly assimilates Ancient Macedonian traditions (in 1991, the symbol of the sun on the coat of arms of Macedonia was replaced with the Vergina star), which is a relatively recent event. The Petrovec airport was named after Alexander the Great and several weeks before, the government in Skopje decided to raise a monument of this great Macedonian, in the centre of the city in the public square, that not long ago bore the name of Marshal Tito.

For Serbia, Macedonians are almost Serbian: in view of the language, religion, and alphabet. In addition, Macedonia, in its current form, would have probably never existed politically, if Serbia didn't allow the formation of such a federal republic within the framework of Yugoslavia.

For Bulgaria, the Macedonian language is just a dialect of Bulgarian. For the Albanians, Macedonia is one of the countries they want to incorporate into a Greater Albania – a large part of the people in this country are Albanians, and the demographic trends show that the Albanians may soon be a majority in Macedonia.

The linguistic picture of the Macedonian // Macedonians in recent history as well as in the works of contemporary researchers, is conceptualized in the form of the same ethnonym that is determined by at least five prototypical profiles:

1. the notion of the Macedonian in ancient history – Herodotus,
2. the notion of the Macedonian Slav – a profile that dominates in the system of knowledge,
3. the notion of the Macedonian as a representative of the non-Slavic or "pre-Slavic" population,
4. the notion of the Macedonian from the advent of the Macedonian nation in modern history,
5. the notion of the Macedonian as a citizen of today's Macedonia, as a continuation of the ancient Macedonian ethnos.

What is the conceptualization and what is the profile of the Macedonian who succeeded during the XXI century, in the Macedonian common and scientific discourse, remain open questions. However, this does not depend only on the development of archaeological, historical and linguistic research, but also on the rivalry between the two main contemporary notions of the Macedonian: the Slav and the Macedonian as a continuation of the Ancient Macedonian ethnos. This rivalry is strongly dependent on political disputes and controversies, as well as the general knowledge of the Macedonians and accomplishments of Macedonian philological and historical science.

2. The Notion of the *Macedonian Language* in Scientific Discourse

Language matter is a subject of study of linguists; historical events are analyzed by historians; sociological matters are studied by sociologists etc. In scientific texts intended for people dealing with specified matters, such situations arise quite often; yet in some works of a general character (interdisciplinary and encyclopedic) or such that incorporate a didactic perspective, as are for example, the histories of nations and peoples, information processed by non-specialists can be accommodated. This usually refers to the processing of cultural information related to historical events (for example history of literature or history of language), if treated on a conceptual level of the work that is a part of the country's or peoples' history, but is not autonomous to it.

I would like to use this opportunity to present the matter pertaining to the notion of the Macedonian language in the Macedonian scientific or historical discourse. I would not delve into the complicated problem related to the interpretation of the notion discourse (there is a wide linguistic and other literature on this topic), but only emphasis that in this context the notion discourse implies the process of building a text in the form of speech acts. Namely, discourses in this work and in scientific literature are the sphere of texts as metadiscourses. Therefore, here we will mainly discuss the form of scientific texts and their contents, and less the historical events and their interpretation, although this cannot be completely avoided.

Macedonian language discourse analysis has several aspects of which the most important are: historical, legal, political, geographical and purely linguistic or other aspects related to particular scientific discipline. All these aspects developing in the text of the *History of Macedonian People* create a global discourse, with a polythematic and dynamic character, as a "discourse of the Macedonian language".

According to Maria Wojtak, this global discourse is comprised of the following parameters:

a) Thematic determination (field) (global and partial thematics and manners of their representation),
b) Ontological determination (field) (relationship between the world of discourse and reality),
c) Functional determination (dominating illocutions i.e., communication purposes),
d) Communication determination (relations between sender and receiver, time and place of communication),
e) Axiological determination (accepted and denied system of values),
f) Determination of genre conventions.[48]

Language determinations as text's surface traits and it's structure – coherence and cohesion – can be added here.

The abovementioned works, from all the abovementioned aspects, contain lot of information contributing to the definition of the Macedonian language. Namely, this work elaborates two historical metadiscourses, one of them in two editions: the three-volume *History of Macedonian People*, published by the Institute for National History (INH) in 1969 and the one-volume *Историја на македонскиот народ* (*History of Macedonian People*) published by three publishing companies: Makedonska kniga, Kultura and Misla in 1988. The second, being an abridged version of the three-volume version, is still not published by the Institute for National History, even twenty years later. The third five-volume set, of the *History of Macedonian People* published in 2005, is not taken into consideration here since some volumes completely lack information on Macedonian culture or the Macedonian language (for example v. 4), in others, information on the language and the literature are elaborated by specialists in philology and therefore, due to formal reasons, cannot be treated as part of the historical discourse.

Both *Histories* mentioned above, encompass the history of Macedonia from ancient times until the end of World War II. In these editions, the Macedonian historiosophy, treated as reflection of the meaning and substance of historical entities and events, is practically completely subordinated to the history of creation of national awareness of the Macedonians. This does not concern only the Macedonian historiography but also other historiographies in which the form and sometimes, the contents, should have been an indispensible element of the creation of national identity. Thus, the peoples see their histories not only as traces, but above all as evidence, of their authentic existence. Similarly, for the people of Southern and Eastern Europe, historism and ethnocentrism

---

[48] M. Wojtak, *Głosy z teraźniejszości. O języku współczesnej polskiej prasy*, Lublin 2010, p. 17–18.

became a matter of the mythologization of their own past, their own symbols, their own name and space, that should have said more about modern problems, than about historical myths.

Relatively much information on the history of the Macedonian language, can be found on the pages of the abovementioned works. The historical discourse on antiquity, speaks about the ancient Macedonians, but not about their language. Nonetheless, it is known that the ancient Macedonians, from this time spoke a Macedonian language that was closely related to the Ancient Greek language. The part pertaining to Byzantium gives information on the Slavic people, but there is no information on their language. Byzantine authors depict the Slavs:

> (...) as people of high stature and unusual strength, simple-hearted and extremely hospitable. They are fed with agricultural products (wheat and buckwheat) and meat of domestic and wild animals and fish. Their favorite drink was mead, as well as barley beer. They loved music. Of the instruments, they were familiar with, was the tambourine. However, they were ruled by blood revenge, didn't respect agreements and their tribes lived in strife, even in hatred. The Byzantines knew very well how to use these weakness (p. 24).

The first information pertaining to the Slavic language in written form can be found in the Chapter titled *Expansion of Christianity and Literature of the Macedonian Slavs*, where the discourse on the events of the XI century reads:

> Even while living in their old motherland, as well as after their arrival at the Balkans, the Slavs used tallies and sketches to record some things they needed. After their Baptism, writes Chernorizets Hrabar, the first advocate of a **Slavic** alphabet and literacy, they were forced to use Roman and Greek letters in the transcription of their Slavic words, but these were not suitable. The difficulty was even greater when they needed to write down those sounds of the **Slavic language**, for which there were no letters in the Roman and the Latin alphabet. This shows that the Slavic people had some literacy, before the **creation of the Slavic alphabet**.
>
> **The first Slavic alphabet** (Glagolitsa) was created by Konstantin (Cyril), and his brother Methodius who, together with the former and their disciples, translated the necessary liturgies from Greek to **the language spoken by the Macedonian Slavs in the surrounding areas of Thessaloniki. This language of the oldest translations is called the Slavic language.** Other Slavic tribes could understand this **old Macedonian**

language, because in this period there were still no meaningful differences between the Slavic forms of speech (p. 31–36).

This is the first time a definition of a Slavic language appeared in Macedonian scientific discourse, and a term that directly refers to the language of day-to-day communication; the text says:

> (...) they were **Macedonian Slavs**, who spoke the language of the surroundings of Thessaloniki (p. 30–310).

At the same time, this was a language, of which in the oldest translation, is called Slavic, and the other Slavic tribes could understand this **old Macedonian language** because in this period, there were still no meaningful differences between the Slavic languages. Further on, the text reads: The first Slavic alphabet (Glagolitsa) was created by Konstantin (Cyril), and his brother Methodius who, together with the former and their disciples, translated the necessary liturgies from Greek to the language spoken by the Macedonian Slavs in the surrounding areas of Thessaloniki.

This very short fragment, but of great importance for the historic discourse, incorporates the complete information on the origin of the Slavic people (adjective – *Macedonian Slavs*) and their *old Macedonian language* as language of the oldest Slavic translations of liturgies from Greek, to the language spoken by the Macedonian Slavs in the surrounding areas of Thessaloniki.

This hypothesis is definitely accepted in Macedonian historic texts and Macedonian historiography, however, not to the same extent in the non-Macedonian, but Slavic historical discourse, even though, if dealing with historical terminology, in Macedonian scientific texts, the Slavic language is defined as old Macedonian not only by Macedonian historians, but also linguists, providing a direct association to the language of ancient Macedonians.

The term "Old Macedonian language," meaning "Old Church Slavonic language" can be found in Macedonian scientific texts. There are historic and geographical reasons for this – the place of the creation of this language can be found on a map of modern Macedonia, and today's Macedonians consider Sts. Cyril and Methodius, to be their historical ancestors.

For example, the Polish Slavic texts do not use the term "język staromacedoński" (Old Macedonian language) in the sense of Old Church Slavonic language so as to avoid an association with the language of the ancient Macedonians. Instead, the term "język staro-cerkiewno-słowiański"

(Old Church Slavonic language), which means old Slavic language meant to be used in church, is used and is accepted in the Polish Slavic discourse. In his "Macedonian Grammar," Horace Lunt uses the same notion and writes about "Old Church Slavonic".[49]

The renowned Slavist and Macedonist, František Mareš, goes even further and writes:

> The Church Slavonic language is simply regarded as a literary language for all Slavs. For the smart and opinioned missionaries, the linguistic norm was something elastic, which, from a modern linguistics stand point, is a positive trait. Language always adapts to its environment. Although it was standardized, originally founded on a single dialect, in the other Slavic areas, the dialect of the Thessaloniki area was not a foreign language that could not be changed because it belonged to other people. It was also a native literary language in Thessaloniki and in Moravia and in Pannonia, as well as in Ohrid and Preslav and the Croatian coast and Russia and so on.[50]

In the chapters pertaining to the cultural conditions of the late XI century (p. 69–74), the Macedonian language is indirectly involved when discussing the important transcription centers in Macedonia:

> (...) various anthologies of sermons of the celebrated orators of the Christian Church, anthologies of Christian poetry as well as short stories and novels were created and transcribed. The work proceeded in several important transcription centers as were the centers in Ohrid, Mount Athos, Lesnovo, Skopska Crna Gora and other smaller centers that existed within many Macedonian monasteries. There are no prominent literary names from this period, although some of the transcribers left behind many transcribed manuscripts. Many novels and short stories, such as the novel on Troy and especially the novel about Alexander, which came from Byzantine and Latin literature in Slavic literature, were transcribed and read in Macedonia (p. 69–70).

Unfortunately, there is no information on the language in which the texts were written or translated. Instead of a term for precise language, the authors use the criterion of the territorial affiliation of the text:

1. *From the monuments of Slavic literacy that were created in Macedonia from the XI to the late XII century...*

---

[49] H.G. Lunt, *Old Church Slavonic Grammar*, 7th ed., Berlin–New York 2001 (1st ed. Mouton 1955).

[50] F.V. Mareš, *Makedonská gramatika*, Skopje 1994, p. 4.

2. *Many novels and short stories were read and transcribed in Macedonia...*
3. *Various records and inscriptions from ancient to the most recent times remain in Macedonia...*

or it is spoken about appurtenances to a certain type of literature:

1. *As in the case with other Slavic literature, many hieroglyphic works belong to Macedonian medieval literature...*
2. *Apocryphal works enter Macedonian medieval literature very early...*
3. *As in the literature of other South Slavic peoples, almost all works that bring joy to man's soul were also present in Macedonian literature* (p. 70).

The term Macedonian spoken language, appears as a special notion in the Macedonian historical discourse related to events from the XV to the XVII century. In the late XVI and especially in the XVII and XVIII century in Macedonia came a period of translation of anthologies with different content, called *damaskini* in which elements of the Macedonian spoken language started to spring up. Yet, further on, this term competes with the notion of a Slavic language as the authors write:

> Along with the opening of monastic schools in the Slavic language, Greek schools also emerged in the cities (p. 99).

The following part of the Macedonian historical discourse on language refers to the events from the second half of the XIX century, related to the development of textbooks in Macedonia. This is the first time the notion of a *Macedonian language* is used without the adjectives "old" or "spoken."

> The struggle to overturn the Greek language and to introduce Macedonian in the schools in Macedonia, was started by a small-numbered Macedonian intelligentsia, at the same time with the struggle against the Greek clergy (p. 115).

Further on, authors describe the idea of the creation of Macedonian literary language, separated from the Bulgarian language:

> The first to introduce practical use of the **Macedonian language** in textbooks, was the Dojran bishop Partheniy Zografski from Galichnik. He wrote two textbooks: *A Concise Holy History of the Old and New Testament Church* (1857) and *An Elementary Education for Children* (1859). However, it should

> be pointed out that the language spoken by Zografski is a dialect from the surroundings of Galichnik, and besides, it was the general written language i.e. "the Bulgarian-Macedonian written language" that Zografski envisaged as the language of compromise, with elements of both languages. The same applies to the language in which Grigor Prlichev wrote and being driven by the idea of a single Slavic language and culture, he even tried to be its creator. He writes in a language composed of Macedonian, Bulgarian and Slavic church language, but his attempt is unsuccessful (p. 115, 117).

However, it should be mentioned here that the language spoken by P. Zografski is a dialect from the surroundings Zografski envisaged the general written language i.e., the Macedonian – Bulgarian written language, as a language of compromise with elements of both of them. The same refers to the language used by Grigor Prlichev.

He wrote:

> (...) carried along by the idea of a single Slavic language and culture, he is trying to be its creator, too. He writes in a language comprised of Macedonian, Bulgarian and Church Slavonic, but his attempt is unsuccessful (p. 117).

In the analyzed discourse there are no information on the language of Konstantin Miladinov, except for one sentence, which is about the poem *Т'га за југ* (*Longing for the South*), written in the Macedonian language and about *The Anthology of Folk Songs*, as follows:

> The publication of the *Anthology of Macedonian Folk Songs*, Riddles and Customs, compiled by Konstantin Miladinov, in Zagreb 1861, with the financial assistance of the Croatian Bishop Josip Juraj Strossmayer, was a paramount event for the Macedonian culture as well as the cultures of the other South Slavic peoples (p. 116).

Furthermore, there is no information on the language of the anthologies compiled by Cepenkov and Shapkarev. Regarding these collectors of national folklore, we can read:

> In the cultural field, the tradition established by the brothers Miladinov continued: that is the publishing of the national folklore treasure. Kuzman Shapkarev from Ohrid and Marko K. Cepenkov from Prilep were also prominent in this field (p. 116).

In the period between the two world wars, Macedonian poetry and drama developed in proportions that hadn't been observed before. On the scene enters Kocho Solev-Racin, who during his turbulent and fruitful life managed to publish only one poetry book in the Macedonian language, *Бели мугри* (*White Dawns*), which was illegally printed in 1939 in Croatia. Racin's first literary works are poems written and published in the Serbian language in the period between 1928 and 1934. Kole Nedelkovski (1912–1941) published two books of poems, one after the other, in the Macedonian language: *М'скавици* (*Lightnings*) (1940) and *Пеш по светот* (*On Foot Around the World*). There isn't any detailed information on the Macedonian language, in which these texts were written, except for the following sentence:

> In the language of these writers one can feel the strong influence of folk poetry (p. 268, 117).

The same applies to the language of Venko Markovski for whom we read:

> Venko Markovski in a relatively short interval of time, from 1938 to 1941, published several poetry books and poems: *Народни бигори, Огинот, Огномет, Лулкина песна, Гоце, Илинден, Чудна е Македонија, Бие дванаесет* (*Folk Sorrows, The Fire, The Fireworks, Lullabies, Gotse, Ilinden, Strange is Macedonia* and *It strikes Twelve*, respectively) (p. 268).

Many traces of Macedonian folk poetry influences, can be felt in Venko Markovski's writings.

> Macedonian drama is created and developed with prominent folklore features and the observation of social moments and use of the mother tongue. Vasil Iljoski (1902) first began to deal with the dramatic literature in the Yugoslav part of Macedonia. Anton Panov (1905–1968) is the author of the popular play *Печалбари* (*Migrant Workers*), Risto Krle (1900) wrote three plays with themes of emigration, activities of foreign troops in Macedonia and the commercial ruining of the craftsmen (p. 269).

Here we get information on the language of these plays:

> The plays were written and performed in dialects (the dialects of Kumanovo, Skopje, Galichnik and Struga) (p. 268–269).

The phenomenon of the literary Macedonian language from the period between the two world wars is still waiting for a more serious and deeper elaboration, because the language of the poets Racin,

Nedelkovski, Markovski and the playwrights Iljovski, Krle, Panov influence the form of the Macedonian language and Macedonian literary norm to a decisive degree.

Information on the Macedonian discourse which refers to the World War II pertains only to the Macedonian language, used in culture dissemination and the enlightenment of people in which newspapers, bulletins, radio news and other means of information in the Macedonian language occupy a special place. Thus, during the National Liberation War, almost all party organizations, military units and partisan detachments issued their own newspapers, bulletins, etc.

A conceptualization of the notion of the Macedonian language... Macedonian language discourse, is largely objective, but to the same extent ethnocentric. In the case of Macedonia and its Slavic language, the first phase of national form creation was the struggle for national culture and its foundation, the Macedonian language. This caused a compensatory response, an increase of the sense of national singularity and, in the end, ethnocentrism.

V. The Macedonian Language versus other Languages in Macedonia

The majority of the Republic of Macedonia's – a state in the South Eastern region of the European continent – population speaks the Macedonian language (65%), recognized as an official language. In addition, the Albanian language is used by 25% of the population as well as the Turkish and Serbian languages and other languages. Orthodox Christianity is the predominant religion in the Republic (64% of the population), but Muslims are also an important part comprising ¼ of the society (more than 500,000). This number also includes Orthodox Albanians, of whom the majority are concentrated in the region of Dolna, Mala and Golema Reka (Lower, Small and Big River) in 17 villages. The people who live there are known as Mijaks (Macedonian: Мијаци, *Mijaci*), Mijacs – Orthodox or Muslim Macedonians whose mother tongue is the Albanian language and they are Orthodox Christians. A portion of these ethnic Macedonians are referred to as Shkreti.[51]

In the family of Slavic languages, the Macedonian language, together with the Bulgarian, Serbian, Croatian and Slovenian languages, belong to the South Slavic language group. Today, it is the official language of Macedonia, and yet, in accordance with the constitutional amendments and with the Framework Agreement signed in Ohrid in 2001 t. 6.5 and 6.6:

> Any other language spoken by at least 20% of the population is also an official language in terms of local government, in municipalities where

[51] The Macedonian word *Шкрет* (*Shkret*) originates from the Gheg (Albanian) expression *Шкја* (*Shkia*) meaning Slav. A large part of Macedonians living in Western Macedonia – today's Shkrets – were Islamized beacause, as Christians in the Ottoman Empire, they were terrorized by the Islamized Albaninas, and those who stayed true to their ancestorial faith, accepted the Albanian language in the 19th century. Today, Islamized Shkrets form Gorna Reka are considered to be Albanian, although their ethnic origin is purely Macedonian. Recently, a public request was made for the church Mass to be held in the Albanian language, which was accepted by the suffragan of the Macedonian Orthodox Church.

a certain community comprises at least 20% of the population of the municipality, the language of that community will be used as an official language in addition to Macedonian.

It is estimated that the Macedonian language is spoken by 2 to 2.5 million people, including the Macedonian diaspora.

The legal status of languages in Macedonia, the Macedonian language, as an official language, as well as other languages, other than Macedonian, was established by Amendment V of the Constitution of Republic of Macedonia:

AMENDMENT V

1.

The Macedonian language, written using its Cyrillic alphabet, is the official language on the whole territory of the Republic of Macedonia and in its international relations.

Any other language spoken by at least 20 percent of the citizens is also an official language, written using its alphabet, as specified in this Article.

Official personal documents of citizens speaking an official language other than Macedonian shall be issued in the Macedonian language, as well as in that language in accordance with the law.

Any citizen living in a unit of local self-government in which at least 20 percent of the citizens speak an official language other than Macedonian may use any of the official languages and their alphabets in communication with the local office of the central government.

The local offices with competencies for these units of local self-government shall reply in the Macedonian language and its Cyrillic alphabet, as well as in the official language and alphabet used by the citizens.

Any citizen may use any official language and its alphabet to communicate with the Ministries, which shall reply in the Macedonian language and its Cyrillic alphabet, as well as in the official language and alphabet used by the citizen.

In the organs of the Republic of Macedonia, any official language other than Macedonian may be used in accordance with the law.

In the units of local self-government, the language and the alphabet used by at least 20 percent of the citizens is an official language in addition to the Macedonian language and the Cyrillic alphabet.

The bodies of the units of local self-government decide on the use of the languages and alphabets spoken by less than 20% of the citizens in that unit of local self-government.[52]

---

52 Constitution of Republic of Macedonia, http: // www.sobranie.mk/ustav-na-rm.nspx (accessed on: 15 February 2015).

Macedonians and Albanians, Turks, Roma, Vlachs (Aromanians called Kucovlachs) and other national and ethnic groups, live in this country with population of 2.5 million people.

The statistics, which indeed, never reflect the factual situation, present the following data (from the 2002 census):[53]

Total	**2,022,547**	
Macedonians	1,297,981	64.1%
Albanians	509,083	25.1%
Turks	77,959	3.85%
Roma	53,879	2.66%
Serbs	35,939	1.77%
Vlachs	9,695	0.48%
Bosniaks	17,018	0.84%
other	20,993	1.03%
of whom		
Orthodox Christian	1,310,184	64.7%
Muslim	674,015	33.3%
Catholic	7,008	0.34%
other	30,820	1.52%

The census also included data regarding the mother tongue, but there are not many differences in this regard compared to the data on nationality. Those who declared they were Macedonian speak the Macedonian language, Albanians speak the Albanian language, and Turks speak the Turkish language. There are differences only in regards to the Roma people. Out of a total number of 53,879 people, 38,528 speak the Roma language. The total number of Serbs is 35,939, among whom 24,773 speak the Serbian language. Among the 17,018 Bosnians, 8,560 can speak the Bosnian language and among the 9,695 Vlachs, 6,884 speak the Aromanian language.

In this county of two and a half million people, together with the Macedonians, also live Albanians, Turks, Roma, Vlachs (Aromanians called Kucovlachs) as well as other communities. All these groups speak their own mother tongue but they are also familiar, more or less, with the languages of their neighbors. So far, however, there are no statistical data to point out how many languages were and are spoken in Macedonia. It is solely by following population statistics that we can indirectly draw conclusions in regards to this question. However, it never

53 *Census of population, households and apartments in Republic of Macedonia, 2002*, Skopje, May 2004, p. 581 and 591.

actually reflects the actual situation. It doesn't necessarily mean that Macedonian is spoken only where Macedonians live.

In the history of the Macedonian language, after World War II, situations and necessities arose when the destiny of the Macedonian linguistic norm was dependent on decrees and decisions issued by linguistic committees that were formed at the time. The extra-linguistic conditions of this phenomenon were particularly noticeable in the Balkan reality, during the period when the fate of the Macedonian standard was influenced by a few, but influential scientific elites, who implemented a language policy in accordance with the prevailing political option. Given the conditions in this federal republic, subordinate to Belgrade till 1991, this was not a difficult task.

In sociolinguistics, the notion of language policy represents a group of directives which concern the formation of a relationship between society and language. This standpoint is characteristic for the situation of the Polish language and Polish society, which is almost unilingual and where Polish is the dominant language. However, in a majority of European states, the situation differs from the one in Poland. This is especially true for those states populated by cultural, ethnic and national communities, who speak different languages. Macedonia can also be counted amongst these states.

The state language policy played a great role at the dawn of Macedonia in the 20th century, and according to this policy, the Macedonian language was to be acknowledged, and a Macedonian standard to be developed and disseminated in all spheres of social life. Political activists, who were also specialists in the field of linguistics or literature (writers), were entrusted with this task. In Macedonia, the task was assigned to Blazhe Koneski, who was a young activist educated in Belgrade and Sofia, a poet and man of letters who at the time, in the 1940s, codified the Macedonian language. In this regard, the modern French Balkanologist, Bernard Lory,[54] in 1998 wrote that:

> Le choix des normes du macédonien répondait à des critèries linguistiques et politiques.
> (The choice of standards meets Macedonian linguistic and political criteria.)

Macedonians who are proud of their literary and language tradition can hardly agree with such a hypothesis. With great confidence,

---

54 B. Lory, *Approches de l'identité macédonienne, La République de Macédoine: Nouvelle venue dans le concert européen*, Sous la Direction de Christophe Chiclet, Bernard Lory, Paris 1998, p. 22.

they call upon the genetic connection of modern Macedonian literature with Church Slavic literature, and yet, now they search for their linguistic roots in their ancient culture, in the common territories, in the identity of the biblical and mythological archetypes and topoi.

During the past centuries, the Balkan peoples did not have their own standardized languages and spoke dialects with adopted language features of the languages spoken by their neighbors. This is how the Balkan language union was formed and was defined as a group of genetically unrelated Balkan languages which, nonetheless, had a similar grammatical structure created during a period of mutual historical and societal coexistence. These languages were subdued to interference processes on a grammatical and lexical plan, and they are characterized by bilingualism and multilingualism. Bilingualism, characterizing the Macedonian and the Albanian language environment of the Macedonians and the Albanians, respectively, as the most numerous language communities, is the most characteristic phenomenon in Macedonia today.

During the period when Macedonia was part of the Ottoman Empire, the official and most prestigious language was Turkish (15th–19th c.), whereas in the first half of the 20th century, the Serbian language was the official language of the Kingdom of Yugoslavia. During this time, the Serbian language was the most prestigious and official language in Macedonia. Moreover, the complete Macedonian lexical corpus was taken from the Serbian language. The interference primarily concerned oral communication, and secondly the uncodified written language. Until the break-up of Yugoslavia, the Serbian language was an intermediary language for the introduction of internationalisms in the Macedonian language. After World War II, in the newly formed Republic of Macedonia, as part of the Federal Republic of Yugoslavia, the so-called Serbo-Croatian language functioned as a universal state language, and the Macedonian language was the official language in the Republic of Macedonia. This linguistic situation further contributed to the fact that the Serbian language was used in churches and education until the Bulgarian occupation in April 1941, when the Bulgarian language took over and dominated, until the capitulation of Bulgaria. After World War II, teaching was conducted in the Macedonian language, however, studies of the Serbo-Croatian language were compulsory in elementary education. In addition, the relatively small language territory of Macedonia, was dialectically divided.

This especially concerned the south-western part of the Macedonian territory, which in its larger part is inhabited by Albanians. This territory includes the following Macedonian dialects: Prilep-Bitola, Poreče-Kičevo, Ohrid-Prespa, Debar, Reka, Lower Polog and the Upper Polog dialect. Moreover, the Albanians who live in this territory also have their own dialects. There are also Turks and Aromanians, who have lived there since the time of the Ottoman Empire.

Therefore, a new problem of diglossia and polyglossia emerged in Macedonia. Macedonian linguistic circumstances include diglossia between the prestigious official language used for official communication and the native language (which generally includes the dialects used by native speakers for unofficial communication). In different historical periods, before and after the independence, there existed a Turkish-Serbian-Macedonian diglossia among Macedonians, and Turkish-Serbian-Macedonian-Albanian polyglossia among Albanians.

From the perspective of the language policies implemented by the communist government of the former Yugoslavia towards the Macedonian and the other languages used by the peoples of this republic, Macedonia was ethnic state of the Macedonian people. In accordance with this hypothesis, the Macedonian language was the official language. National minorities (nationalities) could use their language in the private sphere as well as publically, in the territory on which they lived.

After the breakup of Yugoslavia and the formation of the Republic of Macedonia, the functions of the Macedonian language broadened. It gained all functions of the previously prestigious Serbo-Croatian language, and became a means for communication in foreign relations and in the army. Some researchers claim that in the Republic of Macedonia, the Macedonian language became a means for assimilation of the minority groups who lived in this territory, especially the Christian non-Slavic peoples (Aromanians) and the non-Muslim Albanians.[55]

[55] See: V.A. Friedman, *Charakterystyka socjologiczna współczesnego języka macedońskiego*, "Socjolingwistyka" 1993, XII–XIII, p. 183–197.

VI. In the Circle of Politics and Linguistics

At the dawn of Macedonia in the 20th century, language politics had a very important role to play. The Macedonian language was to be recognized, and a Macedonian standard was to be developed and disseminated in all spheres of life. This task was entrusted to those people who were politically active at the time, and were also specialists in the field of literature and linguistics. Language commissions led by social activists, writers and linguists, were appointed to work on the codification of the Macedonian alphabet. After fierce discussions, a Macedonian alphabet was established and the central Macedonian dialects were chosen as the basis for the standard language.

The language policy of the country played a great role here, especially with regards to the codification of the Macedonian alphabet, which – in accordance with the will of its authors – should have increased the difference between the Macedonian and the Bulgarian languages, and decrease the differences between the Macedonian and the Serbian languages. The Bulgarian Cyrillic alphabet is closer to the Russian alphabet, but the Macedonian Cyrillic alphabet is under significant Serbian influence. The Bulgarian alphabet includes letters to represent, for example, the half voiced sounds – in the Old Slavic language; these sounds were reproduced and were represented with the corresponding letters: the front and back yer – were eliminated from the phonological system and the Macedonian alphabet. In the Orthography of 1945, the half voiced sound was granted a graphic representation in the form of an apostrophe. *Љ, њ, џ* were introduced in the Macedonian alphabet in accordance with the Serbian letters,[56] as well as the Latin *j*, after Vuk Karadžić.

After World War II, the Macedonian language was recognized as an official language of the newly formed Republic of Macedonia, as part of the Yugoslav Federation. Although the Macedonian language was recognized as an official language of the Republic, in practice, the

---

[56] Vuk Karadžić carried out a reform in orthography in the first half of the 19 century. He removed the letters ъ, ь, and introduced *љ, њ, џ* as well as the Latin letter *j*.

role of a dominant language – higher ranking, from the perspective of prestige and functions – was performed by the Serbo-Croatian language. Some researchers, including Ch. Voss,[57] are on the opinion that the Serbo-Croatian language influenced the Macedonian standard so strongly, that the larger part of the population in Greek Macedonia, stopped feeling their mother tongue, leading to a quick Hellenization of this population.

1. The Macedonian Language and the Framework Agreement (*Рамковен договор*)

Since independence in 1991, the Macedonian language has essentially been the sole official language of the Republic of Macedonia, overthrowing, at least constitutionally, the predominance of the Serbian language. A large part of Macedonia's inhabitants, according to some estimates 20% to 40% with a tendency for growth, is composed of Albanians who have so far had the status of a nationality. The majority of them are Muslims, and the minority are Catholics, however, these religious groups are characterized by a very fast growing birthrate with ever increasing political aspirations. Since the very beginning of Macedonian independence, unsatisfied by their status, the Macedonian Albanians have demanded changes, especially regarding matters concerning the Albanian language and its equality with the Macedonian language.

In the fall of 1998, parliamentary elections were held in Macedonia and the coalition of VMRO-DPMNE[58] and the Democratic alternative won the elections. The coalition was then broadened by the Democratic Party of the Albanians (DPA). When the Albanian party entered the government as part of the coalition, it's politics were moderate and it wanted to solve all Macedonian – Albanian conflicts by means of negotiations and agreements. Such politics were not appealing to all Albanians. Some considered that the Party's leader, Arbën Xhaferi, did not care about the Albanian minority but realized his own private interests.

---

57 Ch. Voss, *Great Macedonia as a "mental map" in the 20th and 21st century*, "Sprawy Narodowościowe" 2007, 31, p. 163–169.

58 ВМРО-ДПМНЕ, mac. Внатрешна македонска револуционерна организација – Демократска партија за македонско национално единство (Internal Macedonian Revolutionary Organization – Democratic Party for Macedonian National Unity).

The Albanian group, increasing in numbers, in Macedonia radicalized their demands.

At the beginning of 2001, units of the UÇK[59] with approximately 5 thousand fighters, started armed actions against police stations of the Macedonian police, and against military units and communication networks for destruction of hydro-energetic system and the complete disorganization of life in the Republic of Macedonia, while the Macedonian population in those territories with majority of Albanians, was forced to leave their homes.

There were casualties on both sides, and foreign intervention was needed to put an end to the armed conflict – via pressure and mediation from the European Union and NATO.

From the 15 to the 25 June 2001, negotiations were opened for granting Albanians a more extensive autonomy, however, they ended without any results. On 24 June, Javier Solana managed to establish a ceasefire and NATO troops evacuated armed UÇK units groups from the village of Aracinovo near Skopje. Negotiations between Macedonian and Albanian representatives began on 20 July 2001. However, fighting ceased only after the signing of the *Framework Agreement* (мас. *Рамковен договор*) on 13 of August 2001. The Albanian language was granted a principal position in this political settlement by compromise. The status of the Albanian language was raised, however, it was not aligned with the position of the Macedonian language in the country. Both languages formally perform the function of official languages and are both used for the publication of state documents. However, the Macedonian language remains the universal state and working language.

The standpoint accepted with the Framework Agreement led to an even greater linguistic and ethnical instability in the Macedonian state, as a dual-national state. In certain Macedonian municipalities, where the Albanian population is more numerous (Tetovo, Gostivar), students in elementary schools protested because they didn't want to attend lectures in the Macedonian language, and demanded to be allowed to have their lectures in the Albanian language.

The situation gets even graver because there are no mechanisms for the integration and assimilation of Albanians with the Macedonians, and this brings Macedonia closer to the status of dual-national, bilingual state, which today is still an unacceptable vision from a political standpoint, however, from a linguistic one, it has already become a reality.

---

59 UÇK – National Liberation Army (alb.: Ushtria Çlirimtare Kombëtare).

2. *За македонцките работи* (*On Macedonian Matters*) by Krste Petkov Misirkov i.e. How A Political Discourse is Created

The scientific work of Krste Petkov Misirkov, according to one available bibliography included in the phototypic edition of *За македонцките работи*[60] from 1974, comprises 21 of the more important works of different character. These mainly elaborate cultural problematic and the majority are published in Sofia; two are in the Russian language and are published in Odessa, and for several works, place of publishing is unknown. At the bottom of all these analyses, the book titled *За македонцките работи* (*On Macedonian Matters*), published in Sofia in 1903 for the first time, can be conspicuously singled out. Several Macedonian editions of the work have been published so far – the last one in 2003[61] by the Tabernakul publishing house in Skopje. The same year, the Macedonian Academy of Sciences and Arts published a parallel Macedonian – English version of Misirkov's work,[62] for the 100th anniversary of the first edition.

In comparison to the numerous different jubilee editions of K.P. Misirkov's work, the work's critical analyses are small in number, given the importance these texts are prescribed in Macedonia. Here, primarily, we should single out the work of B. Korubin, *Јазикот на Крсте П. Мисирков* (*Krste Petkov Misirkov's Language*) from 1956, three articles by T. Dimitrovski and one on Misirkov's geographical system by T. Stamatoski.[63] In this regard, the urgent need of substantial linguistic elaboration of all Misirkov's texts emerges, not only regarding lexis

---

60 See the following editions: К.П. Мисирков, *За македонцките работи*, II – издание, Предговор кон II-то издание: Д. Џамбаз, Скопје 1946; К.П. Мисирков, *За македонцките работи*. Јубилејното издание по повод на стогодишнината од раѓањето на авторот, Скопје 1974. Only 2009, on the occasion of 135 years of Krste Petkov Misirkov's birth, NUB „St. Kliment Ohridski" published a personal biography on this national ideologist, slavicist, folklorist and publicist. The bibliography *Krste Petkov Misirkov* includes six references for monographic publications and articles in anthologies and magazines by Misirkov and on Misirkov. *Крсте Петков Мисирков, Библиографија*, Скопје 2009.

61 К.П. Мисирков, *За македонцките работи*, јубилејно издание, Табернакул, Скопје 2003.

62 К.П. Мисирков, *За македонцките работи*. Фототипно издание по повод 100-годишнината од излегувањето на книгата; *On Macedonian Matters*, приредил Блаже Ристовски. Transl. by A. McConnell, Скопје 2003.

63 See: Т. Димитровски, *Избор од библиографијата за К.П. Мисирков*, in: К.П. Мисирков, *За македонцките...*, p. 173–175.

and graphics, but also morphology, syntax and cohesion[64] of expression together with the author's style. To enable these analyses, a full critical edition is necessary, not only of Misirkov's work *За македонцките работи*, but also of all his texts, and not only by use of samples of the original versions (*editio princeps*) (phototypes), since these are already discovered in Macedonian philology, but all versions of the texts (*editio ne varietur, editio posthuma, editio purificata*), historical and linguistic commentary and glossary.

The publishing of Misirkov's work *За македонцките работи*[65] in Sofia in 1903, is considered a historical event in Macedonia. In his work, the author presents his political credo regarding national questions, and above all else, engaged the issue related to the creation and codification of the Macedonian literary language. This part of the discussion is proceeded by: an introduction of five separate texts, named:[66]

1. Шчо напраифме и шчо требит да праиме за однапред?
   (What have we already done and what we ought to do in the future?)

2. Имат ли се нужда од македонцки национални научно-литературни другарства?
   (Is there a need for Macedonian national scientific, scholarly and literary societies?)

3. Националниіот сепаратизм: земіишчето на коіе се имат развиіено и ке се развиіат за однапред.
   (National separatism: the soil on which it has grown and it will vontinue to grow in the future.)

4. Состауала, состауат и можит ли Македониіа да состауат от себе оддел'на етнографцка и политична іединица.
   (Can Macedonia turn itself into a separate ethnographic and political unit? Has it already done so? Is it doing so now?)

---

64 Л. Минова-Ѓуркова, *Дистрибуцијата на што и кој(што) во релативната реченица кај Мисирков*, "Литературен збор" 1974, 21 (2), p. 26–34; *Некои карактеристики на релативната реченицаа во јазикот на К.П. Мисирков*, "Македонски јазик" 1974, 25, p. 181–193.

65 К.П. Мисирков, *За македонцките работи*, II – издание...; К.П. Мисирков, *За македонцките работи*. Јубилејното издание по повод на стогодишнината од раѓањето на авторот...

66 К.П. Мисирков, *За македонцките работи*. Фототипно издание...; *On Macedonian Matters*. (All quotes are taken from this abridged edition.)

5. Неколку зборои за македонцкиіот литературен іазик.
(A Few Words on the Macedonian Literary Language.) (p. 311)

Four of the texts listed by the author are thematically related, although two of them were given as speeches at different times (the first on 21 September the second on 28 September 1903, and the third in October of the same year), all three at the forum of the Literary and Scientific Association "St. Kliment Ohridski" in St. Petersburg. Four of the five chapters are actually Misirkov's speeches that he read at meetings of the Macedonian literary circle in Russia.

The last text included in the chapter titled *Неколку зборои за македонцкиот литературен іазик* (*A Few Words on the Macedonian Literary Language*) contains, as stated by the scientific literature, the first well-argued and conceptually well elaborated project on the codification of the Macedonian literary language. Although all texts are published chronologically and are separately gathered in one volume, this fact is constantly emphasized at the beginning of the text on the language. The other texts, even though they are not related to the language issue, are filled with a web of political theses. This is not a coincidence, given that the entire text meets the genre condition, which we may call political discourse.

At the end of the XX century and the beginning of the XXI century, the concept of discourse began to be current and contemporary, and especially popular in the humanities. However, this notion was also vaguely and ambiguously defined.

It is interesting, that the notion of discourse is related to new tendencies in linguistics for the first time having larger and more complex linguistic structures, such as texts and expressions not only of traditional types of such units as their subject matter. These include: phonemes, morphemes or sentences (simple and compound). A description of language as a static product of the speaker is denied in research in favor of analysis of dynamic communication in cultural, societal and other aspects. In this context, the concept of discourse as a communication event, which sometimes refers to specific individual cases – single speech acts or generally, for specific collections and types of language events, is introduced.

The analysis that needs to be used to treat Misirkov's text as a political discourse, generally refers to the last fragment of his book, titled: *Неколку зборои за македонцкиот литературен іазик* (*A Few Words on the Macedonian Literary Language*).[67] This text is comprised of two

[67] This part was first published as a separate book in 1948 by the State publishing of Macedonia, Skopje 1948, under the title: *Неколку зборои за македонцкијот*

parts – the first, a political part, in which the author states his opinion on the Macedonian national question and the second, in which he talks about the codification of the Macedonian literary language.

From a formal point of view, the most important characteristic of this non-scientific discourse is the fact that on an informational level, rhetorical means are more often used than scientific methodology. Moreover, logical argumentation is clouded by a strong tendency of persuasion.

In Misirkov's text, besides the division on thematic microstructures, political and linguistic, segmentation of opinions can be singled out, logically and substantively dividing the text in two – metatextually. The second contains four introductory stances, which are metatextual and only introduce the discourse content:

> 1. Во четирите горни статиіи на оваа книга іас сакаф да обрнам погледите на моіите сонародници на нуждата од іедно корено изменуаін'е на досегашниіот процес на нашето дуовно развиіаін'е, као и на тоа, да моіите возгледи во тоі случаі не сет нешчо ноо и безосновно, а сет само чекор напред во досегашното развиіаін'е на нашето национално самосознаін'е и да сет затоа сосем природни и основател'ни.
> (In the previous four sections of this book my aim was to drew the attention on my compatriots to the need for making a radical change in the process of our spiritual development to date and also to point out that in this respect my views are by no means something new and unsubstantiated but merely a step forward in the development of our national self-awareness, and hence perfectly natural and justifiable.)

> 2. Се разбират, оти во іедна мала книга, као шчо іет оваа моіата, не се можат подробно да се разгледаат сите задирнати прашаін'а. За секоіе од ниф би се можела да напишит по іедна цела книга. Но сега за сега от таквиіа подробни разгледуаін'а за задирнатите питаін'а се немат ушче голема и неотложна нужда; за тоа требаше за сите од ниф да се кажит по неколку зборои, зашчо они іедно без друго сет неіасни и неразбирливи. Осем разгледуаін'ето на сите задирнати прашаін'а, за да бидит іасно поіауаін'ето на книгата, сега ке

литературен јазик со предговор на Крум Тошев (*A Few Words on the Macedonian Literary Language* with a preface by Krume Toshev). The commentary of this edition made by editors is interesting to mention: "Misirkov's language is completely preserved. If there had been any inconsistencies in orthography, they were not corrected. For technical reasons, the sign i used by Misirkov where we use j was replaced with 'j' throughout." (p. 11).

> требит да се кажит неколку збори за своіевременоста на книгата и нашиіот литературен іазик.
> (It is, of course, in a book as small as this to enter into a more detailed consideration of all the questions involved, for each by itself might merit a whole book. At present, however, there is no great or pressing need for such detailed consideration of these matters; nevertheless, it has been necessary to say a few words about each of them, because if they are taken independently of one another, they become unclear and incomprehensible. But if the appearance of this book is to be justified, we must now, in addition to considering these matters, say a few words about the topical importance of this book and about our literary language.)
>
> 3. Мнозина, можит, ке речат, оти вистина арно іет чоек да се позамислит над прашаін'ата, задирнати во таіа книга, но сега ушче не му іет времето. Со оваа книга, ке речат они, се носит раздор и разіединуаін'е мег'у нас, на место соіединуаін'ето, коіе сега за сега ни іет така нужно. За македонцка народност, македонцка литература и литературен іазик ниіе ке можиме да му мислиме само, кога ке заживеіеме іеднаш слободен политичен жиот; а до тогаі нам ни требит, ниіе да сме соіединени и да остаиме на страна националното прашаін'е.
> (Many people will perhaps say that although the problems raised in this book are indeed worthy of consideration, the moment is not yet opportune. For this book, they would say, brings us strife and discord instead of the unity which we so dearly need at present. We can start thinking about the Macedonian nation, Macedonian literature, and the Macedonian literary language only when we finally begin to lead a free political life, and until then we ought to be united and leave aside the national question.) (p. 282–283)

Misirkov continues Chapter 4 in the same manner – he replies by using interrogative sentences of the already initiated discourse:

> 4. На тоа іас можам да одгоорам само ово: по моіето мислеін'е, сегашните, т. е. міурштегцките реформи сет максимум, шчо можа да ископчит од Европа револуциіата. Револуциіата на пролет ке бидит наі глупаото, шчо можиме ниіе да напраиме. Со револуциіата на пролет ке се користат само нашите неприіатели, коіи си имаат само есапи, противни на нашите национални интереси. Револуциіата на пролет само ке ни унишчит совршено нас и ке унишчит плодоите, добиіени од неіа до сега, оти она ке бидит

напраена не против Турцко, а против него и Реформаторцките Сили, и оти тоа ке бидит не по наши есапи, а по есапите на некоіа Голема Сила и некоіи мали балканцки држаіи, коіи ке не натераат нас да се дигниме, а после ке не остаат на стред пат; наі после, оти ниіе, ако против сите аргументи на здравиіот смисл пак подигниме востааін'е, ке бидиме само осноа на дипломатцка, борба мег'у реформаторцките држаи и некоіа трек'а, коіа борба ке се свршит само нашето понишчуаін'е. За тоа ниіе, требит, да се откажиме от секоіа мисл'а за революциіа на пролет, ушче поеке, шчо реформите ке се воведат, зашчо со ниф іет врзана честта на две Големи Сили, коіи сет во стаін'е да постаат се́ на своіето, – и да се зафатиме за ноа т.е. културна борба, во коіа прво место, ке требит да зимат прашаін'ето за нашата народност и нашето национално – религиозно развиіаін'е. Значит, истом сега му іет времето да се мислит за іазико наш, нашата национална литература и воспитааін'е во национален дух.
(In answer to this I can only say that it in my opinion the present, i.e., the Muzstag, reforms are the most that the revolution can hope to get out of Europe. The most foolish thing we could do would be to launch a spring revolution; it would be of benefit to no one but our enemies who are working against our national interests. A spring revolution would only bring about our total ruin and destroy all that has been so far achieved, because it would be directed not against the Turks but against the Reform Powers. For this would all happen not in accordance with our interests but in compliance with the calculations of some Great Power and certain of the small Balkan slates which would force us into action and then abandon us in the middle of the road. And finally, if, in spite of all the dictates of common sense, we were to launch an uprising we would simply become the basis for a diplomatic battle against the reform states and some third force, and this would result in our destruction. This is why we should give up all idea of a spring revolution, all the more so since the reforms will be introduced, because they are bound up with the honour of two Great Powers who are capable of arranging everything as they think fit. And this is why we should rather engage in a new, cultural struggle in which priority should be given to the question of our nationality and our national and religious development. So, then, now is the time to start thinking about our language, about our national literature and about education in the national spirit. Now is the time for interest in national and religious questions.) (p. 284–285)

Here, Misirkov's discourse on the language reaches its culminating point in the substantive and linear flow of logical argumentation. Here, the author expresses his first main thesis in the discourse construction in form of the following macrotopic:

А.

За тоа ниіе, требит, да се откажиме от секоіа мисл'а за револуциіа на пролет...
(This is why we should give up all idea of a spring revolution.)

At the same time, this is the main macrostructure of the discourse – realized and repeated phrase in different textual variants as a basic rhetorical means in the process of persuasion:

1. ...міурштегцките реформи сет максимум, шчо можа да ископчит од Европа револуциіата.
(...the Murzstag, reforms are the most that the revolution can hope to get out of Europe.)

2. Револуциіата на пролет ке бидит наі глупаото, шчо можиме ниіе да напраиме.
(The most foolish thing we could do would be to launch a spring revolution.)

3. Со револуциіата на пролет ке се користат само нашите неприіатели, коіи си имаат само есапи, противни на нашите национални интереси.
(It would be of benefit to no one but our enemies, who are working against our national interests.)

4. Револуциіата на пролет само ке ни унишчит совршено нас и ке унишчит плодоите, добиіени од од неа до сега.
(A spring revolution would only bring about our total ruin and destroy all that has been so far achieved.) (p. 284)

The second main thesis in Misirkov's political discourse is the thought of a cultural revolution and the role of language in it – "our"and "our national literature":

Б.

Да се зафатиме за ноа т.е. културна борба, во коіа прво место, ке требит да зимат прашаін'ето за нашата народност и нашето национално – религиозно развиіаін'е. Значит, истом сега му іет времето да се

мислит за іазико **наш**, **нашата** национална литература и воспитаіін'е во национален дух.
(And this is why we should rather engage in a new, cultural struggle in which priority should be given to the question of our nationality and our national and religious development. So, then, now is the time to start thinking about **our** language, about **our** national literature and about education in the national spirit.) (p. 284)

Here Misirkov used adjectives more often: *our, ours* as synonyms of the words: *Macedonian, native, national,* but above all, *Macedonian,* often *our* represents *Macedonian* in agreement with the thesis: **our** language – **our** identity.

развиіаін'е на **нашиіот** народ
(development of **our** people);

прашаін'ето за **нашата** народност и **нашето** национално – религиозно развиіаін'е
(the question of **our** nationality and **our** national and religious development);

сега му јет времето да се мислит за іазико **наш**, **нашата** национална литература
(now is the time to start thinking about **our** language, about **our** national literature);

револуционерите согледуваа во **нашиіот** народ
(revolutionaries have found in **our** people qualities);

предаін'ата и јазикот на **нашиіот** народ јет важна причина да сме ниіе против делеін'ето
(traditions and language of **our** people that we can give tangible reason for our opposition);

на **нашата** таткоина
(of **our** country);

нашиіот народен дух
(**our** national spirit);

на **нашите** национални интереси
(of **our** national interest).

However, in thesis context, Misirkov's program for the creation of a Macedonian literary language is the most important. What does the author suggest? He takes the central dialects (on the line Veles – Prilep – Bitola – Ohrid) as the basis for a literary language:

1. И така: стремеін'ето на македонците да создадат своі културен центр; тоа, шчо сега Битол'а се чинит престолнина на Македониіа; шчо Битол'а, Орид, Прилеп сет историіцки места за македонците; као и тоа, шчо состауваат они географцки и іазичен центр; сите заіедно праат да се приіимит, као општ македонцки литературен іазик, централното македонцко наречиіе.
   (Thus the aspiration of the Macedonians will create a cultural centre of our own, which will come to be what Bitola now is as the capital of Macedonia, or what Ohrid, Prilep and Bitola have been in the history of Macedonia.) (p. 294)

2. Благодареін'е на приликите сега ниіе си избираме за општ литературен азик, централното македонцко, т. е. Велешко-Прилепцко-Битол'цко-Охридцкото наречиіе.
   (Now, however, thanks to circumstances, we are taking the dialect of central Macedonia (Veles-Prilep-Bitola-Ohrid) as our general literary language.) (p. 300)

On the following several pages of his work, Misirkov states his reasons why he has chosen "централното македонцко, т. е. Велешко-Прилепцко-Битол'цко-Охридцкото наречиіе (the central Macedonian i.e. Veles – Prilep – Bitola – Ohrid dialects)" as a literary language.

Hence, Misirkov insists that the alphabet and the orthography include:

- establishment of orthography based on phonetics, with small exceptions regarding etymology;
- inclusion of new graphemes in the Macedonian Cyrillic alphabet; *і, к', г', н', л'*, which will distinguish it from other Cyrillic script;
- omission of intervocalic sounds в (v) and х (h) (*чоек, жиот, дуот*); anticipation of softness (*ќ* and њ: *браіка, стаіне, коін*); the group шч (*шчо, опшч*); the groups *стр, здр* (in all cases: *стред, здрел*).

He insists on using folklore lexis and the inclusion of elements from all Macedonian dialects and live word-formation models (*благодареін'е*); the suffix *-цки* instead of *-ски* (македонцки) in lexis and word formation.

Yet, the main characteristic of Misirkov's political discourse is the connecting of linguistic and cultural programs for the purpose of achieving political goals.

This is how the complete and synthetically argumented discourse looks in progressive stages:

> Около централното наречиіе требит да се групираат сите наши научни и литературни сили, за да го очистат и обогатат со сокроишча од друзите македонцки наречиіа и да создадат од него іеден убав литературен іазик. На него требит да се создадит іедна богата сколиіцка, научна и убаа литература, за да можит преко ниф да се раширит низ цела Македониіа во вид на литературен іазик, коі шчо ке изместит од неіа пропагандцките іазици. А заједно со изместуаін'ето на пропагандцките іазици и со создааін'ето наш литературен іазик, се изместуваат од Македониіа и интересите на балканцките држаици и нивното место к'е го застапат создадените со іазикот македонцки интереси.
> (All our scientists, scholars, and writers should group themselves around the central dialect in older both to cleanse it and to enrich it from the treasury of the other Macedonian dialects and turn it into a fine literary language. This dialect should serve to create rich and attractive educational, scientific, scholarly, and literary works through which the literary language may be spread throughout Macedonia, thus displacing all the languages of the propagandists. And while eradicating the influence of the languages of the propagandists from Macedonia and establishing our own literary language we will also force out the interests of the small Balkan states and replace them with a language embodying the interests of Macedonia.) (p. 296)

As it seems, Misirkov's illusory program created and existing only in the political discourse as its interlinguistic creation, to a great extent, received its implementation in the second half of the 20th century.

In the history of peoples, political freedoms have never before been conditioned by the development of culture, literature and art, quite the contrary. However, here, thanks to this strategy comprised of the exemption of solid (logical) argumentation in favor of contemplation based on analogy and discursive rhetoric, it was important to point out that

> (...) заіедно со изместуаін'ето на пропагандцките іазици и со создааін'ето наш литературен іазик, се изместуваат од Македониіа и интересите на балканцките држаици и нивното место к'е го застапат создадените со іазикот македонцки интереси.
> (...) while eradicating the influence of the languages of the propagandists from Macedonia and establishing our own literary language we will also

force out the interests of the small Balkan states and replace them with a language embodying the interests of Macedonia.) (p. 296–297)

Faith in the pragmatic (illocutive) power of discourse is surprising here, especially its creative strength deriving from historical and political changes, principally when it comes to the second part of Misirkov's program, i.e. the role of the Macedonian language in those historical conditions – a phenomenon which, in this magnitude, has not yet emerged in South Slavic political texts.

3. A Macedonian Discourse on Monuments and Statues

The term discourse, which today is very much present in humanistic and societal sciences as well as in the media, is still a category with great meaning and it has also become a subject of linguistic research, especially regarding its tendencies in communications. This is derived from the fact that the current descriptions of semantics and syntax do not take into consideration the communication perspective, which presupposes the speaker, listener, intentions, emotions of the speaker, the context, the basis for communication act, space, time, etc. Speech acts, as basic units of the discourse, are divided into micro and macro acts and classified as discursive genres, for example, literary, political, media (discourse of radio, television, printed media, the internet, etc.), as well as parliamentarian. A book was dedicated to the Polish parliamentary discourse, by Elżbieta Laskowska titled: *Dyskurs parlamentarny w ujęciu komunikacyjnym.*[68] The author in her work used the theory of speech acts, and in their classification used the categories of modality and persuasion, T. van Dijk and L. Martin Rojo[69] dealt with the Spanish parliamentary discourse, from the aspect of a critical analysis of the discourse. The methodology for discoursive analysis provides for three solutions situated on three levels: 1. Linguistic – the discourse

68 E. Laskowska, *Dyskurs parlamentarny w ujęciu komunikacyjnym*, Bydgoszcz 2004.

69 L. Martin Rojo, T.A. van Dijk, *There Was a Problem, and It Was Solved: Legitimating the Expulsion of Illegal Migrants in Spanish Parliamentary Discourse*, "Discourse & Society" 1997, 8 (4), p. 523–566; L. Martin Rojo, T.A. van Dijk, *Habia un problema y se ha solucionado. La legitimacion de la explusion de inmigrantes „ilegales" en el discurso parlamentario espanol*, in: L. Martin Rojo, L.R. Whittaker, eds., *Poder decir o El poder de los discursos*, Madrid 1998, p. 169–234.

is the verbal structure, i.e. a form of language use (system). This research is dominated by the functional perspective (who?, how?, why?, for whom?, when is the text generated?). This is a purely linguistic approach; 2. Communicational and interactive – the discourse is acting by means of words – interaction which is created in particular societal and cultural context with inclusion of situation elements as important condition for successful communication (pragma-linguistic approach); 3. Cognitive – the discourse is a form of communication within a frame of certain determined system of notions and values (worldview), in which the semantic, and even the formal structure of texts is molded with this metal image of the world and with the cognitive processes which are the basis for its familiarity and understanding (cognitivism). Lately, building on the so called concept of critical discourse analysis, the discourse has been proposed to be societal and institutional norm, convention, rules and strategies that would be used in the process of creation of text and expression. The bases on which the discursive expression is to be formulated are the cultural and societal patterns, and their effects are the texts with determined genre traits. In this direction, the Macedonian parliamentary discourse should be considered as defined norm, strategy, convention applied in the creation of the parliamentary text and thus, the parliamentary discourse can be defined by taking in consideration not only the linguistic structures typical for the parliamentary discourse, but also the contextual properties and strategies based on societal and cultural patterns. A parliamentary discourse may include genres, as are for example, debate, expose, decision, declaration, resolution, recommendation and conclusions. Most of these genres are characteristic not only of parliamentary discourse but can also be found outside of it, however, some of these (expose, parliamentary questions and so on) are characteristic only of the parliamentary discourse. Such genres (as are for example, expose, parliamentary questions and so on) have a strategic value because they allow parliamentary control over the work of the ministries or the government as a whole. Parliamentary question in the Macedonian parliamentary discourse can be determined as an additional parliamentary question. Such was the character of the parliamentary question, regarding the state's financial situation, posed during the Macedonian Parliament session of 2004. It developed into the Macedonian parliamentary discourse on monuments and statues. This is the manner in which that investment was named by the government, On Statues and Monuments, or discourse on the statue of the bull and the trendy girl sculpture or Alexander the Great with the horse Bucephalus. "A monument is, for example, a bull, or a trendy girl or the legendary one that we all await for now, maybe it is on a ship, we don't know that, Alexander the Great with Bucephalus," this is how the opposition representative described this investment and we have stenographic records of the 53rd session of the Macedonian Parliament to support it.

> STENOGRAPHIC RECORDS of the Fifty third session of the Parliament of Republic of Macedonia, held on 4th May 2009. The session was held in the Parliament of Republic of Macedonia, hall 1, at 11:31 o'clock. Document 328 КБ – May 5, 2009.
>
> **Т.В.:** Благодарам и јас.
> Дали пратеникот е задоволен од одговорот, односно дали сака да постави дополнително пратеничко прашање.
> Има збор пратеникот господинот Игор Ивановски, повелете.
> (**T.B.:** Thank you.
> Is the MP satisfied by the answer, i.e. does he want to ask an **additional parliamentary question**.
> The MP, Mr. Igor Ivanovski has the floor, you are welcome to it.)
> **И.И.:** Воопшто не сум задоволен, господине претседателе. Кога веќе се навраќаме на многу работи, господине премиере, немојте да отвораме за времето кога вие бивте министер за финансии, кога Македонија имаше -2% раст, имаше воен данок и оставивте дупка која што требаше некој, а тоа бевме ние да ја враќаме 4 години, ама за тоа друг пат ќе разговараме, во друга прилика.
> Втората работа е што навистина веќе не можам ни да бидам зачуден, огорчен сум, со каква леснотија ги убедувате македонските граѓани, дека уште треба да бидат и среќни и задоволни што живеат подобро од тие во Америка, од Италија, од Шпанија, од Романија.
>
> (...)
>
> Почитувани македонски граѓани, кога го слушате македонскиот премиер, воопшто да не се секирате. Вие живеете добро, само уште тоа треба да го почувствувате. Бидејќи господине премиере сакате да се споредувате со сериозни економии и држави и паметни влади, ајде кажете ми еден пример каде што во овие година дена, речиси на економска криза, почнувајќи од САД, завршувајќи со Албанија, се дадени 10 милиони евра за споменици и статуи и објаснете ми кој во Вашингтон постави споменик на пример оној бик, или шмизли или легендарниот што го чекаме сега, можеби е на брод, сега не знаеме, Александар Македонски сосе Букефал и го постави

среде некој сквер, или плоштад во било која европска или друга метропола.
(**I.I.:** Mr. President I am not satisfied at all. If we are looking back to many things Mr. Prime Minister, let us not open matters from the time when you were a Minister of Finance, when Macedonia had -2% growth, a war tax and when you left a hole that someone needed to cover, and this was us, doing so for four years. But this is something we will discuss another time, in another occasion.

(...)

The second matter, which doesn't even surprise me anymore, is that I am embittered by the ease with which you persuade the Macedonian citizens that they should be happy and satisfied because they live even better than the people in America, Italy, Spain, Romania.

(...)

Respected Macedonian citizens, when you listen to the Macedonian Prime Minister, don't you worry at all. You live well, you just have to feel that. Because you, Mr. Prime Minister, want to compare yourself with serious economies and countries and smart governments, tell me just one example where in the past year, almost at the verge of an economic crisis, starting from USA, ending with Albania, have 10 million euros been spent on monuments and statues and explain to me who in Washington raised a monument, for example, of a bull, or a trendy girl or the legendary one that we all await for now, maybe it is on a ship, we don't know this, Alexander the Great with Bucephalus and placed it in the middle of some square or plaza in any European or other metropolis.)
Одговор:
Понатаму, спомнавте дека јас сум кажал дека ние живееме добро, па се обративте на граѓаните итн. Морам да ви кажам дека такво нешто не сум кажал, вие карикирате.
Спомнавте и тоа дека градиме споменици и статуи. Јас ќе ве потсетам дека ова се проекти кои се започнати 2007 година и во 2008 година. Најголем дел од средствата тогаш се префрлени, кога економијата имаше раст од 5,9% во 2007 година, рекорден до тогаш, 2008 година 5% раст.
Во едни такви услови се започнаа проекти за кои што сметаме дека се добри за државата, за кои што сметаме дека се позитивни и тие проекти се започнаа во време кога имаше сериозен раст на економијата.

Така што немојте да карикирате дека токму сега ние започнуваме такви проекти, не е точно. И статуите и спомениците се започнати во периодот од 2007, 2008 година кога навистина имаше една поинаква економска ситуација, многу подобра и тие причини тогаш беше донесена одлука дека Владата може да ја помогне општината Центар, финансиски, да таа ги оствари тие планови.
Тоа говори дека оваа Влада гради. Можеби некои од тие градби не ви се допаѓаат. Не се по ваш вкус. Меѓутоа, проблем е тоа што во времето кога беше СДСМ, ниту една од овие работи не се градеше. Излегува дека се што треба да се гради и да се содава не било по ваш вкус. По таа теорија не треба ништо да се работи, треба да се седи, да се мирува и да се чека.
Драги пратеници, ние имаме друг концепт. Концепт на градење и создавање. Тоа е разликата меѓу нас.
(The Prime Minister's response:
Moreover, you mentioned that I had said that we live well, and then you addressed the citizens and so on. I have to tell you that I haven't said such a thing, you are exaggerating.

(...)

You have also mentioned that we are building monuments and statues. I will remind you that these projects began in 2007 and 2008. Most of the funds were transferred during this period, when there was an economic growth of 5.9% in 2007, a record-breaking at the time, 5% growth in 2008...

(...)

In such conditions we initiated projects which we considered to be good for the state, for which we considered to be positive and we started these projects at a time when there was a serious economic growth.
So, do not exaggerate that we are initiating these projects now, that is not true. And the statues and the monuments were initiated in 2007 and 2008 when the economic situation was different, much better and these were the reasons why a decision was reached by the Government to help, financially, the Municipality of Centre to fulfill these plans.
It is obvious that this government is building. Maybe you do not like some of the buildings. They are not of your taste. However, the problem is that at the time of SDUM, none of these things were built. It turns out that everything that needs to be built and created is not to your taste. In accordance with this theory, nothing should be done; we should sit, be still and wait.

Dear Member of Parliament, we have another concept. A concept of building and creating. This is the difference between us.)

И.И.: Благодарам претседателе, не сум задоволен.

Господине премиере,

Ве молам, два реда позади вас, е министерката за култура, да ве потсети дека парите за спомениците на општина Центар ги дадовте во декември 2008 година, со трансфер, преку ребалансот на Буџетот на Министерството за култура на Советот на општина Центар. 8,5 милиони евра, декември 2008 година Кога ни ги носевте мерките, овие што не профункционираа, што беа катастрофа, меѓу другото, молчешкум 8,5 милиони евра дадовте и за тоа постојат документи во општината Центар. Можете слободно да ги проверите. Сте знаеле дека има криза, конечно потврдивте тогаш. Наводно ја манипулиравте јавноста со некакви 10 мерки, што беа 10 анти мерки и беа празен воздух и покрај тоа, 8,5 милиони евра сте испорачале на општината Центар за бикови итн. И, на крајот на краиштата, господине, благодарам премиере, што го дадовте одговорот. Осумте милијарди се ветер и магла. Благодарам. Немам дополнително прашање.

Кон основните контекстуални црти карактеристични исклучиво за парламентарната дебата како макродискурс припаѓаат: институционална средина (собраниската сала), учесниците (пратениците), политичките сознанија и цели.

(I.I.: Thank you Mr. President, I am not satisfied.

Mr. Prime Minister,

Please, two rows behind you is the Minister of Culture; let me remind you that you spent the money for the monuments in the Municipality of Centre in December 2008, by a transfer, through rebalance of the Budget, from the Ministry of Culture to the Council of the Municipality of Centre. 8.5 million euros in December 2008, when you brought us the measures, those that did not work out, which were a catastrophe, and above all else, you gave away 8.5 million euros quietly and there are documents in Municipality of Centre that can prove this. Feel free to check them out. You knew about the crisis, which you confirmed at the time. Supposedly you manipulated the public with some 10 measures, which were actually 10 anti-measures and smoke and mirrors, and in addition, you have delivered 8.5 million euros to the Municipality of Centre for bulls etc.

(...)

And at the end of the day, mister, thank you Prime Minister for your answer. Eight billion are smoke and mirrors. Thank you. I have no further questions.)

The following belongs to the basic contextual traits exclusively characteristic for the parliamentarian debate as a macro discourse: the environment (parliamentary hall), participants (MPs), political awareness and goals.

Thus understood, the Macedonian parliamentarian discourse on monuments concerns not only historical persons, but also statues of animals (a bull, cat, etc.) or people of the everyday life (trendy girl, shoe cleaner...) that have recently appeared on the public squares and streets of the capital of Macedonia, Skopje. This gave rise to discourses and polemics, not only in the media, but also in the Macedonian families, and also in the Macedonian parliament (for example, the discourse on the bull or the discourse on Bucephalus that was placed on the central square in Skopje). In such a discourse, the language mechanisms are exclusively in the service of expression organization, however, the discourse itself is in the sphere of concepts and ideas that propagate or disavow monuments which are not always directly related with the history of the Macedonians.

The Macedonian discourse on monuments and statues is present not only in the media, within families and on Macedonian streets, but also in the parliament, can be considered as an element of the creation of a national memory and constituent of collective identification and the symbol of monumental history. This kind of discourse is closely related to the notion of *text of culture*, which was introduced in science by the Polish semiotician Stefan Żółkiewski.[70] He defines it as an arranged sequences of signs which are an objectification of certain properties of a semiotic system, a system of signs. A similar definition can be found in the works of Maria Renata Mayenowa according to whom: "the text is informative wholeness, a subject with a sign-character, organized in such a way that it has a beginning and an end, that conveys information which is complete from the stand point of its creator."[71] Thus can be considered the Macedonian discourse on monuments and statues. Setting monuments and statues in urban space can be considered as a kind of political discourse – text of culture. This discourse is in the service not only of the current political goals, but also of the creation of emblemic (symbolic) mind regarding the past. In a very short period, monuments of national heroes (more recent as well as ancient ones) are being built in numbers which, so far, have not been encountered in Macedonia and thus this

70 S. Żółkiewski, *Teksty kultury. Studia*, Warszawa 1988, p. 5–37.

71 M.R. Mayenowa, *Posłowie: inwentarz pytań z teorii tekstu*, in: *Semantyka tekstu i języka*, ed. by M.R. Mayenowa, Wrocław 1976, p. 292.

discourse should confirm the very rich and national tradition. This new phenomenon-creation of monuments as elements of the new codex in the universal and the intercultural discourse is an expression of the quest for additional and inconsistent linguistic markers of national identity and national uniqueness.

4. Discourse on the Name of the State (1990–1999)

In recent European history, two state name disputes are prominent: the first chronologically began in 1990, and the second, known as the "The Hyphen War", (cz.) *pomlčková válka*, (sl.) *pomlčková vojna* concerning Czech-Slovakia, began in 1991 and ended in 1993. It is connected with the creation of two states – the Czech Republic and Republic of Slovakia. The second refers to Macedonia and has got nothing to do with the state's division, but, it mainly concerns its international affirmation. It is still on-going and there are no indications that it will be over soon.

In 1989, right after the fall of the communism, the official name of Czechoslovakia was the Czech-Slovak Socialistic Republic (*Československá socialistická republika – ČSSR*) or the Federation of Czech-Slovakia (*Česká a Slovenská Federativní Republika – ČSFR*) i.e. as it was the state's name during the periods of 1918–1920 and of 1938–1939. The abovementioned dispute shows the basic differences in the attitude of the Czechs and the Slovaks towards the idea of common state and it finally ended with the fall of the federation and the creation of two separate states on 1st January 1993, the Czech Republic and the Republic of Slovakia.

Similar problems – although not of such magnitude and such political consequences – were also encountered by other countries. I would not give any more examples but only quote fragments of an interview with the special UN representative, Matthew Nimitz, for the daily newspaper Nova Makedonija of September 1995, who among everything else, stated:

> The Constitutional name of the country we refer to as the Former Yugoslav republic of Macedonia is the Republic of Macedonia. So, the state adopted its name. Greece stands against that name for historical reasons. The UN admitted the country, but did not change its name, neither added anything to it. They use a reference, which reads as follows: In the UN this country will be addressed as the Former Yugoslav Republic

> of Macedonia, a formulation that I'm not glad to use when I use it. It is as if you would call the US the "former British colony of America." This is not a name. It is just a reference. It is as if you say the name Zimbabwe, the "former Rhodesia." It is not a name, but a reference used to address when you don't want to say "Zimbabwe." So, to this country we address in that way, but it is not its name, avoiding in that way all the possible remarks about the name's use. In a certain way it is very philosophical, but it is the reality. Such name problems exists between Great Britain and Ireland. I don't know if you are familiar to that. The Irish do not recognize the name the "United Kingdom of Great Britain and Northern Ireland." They do not use that in any document, and as I understood, the agreement is not on paper, because Ireland did not recognize that name. Also, the British do not accept the "Iri" (Eire), that is the pronunciation on the word "Ireland" in the Irish language, and instead use the formulation "Republic of Ireland," and not "Iri" (Eire) referring to entire Ireland (including Northern Ireland). It is since the year 1920. However, both countries cooperate very well, although technically, formally they have not settled their names. There are other places in the world with a similar problem: Both China(s), for instance, since Taiwan is named the "Republic of China" which we don't recognize as a name, so this country can be included as a country under the name of "Taiwan." There are also other countries with similar problems, but they all work on to overcome them.[72]

The author of this statement refers to this phenomenon as somewhat illusionary – or as he puts it – "philosophical" difference between the name and its reference. Essentially, in his philosophy of language, G. Frege makes a difference between Sense (*Sinn*) and reference (*Bedeutung*). For example, the sole name "Carl Ludwig I" expresses the sense – "emperor of a state" and also has a precise meaning (physical person, who exists). Yet, what is defined as a meaning in Frege's philosophy, in linguistics, corresponds to the notion of reference. The difference between sense and meaning can be seen in cases of expressions which have the sense but have no meaning, as for example, "The man on Mars." The sense of this expression – the first man who was on Mars – can be understood by any speaker, although such meaning does not exist – such person does not exist. Yet, it is difficult to understand what Nimitz meant when he was saying that the name "'Former Yugoslav Republic of Macedonia' is just a reference." The author probably

---

72 Стенограм; Нова Македонија, 24 September 1995 (Stenograms, Nova Makedonija, September 24, 1995).

wants to tell us – referring to the philosophical difference between the name and its reference – that when we say the "Former Yugoslav Republic of Macedonia" the sense of this name has no meaning, which, in turn, means that such a country does not exist. According to Nimitz'[i]t is as if you were to call the US the "former British colony of America." This is not a name. It is just a reference. It is as if you say the name Zimbabwe for the "former Rhodesia." It is not a name, but a reference used to address when you don't want to say "Zimbabwe." So, this country we address in that way, but it is not its name. However, the difference is that in all the examples given by Nimitz, the states in question essentially exist, contrary to the reference "The First man on Mars," since in reality such person does not exist. As we can see, philosophy of language cannot help solve the onomatopoeic disputes, but it is in the service of the political rhetoric.

The second – let's say, conditionally – Greco-Macedonian discourse began in 1991 when Macedonia declared its independence. At the time, Greece caused this country to enter the international scene after agreeing to accept the absurd name of FYROM. For internal use, the country uses the name Republic of Macedonia, however, in the United Nations and other international organization it is renamed in Former Yugoslav Republic of Macedonia. The practice varies when it comes to relations between Macedonia and other countries: some use the name FYROM, others, do not.

However, the major difficulty of the dispute between Greece and Macedonia is not only in the sphere of the philosophy of language, but in politics, in the language of politicians and their statements, and also in the fields of data – fields of the media and linguistics. The media create relations out of the politicians' speeches, although there is not much merit in what they have to say. Media relations concerning the name dispute contain all the most important elements that serve to create and increase its importance: geographical, historical, cultural, political, ethnical, etc. The linguistic aspect is not even considered as an aspect that bears merit in the name dispute. When renowned linguists and balkanologists are interviewed by the media, they claim that there is no dispute: Absolutely not. Even Nimitz himself knows that there are no legal, lawful grounds for the so-called dispute. There is no dispute.[73]

Since it has such a major political importance, the dispute is primarily discussed by politicians. Tadeusz Mazowiecki, a special representative of the UN in the former Yugoslavia, in his interview for the

[73] http: // www.dnevnik.com.mk/default.asp?ItemID=48F8FA0715BF074CBD4AFF00363D22FF (accessed on: 7 April 2014).

Skopje daily newspaper Nova Makedonija, on 29 March 2004, emphasized the following.

> International public opinion owes a great debt to Macedonia. A great injustice has been inflicted to this country at the time when it gained its independence and was to accept the absurd name of "Former Yugoslav Republic of Macedonia."[74]

The, now late, first president of independent Macedonia, Kiro Gligorov, in a diplomatic notice sent to the heads of diplomacy of the European Union, on 10 May 1992 wrote: "We are asked not to use the term Macedonia as a name for our country, even though our country has borne this name for half a century, and besides, this name is connected to the name of the people."[75]

Despite of it, and perhaps because of it, the dispute lasts independently of whether there are political grounds or not. The disputed resolution is not facilitated by linguistic-legal manipulation of the type *Interim Accord* or lingo-legal tricks – reads the statement by M. Nimitz, which only prolong the time for principled decisions.

All these facts have led to a situation where in order to resolve the linguistic "name dispute" in the media, in the social communication, and in the political discourse, a large amount of completely new or only modified determinations of the Macedonian state emerged, which in a way are weakening the Macedonian national identity that has so far been sustained by a sense of the unique // exclusive character of the current state name. Their complete registry from 1990–1999 containing 240 entries, together with linguistic and political determinants, was published in the work of Ahil Tuntev under the title *Republic of Macedonia. The first decade 1990–1999.* In addition to the political and legal importance, the material is of greater linguistic (onomastic) interest. Unfortunately, the major parts of the samples in the material have been translated from other languages and are of an offensive nature. Some of them are comic or absurd, reminding one of word games or puns, and rhetoric-eristic means are used for the creation of others, making them not worthy of scientific analysis. However, the material has an acknowledged value and testifies to the great inventiveness of the authors of the texts collected by Tuntev, presenting such curious examples as are: *Nameless country, Great Ancient Macedonia, Former*

---

74 "Utrinski vesnik" 2004, 29 March.

75 А. Тунтев, *Република Македонија. Прва декада (1990–1999)*, Скопје 2005, p. 277.

Republic, Skopje, the second page, Republic of Two Peoples, Republic of Fufuts and so on.

The authors of these terms are mainly Greek politicians, Greek media, but Serbian and Bulgarian sources are dominant. However, there are also samples which do not have a character of a parody or aptness. These are mainly used in the United Nations, some European media and the State Department. Among the 240 terms, the largest group consists of those which contain the noun *Macedonia* and the adjective *Macedonian* and are used in different European languages. They are divided in two groups.

I GROUP

In the public local Macedonian and international discourse, the name of the Macedonian state appears in three basic official variations.

1. The state name accepted in the Macedonian Constitution: Republic of Macedonia.
2. The form which is most frequent – (Mac.) Македонија, (Eng.) Macedonia, (Ger.) Mazedonien, (Fr.) Macedoine, and (Pol.) Macedonia, etc.
3. Former Yugoslav Republic of Macedonia – FYROM, (Mac.) Поранешна (или бивша) југословенска Република Македонија – ПЈРМ (БЈРМ).

(The last form does not appear on its own in the Macedonian language, but as a translation from the English language.)

II GROUP

The second group of examples of the name of Macedonia is a result of creative paralinguistic activity of politicians and different media who participated in the Greek protest related to the name of Republic of Macedonia. This fact caused the current creation of *ad hoc* new terms on the international political scene and in the media aimed at "facilitating" the resolution of the Greek Veto with regards to the name of Macedonia.

Thus, in the political and media discourse, a potential and, in the history of modern Europe, unprecedented case was created as was the possibility for Macedonians to accept a name for their country, different from the Republic of Macedonia.

Could it be expected that during the resolution of this problem, the rhetorics and eritics had replaced the diplomats' and politicians' or journalists' common sense in favor of the inhabitants of Macedonia? For now, at the beginning of the second decade of the XXI century, the end of this paralinguistic and quasi-political name dispute of the Macedonian state is not near.

From the media language on the Republic of Macedonia's name dispute, several factors can be distinguished: geographical, historical, cultural, political, medial and at the end, linguistic. On one hand, naming fragments of reality is a convention and societal agreement. On the other hand, the real world is represented (created) in the media by linguistic and visual means. In this regard, we can differentiate between two discourses: the media (or virtual) and public (or real, i.e. political discourse). It means that the dispute's substance greatly depends on its image in the media and the manner in which this discourse is expressed in the language of newspapers, radio, television or the Internet, and rarely vary in scientific literature.

VII. Forms of Address in Contemporary Macedonian Language

Today, the Macedonian language is developing spontaneously. It changes in accordance with the habits of the interpersonal communication as the number of authors and poets who write original works increases. However, it should be emphasized that this hastened development is under constant linguistic and ethnic pressure imposed by the Albanians. After the announcement of independence in 1991, the Macedonian population was indeed more numerous, however, it represented just over 64% of the population in the republic. The Macedonian language was also the main language in the state, liberating itself, at least legally, from Serbian domination.

A large part of the population – according to some estimates, from 25 to 30% with an increasing trend – are Albanians, of whom the majority are Muslims, a small number includes Catholics, however both these religious groups are characterized by a fast population growth and increase of political aspiration. Even in the early phases of Macedonian's road to independence, unsatisfied by their current situation, Macedonian Albanians asked for changes especially concerning the Albanian language, i.e. its agreement with the Macedonian language.

The Framework Agreement [Рамковен договор][76] was signed after the Albanian rebellion on 13 August 2001. Besides concerning important political questions, the Treaty also refers to the Albanian language in Macedonia, which gained the status of an official language in the Parliament, the State Administration and municipalities where the number of the Albanian population was over 20%.

---

[76] Ohrid Framework Agreement, http: // www.ucd.ie/ibis/filestore/Ohrid%20Framework%20Agreement.pdf (accessed on: 7 March 2016).

1. Basic Forms of Address in the Macedonian Language

During the past several years, the Macedonian language changed and the literary standard was also modified and crystalized. Forms and manners of establishing linguistic contact between interlocutors evolved exponentially. Today, as the distance in interpersonal communication increases, and hence new forms appear and old ones reappear, which – as it seemed during the Yugoslavian communist era – irretrievably disappeared. Such forms of address include *господин* // *госпоѓа* (Mister // Madam) or official phrases used in official meetings including *дами и господа* (ladies and gentlemen) or politically colored phrases including *другари* // *другарки* (comrades). At the same time, the tendency of decreasing the distance between interlocutors in public communication supervened – the tendency to use the addressing form ТИ (singular You) became widespread, not only among citizens of rural regions, but also among those in urban regions, and it is increasingly more accepted in everyday communication. The phenomenon of language mediatization promotes this – the Internet, different forums, and direct and indirect comments throughout the media are dominated by the use of the form of address ТИ, regardless of gender, age and social origin, which is due to the influence of the Internet's anonymity. Since 2012, on the Internet, and especially on social media, the decline in the use of the form ВИЕ (plural YOU) is obviously in favor of the use of ТИ (singular YOU) in most European languages including French[77], German, and Polish, reasoned by the fact that these communication platforms are dominated by the philosophy of equality, independent of formal distinctions.

Recently, there are some forms of address, not so widespread before, that appear in different language registers in Macedonia including *господин* // *госпоѓа* (Mister // Madam) in (most often in the vocative[78])

---

[77] R. Lawn, *Tu and Twitter: Is it the end for 'vous' in French?*, "BBC News Magazine" 2012, 7 September.

[78] In the Macedonian language, the form of address is the vocative case. Remnants of this form usually appear in relation to nouns denoting a human being, for example, *жено, господине* (woman, sir). In nouns of masculine gender, the form of address is created by infliction of suffixes *-у* or *-е*. The suffix *-у* can be found in polysyllabic words and the suffix *-е* in monosyllabic ones, and some nouns can take both inflections interchangeably, for example, *маж – мажу, вол – волу, коњ – коњу, професор – професоре, годподин – господине*. Personal names ending in vowel do not have vocative form, and those ending on consonant take the suffix *-е*, for example (*Стојане, Зоране*). In nouns of feminine gender, the form of address is formed by the suffixes *-е* and *-о*. The suffix *-е* is more often used with polysyllabic words ending in *-ица* or *-ке* (*Милице, директорке*), while others are formed by use of the suffix *-о* (*ќерко, сестро*).

form of an appeal used together with the name, title of dignity or last name of the person being addressed:[79]

> Господине Поповски повеќе од провидна е Вашата загриженост…
> (Mister Popovski, your concern is more than obvious…)

> Прво, господине претседателе, на барање на нашиот колега…
> (First of all, Mister President, on the request of our colleague…)

> Ви благодарам господине претседател, почитувани колеги…
> (Thank you Mister President, respected colleagues…)

Forms of address in the contemporary Macedonian language can be divided in two types – generally in view of the societal conditions in which the communication is directed towards establishing a contact. These forms were and are the constant expression of a society that is changing together with the dynamics within the frame of one group, to which one can feel they belong to. However, the form **ТИ** is mainly used within the family and among closest friends.[80]

Use of the form **ТИ** can be particulary offensive in the modern political discourse when an adversary from a political party addresses his interlocutor by using the humiliating form **ТИ** in the media.

> **a)** …по овој разговор можам да ти се обраќам само на „ти". Ти си обичен насилник…
> (…after this conversation, I can address you by "ти." You are just a thug…[81])

The forms **човек // абе човек // овој човек** can also be used in the function of the offensive **ТИ**:

> **b)** Го гледам пред некој ден така засилен и раскомотен малку, подолабавена кошулата, демек неформален е. (…) Слушам не ми се верува, враќам назад, пак слушам, стварно тоа го збори, си велам абе

---

[79] All examples are taken from different transcripts of the sessions of Macedonian Parliament; http: // www.sobranie.mk/ext/sessions1.aspx?Id=47F95433-B52C-465A-AA84-43187C262B4C (accessed on: 12 December 2012).

[80] Sometimes, the form **Ти** can be offensive since it may express disrespect. When few years ago, one famous television speaker addressed a police officer using **Ти**, the case ended up in court. In his defense, the speaker stated that address on **Ти** is his normal form of communication. The Court followed this argumentation, otherwise he would have had to pay a 500 euro fine.

[81] http: // www.novamakedonija.com.mk/NewsDetal.asp?vest=4201593738&id=9&setIzdanie=23448 (accessed on: 12 May 2015).

човек, седи мирен и не си играј играчки, тешки зборови кажуваш, не си играј играчки, да не те лаже ѓаволот да правиш глупости, зашто ако седиме мирно и те пуштаме на глава да ни се качуваш, не значи дека ќе дозволиме и граѓански конфликт да направиш.[82]
(I saw him the other day, stepped-up and little bit cosy, his shirt loosened up, supposedly acting informally. He says proudly that if need be, blood shall be spilled, too. (...) I hear him and I can't believe it. I go back and listen to him again, but he says the same thing. So I think to myself, oh man, stay put and do not play games, you are saying big words, do not play games. Do not let the devil deceive you and make you do foolish things because if we stay put and let you do as you please, it does not mean they we will allow you to create a civil conflict....)

I am listening to him and I can't believe it. I go back and listen to him again, but he says the same thing. So I think to myself, oh man, stay put and do not play games, you are saying big words, do not play games. Do not let the devil deceive you and make you do foolish things because if we stay put and let you do as you please, it does not mean thay we will allow you to create a civil war...

c) Овој човек на секој два дена зборува тотално спротивни работи. Не е чудо што ова не им успева.[83]
(This man says completely opposite things every two days. Small wonder this does not work for them.)

In **b** and **c**, the stylistic coloration of the speaker's manner of address is very important because he is using rhetorical irony[84] to portray his political adversary as someone who is not a serious man, **man** only dressed in loosened up shirt, cozy, informal, in one word, we can now freely address him by – **абе човек** (oh, man).

Particularly offensive and humiliating can be the juggling with different forms of address in an eristically colored discussion or polemic. These start with the implication that the interlocutor does not understand a thing and this is why we can freely address him as ТИ, as first and last name and an the end, as sir.

---

82 http: // www.telegraf.mk/aktuelno/makedonija/263841-gruevski-zaev-ne-si-igraj-da-napravis-gragjanski-konflikt (accessed on: 12 May 2015).

83 Ibidem.

84 See: S. Neshkovska, J. Lazarevska-Stenchevska, *Verbal Irony in Political Discourse*, in: Proceedings of the International Applied Linguistics Conference: *Practice in Language, Language in Practice (PLLP)*, 7–8 June 2013, Skopje 2014, p. 26–34; http: // www.fon.edu.mk/files/ZBORNIK_lingvistika.pdf (accessed on: 15 May 2015).

Кутриот не сфаќа или не сака да сфати...
(Poor thing, he does not understand or does not want to understand...)

Својот дилетантизам **С. Поповски** го покажа уште во првата реченица во својот текст...
(S. Popovski shows his dilettantism even in the first sentence of his text...)

Не, **г. С. Поповски** процесот на прифаќањето на оваа теза почна...
(No, Mr S. Popovski, the process of acceptance of this thesis began...)

Госп. Стојан Поповски, во 1944 година почна само официјално прифаќањето на...
(Mr Stojan Popovski, in 1944, only the official acceptance of... has begun.)

The author of the polemics purposely mixes the forms ТИ, *господин* (mister) (abbreviation: *г.* и *госп.*) with his adversary's name and last name in order to offend him, although he knows very well that he, himself, is a professor by title.

The Macedonian language has two basic forms of address: official and unofficial. In case of official circumstances, the forms *Вие и господин* // *госпоѓа* (plural You and mister // sir // madam) are used. In less official and unofficial (private) circumstances, the form ТИ is used. In the Macedonian language, the sphere in which the form ТИ is used is usually much wider than it is in other Slavic languages, for example in the Polish language. Without exception, ТИ is used as a form of address by young people who are the same or similar age, for example, students, but also, is used in more formal circumstances (the same applies for foreigners), for example. In local stores, the shop keeper would readily address a young person or a person of similar age by use of *Ти* and vice versa – in conversation regarding the quality or price of goods – while *Вие* (formal YOU) is used when there is a relationship of superior – subordinate, for example, professor – student, employer – employee on a lower position, which is even the case in everyday communication and informal contacts.

Today, the use of the form *Ти* in the Macedonian language is much more liberal than it used to be. The form *Ти* is especially dynamic when used in commercials:[85] marketing experts, who naturally want the best for their clients, identify themselves with them by using the universal form *Ти*, but rarely *Вие*, for example:

---

[85] In Scandinavia, *Ти* (YOU) is used consequently even in commercials.

1. И ти си лицето на твојата земја, од туризмот сите добиваме.
   (You are also the face of your country, we all gain from tourism.)
2. Вклучи се во најголемото истражување за социјални мрежи во светот и свој Acer таблет.
   (Get involved in the biggest social media research in the world and win your Acer tablet.)
3. Еј... супер што го посетуваш Црнобело форумот! Слободно регистрирај се приклучи и се во дискусиите!
   (Hey... it's great you visit Црнобело forum! Register for free, join us in our discussions!)

ТИ is used as a form of address by young people at the same or similar age, for example pupils, students, but also this form dominates in more official circumstances to address people who are not well known, for example when buying goods in a store or a the market place where the shopkeeper can address a young boy or a girl by using the form *Ти*:

Имаш банани?
(Have you got any bananas?)

Имаш тази бурек?
(Have you got freshly made burek?)

Similarly, a young shopkeeper can address a customer of a similar age by the use of *Ти*. There is a full symmetry here. However, if there is an asymmetry concerning the age of one or the other party, such a form of address is officially impossible because it creates a sense of overpowering. Regardless, nowadays, it has become more often the case when irrespective of their age, all shopkeepers and customers mutually use the form ТИ.

Young and older people address the waiters using ТИ or more often *дечко* (boy) in the function of *Ти*.

Дај ми едно пиво!
(Give me a beer!)

Дечко, донеси едно пивце!
(Boy, bring me a beer!)

But obviously, official forms exist:

Ве молиме пиво // Едно пиво Ве молам.
(Please, a beer // One beer, please.)

In the Macedonian language, words referring to young women and men can have the same function, for example: *моме* or *чупе* (girl) and a young man aged 30–35: *дечко* (boy), which is usual, or *момче*. This is rather common, not only in the Macedonian language, but it is also related to the expression of domination and control in acts of interpersonal communication. According to J. Lyons[86] there is no language in which this dimension – or lack of symmetry in the use of the forms of address – is not more or less present. This is especially true when the sender uses his social position by means of use of these forms at the beginning of a conversation in order to demonstrate power over the receiver.

In language science, the essence of address forms is in the sphere of linguistic functions, among which the function of appeal, known as impressive or conative function, can be singled out. This category is used to address the addressee directly or indirectly. In scientific literature, according to K. Bühler[87] we can single out: pure appeal – speaker calls and asks the addressee to establish and maintain contact, for example: *Докторе, се случи несреќа* (Doctor, there's been an accident) addressing others when contact has already been established, and the nominated group is used for the purpose of its maintenance: *Знам, сестро моја, знам!* (I know, my sister, I know!) or by use of predicative phrases, when the speaker uses certain nominal groups to characterize the addressee, for example:

Злато мое!
(My darling!)

Партал низаеден!
(You're worthless!)

According to Edward Tomichek, two categories of forms of address can be determined in the Macedonian language, just as in the Polish, French or German languages, a group of pronominal forms – *Тој // Таа, Ти, Тие, Вие* (He // She, informal You, They, formal You) and a group of nominal forms: I – name, N – last name, T – title.[88] All these structures are also present in Macedonian, however, with different prevalence

---

[86] J. Lyons, *Semantyka*, transl. by A. Weinsberg, Vol. 2, Warszawa 1989, p. 191–192.

[87] K. Bühler, *Teoria języka. O językowej funkcji przedstawiania*, transl. by J. Koźbiał, Kraków 2004.

[88] E. Tomiczek, *System adresatywny współczesnego języka polskiego i niemieckiego. Socjolingwistyczne studium konfrontatywne*, Wrocław 1983.

in official communication as unofficial contacts are dominated by the class of pronominal forms: 2nd person singular – ТИ (you) and 2nd person plural – *Вие* (you). This is in agreement with the majority of systems containing pronominal opposition: *Ти and Вие* (for example – French, Tu – Vous, German, Du and Sie), where Tu is unofficial and informal, and Vous indicates an official contact. Similarly, in the Macedonian language, unlike in the Polish, there is a functionally identical opposition, but differently expressed: *Вие – господин // госпоѓа* (Pan // Pani):

> Дарко, како сте поминале во Македонија? (слушнато)
> (Darko, did you have a nice time Macedonia?) (heard)

Forms of address functioning in the Macedonian language have been borrowed from materials of official texts – minutes of meetings of parliamentary sessions, media articles and interviews taken from Macedonian Television and private conversations. Part of the material includes texts from Macedonian literature, especially the stories of Zhivko Chingo,[89] whose style is very similar to the spoken language.

Basic function of forms of address is to identify the addressee, establish contact with them and include them in a situation of communication. However, before continuing towards a more developed dialogue, it it important to point out that the function of the most official form of salutation in the Macedonian language is performed by the expression *добредојде // добредојдовте* (welcome) or sometimes by *добродојде // добродојдовте* [with the variant *Здраво* (hello)] with the compulsory and ritualistic replies: *добренајде // добренајдовне* or *добродојде // добродојдовте* with a private variant of the reply *добро ве најдов* (fine) // with the variant *здраво* (hello) //. Usually, this form is used in situations when first contact is made before an introduction of name and last name. When entering a Macedonian house, the host addresses the guests with the official words: *добредојдовте // добродојдовте* (welcome), then the appropriate answer is: *добренајдовме // добронајдовме* (it's good to be here // wel(l) found). In addition to the compulsory greeting ritual, the forms *добредојде // добродојдовте*, guests are also welcomed by offering them homemade pudding // jam together with a glass of water or juice.

---

89 Examples indicated with Ч and a page number are from: Zh. Chingo, *Големата вода* (*The Great Water*); *Сребрените снегови* (*Silver Snows*); *Ал*, Скопје 1992. Although stylistically colored, they are in close relationship – especially in Chingo – with informal language.

– Добредојде Наталија, те чекаме у мкд во брзо време.
(– Welcome Natalia, we expect you in Macedonia soon.)

– Здраво Наталија, те чекаме во Македонија во брзо време.
(– Welcome Natalia, we expect you in Macedonia soon.)

– Добре дојдовте! Прв подаде рака умниот стрико Лефтер...
(–Welcome! Wise uncle Lefter reached out first...)

– Добре дојдовте!
(– Welcome!)

– Прво се ракуваа со мудро чичко Lefter...
(– They first shook hands with the wise uncle Lefter...) Ч // 148

Vocative, as pure form of appeal, acts as basic semantic variant of address forms. In many languages, as in the Macedonian language, this function is dominated by the vocative form, for example:

Што работиш, Кејтенов **сине**?
(Son of Kejten, what are you doing?) Ч // 129

Мартине – му се обратија луѓето на стрико Мартин...
(Martin – people addressed uncle Martin...) Ч // 179

Мајко, мајчице мила!
(Mother, dear mother!) Ч // 111

These forms of vocative are still present in the contemporary Macedonian language, besides the fact that it was included by B. Koneski in the *Граматика на македонскиот литературен јазик* (*Grammar of Macedonian Literary Language*):

Вокативната форма во нашиот јазик сè уште здраво се држи, но од друга страна се гледа дека таа веќе е опфатена од процесот на постепено исчезнување.[90]
(The vocative form in our language is still widely present, however, on the other hand, it is obvious that it is being affected by a process of gradual disappearance.)

90 Б. Конески, *Граматика...*, p. 240–241.

B. Koneski also drew attention to the existance of different vocative forms for one and the same noun – *брат* (brother), *брате, брату* – used for the determination of semantic shades. The latter form, according to the author, is used when we directly address someone who is not our brother by birth, but only a friend or a stranger. It is rarely the case when the nominal form, the vocative form without inflection, is used to address our own brother, for example:

...Ами ти, бре брат, оти ич мукает не се чиниш.[91]
(But you, oh brother, why don't you take care of yourself at all.)

In function of the vocative form, in the Macedonian language: name, nickname, hypocoristic forms of the name, and other names with general meaning defining the social status of work and official titles, functions, words conveying respect, and family names are used. The system of names of relatives is especially widely developed and it is used as an integral part of forms of address among which there are about ten precisely defined closest family relations. These are just a small part of the more than one hundred lexicalized names of Macedonian family relations. The following are the most important: *татко*[92] (father), *мајка* (mother), *син* (son), *ќерка* (daughter), *брат* (brother), *сестра* (sister), *маж* [сопруг] (husband [spouse]), *жена* [сопруга] (wife [spouse]), *баба* (grandmother), *зет* (son-in-law), *девер* (bridesman), *деверица* (maid of honor), *јатрва* (sister-in-law), *золва* (sister-in-law), *золвин* (brother-in-law), *внук* (nephew), *внука* (niece), *сват* (inlaw), *сваќа* (mother-in law), *стрина* (aunt), *стрико, чичко* (uncle), etc. Some of them are also used when addressing a person with whome there are no family relations, for example *стрина* (aunt) – addressing an older lady or *стрико* (uncle) – addressing and older man.

Some of them are also used to address a person who is not related to the interlocuter, for example, *стрина* (aunt) or *стрико* (uncle) for addressing an elderly woman or an elderly man, respectively.[93]

91 Ibidem.

92 Е. Стоевска-Денчова, *Именување на роднинските односи во македонските дијалекти од словенски и балканистички аспект*, Скопје 2009.

93 According to V. Drvoshanov, "In the Gorani dialect, the lexeme *бабо* means 'father.' (...) The term *бабо* is borrowed from the Turkish language, 'баба, татко, прадедо, старец, добар човек' (baba, father, great grandfather, old man, good man, respectivelly) and represents Balkan Turkism." See: В. Дрвошанов, *Турски лексеми од роднинската терминологија во горанскиот говор*, "Македонски јазик" LXI, Скопје 2010, p. 144–145.

The most interesting, is the use of kinship names in an addressing function. Here we can mention situations in which the father or the mother in Macedonian families address their daughter as *mame* or *сине*[94] (daddy or son), emphasizing the particularily strong emotional relationship with their children, for example:

> И така еден ден ќе ѝ раскажуваш на ќерката, на скопски: сине, татко ти во тоа време беше еден транзициски фраер. Ех, транзициски, ама фраер.[95]
> (And so one day you will tell your daughter, in the Skopje dialect: son, at that time, your father was a transitional cool guy. Ah, a transitional but cool guy.)

This is related to the increasingly common manner for the parents to address their children as *сине* (son), regardless of the gender, as well as *мама* (mum) // *тато* (dad) for the children according to the manner children address their parents. Specifically, the mother addresses her daughter as *мама* (mum) and the father addresses his son as *тата* // *тате* (dad // daddy).

> Дојди, мама // тато, треба да одиме дома.
> (Come mummy // daddy, we need to go home.)

This phenomenon is especially widespread in Skopje and the address by use of **сине** (son) gets a universal dimensional meaning: *моето дете* (my child). It is characteristic that the form of address *сине* (son) is used in families where the parents have only daughters, however, parents usually address them as **сине** (son). This phenomenon might be explained by verbal-psychological mechanism of composition in families which have no male children.

Regarding the position of the vocative form in function of form of address in the Macedonian language, it can be: initial, medial or final.[96] The vocative form position at the beginning of the sentence asks the addressee to be attentive and to engage in receiving information:

---

94 A similar phenomenon is noticed in the Serbian language.

95 https: // twitter.com/MakNBA/statuses/302895809236713473 (accessed on: 2 February 2015).

96 Question discussed by Т. Гочкова, *Именското обраќање во македонскиот јазик*. Магистерска работа. Универзитет „Св. Кирил и Методиј," Филошки факултет, Скопје 1993 (необјавен труд) (T. Gochkova, *Nominal Forms of Address in Macedonian Language*. Master's work. Univeristy "Sts. Cyril and Methodius," Faculty of Philology, Skopje 1993 [unpublished work].)

О, мили деца, бидете среќни што заврши таа проклета војна.
(O, dear children, be happy that the damn war is over.) Ч // 107

О песно, земјо, жено, о живот и смрт ведно се што ми носиш денес сам ќе го испијам жедно.[97]
(Oh you song, earth, woman, oh life and death jointly, everything you bring me today, I will drink ardently.)

Жено, мори, донеси една лубеница.
(Wife, bring me watermelon.) (heard)

The initial position of forms of address can be proceeded by articles, interactions and also pronouns. "Fantastic points," and the pronoun *ти* (you), for example: *о, ајде, де, ја, а, абе, ама, ами, аман, оф, море // мори*, etc.

Ти, ами, ништо не си зеде за јадење.
(You didn't take anything to eat.) Ч // 64

In a medial position, vocative forms, as part of questions, have the function of communication boosters:

За тебе, Мартине, би прилегал ѕвонец од некое старо прчиште.
(For you, Martin, a bell from an old ram would be fitting.) Ч // 186

Ќе престанеш бе, мрснику, или не!
(Will you stop, you scoundrel, or not!) Ч // 121

In the final position, vocative forms mainly have the function to maintain communication, but at the same time they are of an emotional character. They usually appear within structures used to praise someone by means of diminutive form or augmentative form, when used to criticize someone pointing out their wrong action. Thus, the speaker can determine whether the relationship towards the addressee as a communicant is a positive or negative one:

– Приказни, приказни мили мои.
(– Stories, stories my dearies.) Ч // 108

– Тоа е пример, глупаку!
(– It's an example you fool!) Ч // 118

97 А. Шопов, *Црно сонце*, in: *Одбрани дела… Поезија.* Книга втора, Скопје 1976, p. 215.

2. Personal Name, Name and Last Name, Nickname, Title...

The most frequently used form of address in the Macedonian language is the personal name – it can be the name itself, name and last name, nick name, title or diminutive noun. People who use their personal name in interpersonal relations point out that they are in close relationship with the addressee – familial, friendly and sometimes neighboring relationship with interlocutors easily pass to use of ТИ. In the Macedonian language there is also the possibility for addressing by use of the last name. However, this is when the last name is followed by an appellative – colleague, friend, mister + last name including their feminine equivalents: *колешка, другарка, госпоѓа + име* (colleague, friend, madam + last name), for example:

> Господине Богоевски, дојдовме и до Вас.
> (Mister Bogoevski, it is your turn now. What is your opinion?[98])
>
> Знаете, госпоѓо Костова, јас во стартот поинаку би го поставил прашањето...[99]
> (You know, madam Kostova, I woud ask the question differently from the start...)

It is a very rare case when in the Macedonian language exclusively the last name is used as a form of address. This occurs only when the relations between the speaker and the addressee are symmetrical, for example: an order in the military, communication between soldiers and policemen as a high degree of expression of friendliness and solidarity.[100] The same applies to official situations when Macedonians use the form of address name + last name without any context in a form of complementation, as for example:

1. другар, колега, госпоѓа // господин + име и презиме
friend, colleague, madam // mister + name and last name
with its variety;

2. другар, колега, госпоѓа // господин + презиме
friend, colleague, madam // mister + last name.

---

98 *News*, Македонска Телевизија (October 10, 2012).

99 Ibidem.

100 The same situation can be encountered in the Polish language when in jokes or in family relationships, the speaker and the addressee address one another by use of only the last name.

The second (2) type of construction of forms of address, for example, in the Polish language is very rare. This is discussed by Małgorzata Marcjanik in her work *Grzeczność w komunikacji językowej* (*Politeness in Linguistic Communication*):

> In the Polish language, common forms of address are: (Panie Walczak – Mr. Walczak), (Pani Kowalska – Mrs. Kowalska) and are permited only in two situations (...). First, when someone singles out (calls out) someone else from the group. So, a student may be asked:
>
> Mr. Walczak, could you please explain the difference between a vowel and a semivowel.
>
> A participant in an excursion: (...) Mr. Walczak, here are your documents. It is not the forms that are especially elegant, but they are confortable in the given situations because they prevent errors in identifying people. Second, these forms are used by residents of small cities where everyone knows everyone else (sometimes including people from several generations) and these forms are considered to be polite (...) In other situations, these forms are considered to be inappropriate.[101]

In the contemporary Macedonian language such constructions enter the standard as universal forms of address in all regions of the language, but especially the official register, as is the case of almost all European languages.

a. Forms of Address in the Macedonian Public Discourse (based on examples from parliamentary discourse)

Forms of public address can be analyzed based on examples from the Macedonian parliamentary discourse, having in mind the use of expressions, titles and ranks typical for an official language register (style). Discourse should be considered as a norm, a strategy and a convention applied in the creation and organization of language.[102] The result of this strategy, relying on the social and linguistic patterns, are the genres of parliamentary discourse.

Discourse can also be defined in relation to the context characteristics, not only because of the language structures typical for parliamentary discourse. This is related to the institutional ceremony supported

---

[101] M. Marcjanik, *Grzeczność w komunikacji językowej*, Warszawa 2007, p. 46–47.

[102] M. Kawka, *Współczesny dyskurs polityczny na temat pomników (na przykładzie Macedonii)*, in: *Międzycywilizacyjny dialog w świecie słowiańskim w XX i XXI wieku. Historia – religia – kultura – polityka*, ed. by I. Stawowy-Kawka, Kraków 2012, p. 45–58.

by, for example, processes of taking and giving a word during parliamentary sessions.

The discourse itself takes place in separate room intended for parliamentary sessions, the MPs speak from a given place, from a pulpit, someone gives or takes a word, replies, warns when a speaker exceeds the allowed time limit, titles the speakers etc. In addition, a parliamentary debate takes place in different forms – types of speech acts, permitted or restricted by parliamentary protocol and in accordance with session regulations. Among all else, these include: parliamentary questions: answered or not answered (interpellations). Other genres of parliamentary discourse include:[103] debate, expose, decision, declaration, resolution, recommendation, conclusions, etc., which are not as characteristic for parliamentary discourse. The ceremony also includes forms of address used by MPs to address other participants in the parliamentary debate.

Since 3 October 2002, the websites of the Macedonian Assembly publishes archived language material that can be interesting not only for linguists but also for politicians, journalists and other professionals dealing with the modern history of Macedonia. These are authentic stenograms and notes from all sessions of the Macedonian Parliament. The material contains not only language elements, but also non-language ones that appear during the sessions and are recorded in accordance with the adopted schedules for the sessions. These other, non-language – elements, are very simple – raising a hand, hitting with hands, showing fists, getting up from a chair with gesticulations and mimic gestures and leaving the session hall as a sign or protest. In some parliaments, a physical altercation may occur among MPs. The political content of the stenograms, which can be subject to analysis primarily for political science and political scientists, is less interesting for linguists.[104] The complete material includes the period between

---

103 Polish parliamentary discourse has a book dedicated to by E. Laskowska, *Dyskurs parlamentarny w ujęciu komunikacyjnym* (Bydgoszcz 2004). The theory of speech acts is extensively used by the author, and in their description, in addition to their clasification, she also takes into consideration categories such as: emotionality, modality and belief. Spanish parliamentary discourse was a subject of research to: L. Martin Rojo, T.A. van Dijk, *Habia un problema y se ha solucionado...*, p. 169–234.

104 On this occasion, linguistic structures and their function in communication, not political content of MPs' speeches and dialogues, are the subject of analysis. These are stenograms and notes from all the sessions of the Macedonian Parliament, *Стенографски белешки од Четириесет и третата седница на Собранието на Република Македонија, одржана на 5 октомври 2012 година*; http: // www.sobranie.mk/ext/sessiondetails1.aspx?Id=f769ffd3-81d8-4202-8d2a-0ad160485593 (accessed on: 2 November 2014).

2002 and 2008 and is consistent with tousands of pages of stenograms. Here, I would like to indicate some issues originating in the description of this type of discourse, i.e. the Macedonian parliamentary or political discourse concerning the period until 2012 (publishing of recordings made until 2012).[105] This parliamentary discourse as part of the public discourse, since it is placed on the Internet, can also be considered as a kind of media discourse – because it is on the Internet. Thus, through the media, the government wants to communicate with society, and especially through the Internet creates, the illusion that the people reading the stenograms of parliamentary sessions, on a specific manner, can rule the people together with the representatives and the government.

By analysis of the stenograms language, all speech acts can be directly monitored as constitutive parts of the parliamentary discourse, their exponents and their illocutionary strength from this type of discourse. Similarly, from the theory of speech acts we gain instruments that emphasis the MPs' motivation and goals, which they wanted to achieve by use of different strategies, rhetoric and eristic means during parliamentary sessions. Hence, in the description, rhetorics and eristics will be in the center of our attention, and their functions will have the same place in the description of pragmatics and parliamentary discourse.

People who represented completely different professions and eras, politicians, journalists and writers, used mechanisms of discourse and discoursive strategies to achieve and maintain power, and above all, rule others. From this aspect, not much has changed today.

Discourses: historical, political i.e. parliamentary, film, literary, theatrical, media, etc., today, are mostly communication strategies that are mainly aimed at achieving superiority over a verbal opponent in a conversation from different aspects: esthetic, political, media, etc. In a parliamentary discourse, its participants are more aimed at presenting their own rhetoric and experience than at achieving a settlement over a dispute by means of logical argumentation. This aspect is even more radically expressed in A. Schopenhauer's book: *Die eristische Dialektik*, saying:

> (...) in a discussion we usually fight not only for the truth but for the justification of our hypothesis.[106]

---

105 The stenogram, which are similar in form, but, of course, not by content, can be found on the websites of the Polish parliament (i.e. sejm). The first such stenograms were observed and recorded in 1863, during the session of the Galician Sejm in Lvov.

106 A. Schopenhauer, *Erystyka, czyli sztuka prowadzenia sporów*, transl. by T. Kotarbiński, Warszawa 2002, p. 7. (*Eristische Dialektik oder Die Kunst Recht zu behalten*, Haffmans Verlag, Zürich 1983.)

Moreover, an orator (MP on a parliamentary session, politician during a meeting, journalist in the media, teacher at school, writer in a book) always fights for the right to rule the discourse, wants to be a leader of the discussion, warns, threatens, educates, evaluates other people's actions – directly or indirectly – although competences in this aspect may belong to someone else. Thus, he, as a rhetoric (but not necessarily meritorious) master (strategist) of the discourse, is the most important. He organizes and arranges the statement, allows or permits others to speak, interrupts or creates a metatextually richer discourse, and allows his speech, with pauses and verbal hyperboles, to be, for example ironic and superior. In one word – the speaker (in this case the MP) tends to be versatile and competent, and not only from the aspect of merit, but also linguistically, organisationally and above all discoursively. At the discourse's beginning, initial forms, meta-operators, have a mandatory function. They open the discourse. In such a function, forms of address used by the President of the Parliament in addressing the MPs and other guests present (including greetings, warnings, giving and taking a word, pleas, questions and answers, threats, etc.) are compulsory. *На пратениците и другите присутни гости*. These are mostly stereotypical formulas which, except for few exceptions, can be used in parliament or at other official places where the public or political discourse is led, but rarely take place in everyday i.e. informal, language.

Accordingly, any public discourse has got its own procedural order and ceremony: it can be open and led only by the President or Vice president of the session, who initially must say the following obligatory formula:

> Дами и господа пратеници,
> Ја отворам Седмата седница на Собранието на Република Македонија.
>
> (Ladies and gentlemen MPs,
> I open the Seventh session of the Parliament of the Republic of Macedonia.)

In all types of language communication (official and unofficial) in the Macedonian language, the forms: sir, madam i.e. ladies and gentlemen are used to such an extent only in public announcements, public speeches and addresses, however, they are mandatory in the Parliament. They are not much present in the informal, everyday language. People in stores, on the street or in public institutions do not address others as **sir** or **madam**, but the use of the forms ВИЕ (plural YOU) or ТИ (YOU – singular) prevails.

In comparison with the Polish parliament (sejm), where nobody can address their fellow colleagues, without creating a sense of insult – as: *господин Ковалски или господине Ковалски* (Mr. Kowalski), which is often the case in the Macedonian Parliament. In the Macedonian parliament, the forms of address *господин // госпоѓа* are interchangeably used with the form ВИЕ in the same function, as are ranks and titles in the vocative form without the use of the name // last name, for example:

J.M.: Тоа го нема во Деловникот.
(This is not in the Rules of Procedure.)

Претседателе, не се секирајте нема многу да одолговлекуваме...
(**President**, do not worry, we won't be long...)

D.J.: Затоа, викам јас **прстседателе**, да ми дозволите...
(That is why, **president**, I ask you to allow...)

N.P.: Еве јас ќе **те** потсетам **господине Гечовски**, со оглед што ти многу добро памтиш што се случило 1998 година.
(I volunteer, **Mr. Gechovski**, to remind (singular) you, given that (singular) you remember very well what happened in 1998.)

Z.: Зарем, господине Г., во 21 век веруваш дека ќе ја запреш вистината со цензура?
(Indeed, mister G., do you truly believe that in the 21st century you will stop the truth by means of censorship?)

It might be the case that the MPs address themselves only by means of rank and last name in the vocative – **министре** (minister):

B.G.: Министре П., не кажувајте гачки, одговорете кој е предлогот...
(**Minister P.**, do not give us puzzles, say what the proposal is...)

Sometimes, the speakers purposefully mix the forms TI and ON, i.e., second with third person singular and this happens in the presence of the MP the speaker address:

Јас да му објаснувам, па јас имам потполнето формулар, а ако сака да научи како се создаваат пари, фирми, компании за тоа не можам

јас за една минута да му кажам. **Човекот нека дојде да седнеме ќе му објаснам**, тој е млад треба да научи и се што ќе научи ќе му користи, нели? Сега за една минута ептен е многу. Јас тоа го правев 40 години, а нему ќе му треба можеби 100. Благодарам.
(He wants me to explain! Well I have already filled in a form, and if he wants to learn how money, firms, companies are created, I can not tell him that in one minute. Tell the man to come and I will explain to him, he is young and should learn and everything that he learns will be usfull for him, right? It is too damn much to say it all now in just a minute. I did that for 40 years, and it will probably take him a 100. Thank you.)

And at the end, the dialogue that even brought about the changing of a surname (perhaps unintentionally, this is difficult to veryify) and addressing through ON regardless of whether the discourse took place in the Macedonian parliament, or whether the MP in question is present at the session (and he is present):

(Mak.)
Затоа не да велите **Халили** предложил да се одложи оваа точка. Јас предложив прв, во дискусијата. А тој е втор. Да се запише тоа таму. Заради поените. Па утре, можби ќе имам можност во кариерата да напредувам.
Н.П.:
Благодарам, ќе ви запишеме поени.
Господинот Љупчо Јордановски бара збор.
Момент господине Јордановски, господинот Халими бара збор.
И.Х.:
Јас не сум Халили, јас сум Халими.
Н.П.:
Добро, кажете му, седи до вас.

(Eng.)
This is why you should not say **Halili** proposed to defer this point. My proposal was first in the discussion. And he is the second. This should be recorded over there. For the sake of scoring. And tomorrow, I may have the opportunity to advance my career.
N.P.:
Thank you, your score will be recorded.
Mr. Ljupcho Jordanovski requires a word.
Just a moment Mr. Jordanovski, Mr. Halimi requires a word.
I.H.:
I am not Halili, I am Halimi.

N.P.:
All right, tell him, he is sitting next to you.

In the parliamentary discourse, MPs dispute and discuss. These disputes and discussions are dominated not by the means which are not essentially rhetorical, but possess more of an eristic character. However, most frequently this function is featured not only by ironic expressions, but also by the game with addressing formulas.

Here is how MPs addressed among themselves during a session on 5 October 2012 – *членовите на македонскиот парламмент,*[107] *пратеници, министри и други претставници на највисоките органи на земјата (кога гласот го зема еден од пратениците)* – members of the Macedonian parliament, MPs, ministers and other representatives of the highest organs of the country (when one of the MPs has a word):

1. **Почитуван претседателе, почитуван претседател** на **Владата** на Република Македонија, почитувани министри, колешки и колеги пратеници, претставници на медиумите...
   (Distinguished President, President of the Government of Republic of Macedonia, respected Ministers, colleagues, MPs, representatives of the media...)

2. Благодарам, господине претседател...
   (Thank you, Mr. President...)

3. Да ве прашам господине Павле Трајанов...
   (Let me ask you Mr. Pavle Trajanov...)

4. Господине Поповски вие знаете како јас ги бранам ставовите на Македонија.
   (Mr. Popovski you know how I defend Macedonia's policies.)

5. Ги спомнавте Викиликс, **госпоѓо Поповска**.
   (You mentioned WikiLaks, **Mrs Popovska**.)
   Дали во Викиликс пишува...
   (Does WikiLeaks say...)

6. **Господине колега Јани**, всушност слушајќи го вашиот говор за...
   (**Mr. colleague Jane**, acctually, by listening to your speech...)

---

107 All quotation are taken from: *Стенографски белешки од Четириесет и третата седница на Собранието на Република Македонија...*

7. **Почитувана Иванова**, вас посебно ве ценам…
(**Respected Ivanova**, I particularly appreciate you…)

8. Почитуван колега Илија, вие имавте речиси рефрен во вашата дискусија за тоа како опозицијата сака да дојде на власт.
(Respected colleague Ilija, you almost introduced a chorus in your discussion on how the opposition wants to take the government over.)

8a. Почитуван, излези во центарот на Скопје и види на што личи.
(Respected, come in the center of Skopje and see what it is like.)

9. Marjancho Nikolovski: **Колега Димов, бидејќи рековте со господинот Талат Џафери сте биле пријатели**, да ве прашам, што ќе преземете во понеделник да се надмине пародијата на Комисијата за труд и социјала.
(Marjancho Nikolovski: **Colleague Dimov, since you said that you are friends with mister Talat Djaferi**, let me ask you, what will you do on Monday, to overcome the parody of the Commission for labor and social affairs.)

10. Ilija Dimov: **Марјан**, не ми е само Талат пријател, **со тебе пијам** кафе **во** Велес, се гледаме еднаш неделно, немојте така да злоупотребувате, **или не смееш пред** Игор да **кажеш дека сме** пријатели во Велес. **Немојте така, ве молам. Вака** да се **разбереме господине Николов с книга**, светската криза е реалност. **Не можете**, да ја замајувате јавноста дека во Македонија единствено се случува криза.
(Ilija Dimov: **Marjan**, I am not friends with Talat, I **have coffee with you in** Veles, we see each other once a week, do not make such abuse, **or is it that you can't say it in front of** Igor that we are friends in Veles. **Don't do this, please. Let's make something clear Mr Nikolov**, the world crisis is a reality. The European crisis is a realityYou cannot say to the public that in the crisis is only happening in Macedonia.)

11. **Почитувана министерке** за внатрешни тој работи, јас настанот со автобусите воопшто не го спомнав…
(**Distinguished minister** for internal affairs, I did not mention the event with the buses at all…)

These are even all the options for style of address and manner of address in parliamentary sessions in the Macedonian parliament. The first example (1) includes an official title, which in accordance with protocol, it is used in public discourse. Yet, the following two forms catch the eye:

Почитуван **претседателе** (respected **president**) with its variable: почитуван **претседател**.

The first address (1) – **претседателе** (president) with vocative inflection *-е* – refers to a person of lower rank and function, however, the second form (2) **претседател** – refers to a person with higher function – Prime Minister. This a general tendency, a proof of the process of gradual disappearance of the vocative forms in favor of more prestigious expressions without the inflection *-е*.

This is discussed by L. Minova-Gjurkova[108] in *Синтаксата на македонскиот стандарден јазик* (*Syntax of the Macedonian Standard Language*).

In relation to the tendency for the abandonment of vocative forms in nouns, even in adjectives (except in *драг, мил* (darling), etc.) tha characteristics of the noun group, which are used for address in our language, the absence of special forms becomes more frequent in some group members, and sometimes in all of them.

a) Почитувани господине претседателе!
(Respected Mr. President!)
b) Почитуван господине претседателе!
c) Почитуван господин претседателе!
d) Почитуван господине претседател!
e) Почитуван господин претседател!

According to L. Minova-Gjurkova, the least acceptable is the construction a), but b), c) and d) can be seen through the prism of the standard, and the address in e) cannot be accepted as a manner of address, that can emerge in future. From the observation of the gathered linguistic material, it seems that the most often used construction is the one under b). Today, the construction b) is most popular in the Macedonian language: – *Почитуван господине претседател!*

The above listed examples (3–5) show that the Macedonian language ever so more frequently includes constructions such as:

Господине // госпоѓо + име и презиме или Господине // госпоѓо + презиме.
Mister // madam + name and last name of Mister // madam + last name.

---

108 Л. Минова-Ѓуркова, *Синтаксата на македонскиот стандарден јазик*, Скопје 1994, p. 111; Л. Минова-Ѓуркова, *Обраќањето во македонскиот јазик*, Предавања на XXII Меѓународен семинар за македонски јазик, литература и култура, Скопје 1990, p. 13–21.

The following example (6) contains double titles: *Господине колега Јани* (Mr. colleague Jani), showing independence of forms of address as are: Господине // госпоѓо (Mister // madam) as a form exclusively having an emphatic function, without a specific meaning, gaining content only from the form *колега* (colleague).[109] Exclusively specific forms are: **Почитувана Иванова // Почитуван** (Respected Ivanova // Respected)(without name and last name) in sentences 7, 8, 8a, which are similar (especially 8a) to those present in the Russian language as are: *Uważajemyj – delajte sroczno operaciju na glawnogo Sasharikowa iz Szklowa...*[110] This is how the speaker wants to avoid doubt that can depreciate the adversary, since in his further expose he addresses him as ТИ:

> (...) излези во центарот на Скопје и види на што личи.
> ((...) come in the center of Skopje and see what it is like.)

The last example (9) contains mixed use of the forms: ТИ and ВИЕ. Not only that the speaker cannot decide what form he should use, but most probably he does that on purpose:

> **Марјан**, не ми е само Талат пријател, со **тебе** пијам кафе **во** Велес, се гледаме еднаш неделно, **немојте** така да злоупотребувате, или **не смееш** пред Игор да **кажеш** дека сме пријатели во Велес.
> (**Marjan**, I am not friends with Talat, I have coffee with **you** in Veles, we see each other once a week, **do not** make such abuse, or is it that you can't **say** in front of Igor that we are friends in Veles.)

> Немојте така, ве молам.
> (Don't do this, please.)

> Вака да се разбереме **господине Николовски**.
> (Let's make things clear **Mr. Nikolovski**.)

He begins with ТИ – *Марјан, тебе, смееш, да кажеш*...(Marjan, you, may, to say...) when the strength of warning and critics prevails, he turns to the form ВИЕ. This is done purposefully so that the discourse becomes official and the speaker realizes his intention to dominate his political adversary.

---

109 We encounter a similar situation in the Polish language with the use od the form: *Panie kolego!* in some professions, for example, teachers.

110 http: // feduta.livejournal.com/229520.html (accessed on: 12 October 2012).

The last form of address: **Почитувана министерке (respected minister)**, reminds of the form lately discussed in Polish political science literature: *ministra* and *ministerka*[111] (mak. *тинистерка*).

This phenomenon is more closely related to the Macedonian language than to the Polish language. Feminine designations of professions, titles and functions are created in a serial and categorical manner. For example: *министерка* (ministress), *проректорка* (prorector(ess)), which are not unacceptable in the Polish language for now. Yet, only some of the tendencies are listed here: the first, being a result of a democratization of life, is to shorten the distance and widen the use of ТИ (singular YOU); the second, competing with the first, aims at wider introduction and adaptation of official forms of address in colloquial communication. Forms of address like **господине // госпоѓо, (sir // madam)** were rarely used while Macedonia was part of Yugoslavia. More commonly used forms of address at the time were: *другар // другарка + име и // или само име* (comrade + name and // or only name).

It is a relatively new phenomenon, similar to the one which is more common or standard in other European languages, unlike in the Polish language, that is, frequent use of forms of address as are:

> господин (е) // госпоѓо, колега + име (sir // madam, colleague + name): госпоѓо Поповска // господине Николов (Madam Popovska // Mister Nikolov), even – Господине колега Јани (Mister colleague Jani).

This last form, in which a needless accumulation of titles is used, as in the Polish language, has an effect of superfluous intimacy with the addressee (receiver).

What is interesting and very characteristic for Macedonians, are the forms used by parents to address their children. These include **сине**, which is used by parents to address their daughters, especially if there are no male children in the family.

---

111 I. Bobrowski, *Czy Joanna Mucha gwałci język?*, "Język Polski" 2012, XCII, p. 227–230.

B. LANGUAGE IN THE DISCOURSE: MACEDONIAN–POLISH

I. Some Causative Verbs in the Macedonian and Polish Languages

In *Słownik terminologii językoznawczej* (*Dictionary of Linguistic Terminology*) edited by Z. Gołąb, A. Heinz and K. Polański, the term causativum is defined as follows:

> One of the so-called kinds or types of the action, the word-forming category of transitive verbs denotes the fact that a subject of a verb causes (lat. causare 'cause') completion of a given action or acceptance of a given standpoint or state by its object. Slavic languages include only traces of this category of verbs, as are: Pol. *pić* (Мак. *пие*, Eng. *drink*) as opposed to *poić* (Mak. му дава некој // некому да пие, Eng. to give drink to), *mrzeć* (Мак. *умре*, Eng. *die*) as opposed to *morzyć* (Мак. доведе некого да *умре* // *умира*, Eng. causes someone to die).[112]

A similar definition can be found in the *Encyklopedia językoznawstwa ogólnego* (*Encyclopedia of general linguistics*), however, the authors have added that:

> (...) in the Polish language as well as in other Slavic languages or the newer Indo-European languages there are only remnants of this word-forming category. However, in Pre-Indo-European languages, this category belonged to productive formations created from basic verbs by means of vocal alteration of the basic vowel and the suffixes **-ejo-* // **-ī-* // **(-j-)*.[113]

Yet, the most suitable definition of causation can be found in *Semantics* by J. Lyons, who connects causation to the hypothesis on lexical

---

[112] *Słownik terminologii językoznawczej*, ed. by Z. Gołąb, A. Heinz, K. Polański, Warszawa 1970, p. 90.

[113] *Encyklopedia językoznawstwa ogólnego*, ed. by K. Polański, Wrocław 2003, p. 81.

distribution (component analysis). According to the author, valency as well as verb semantics, for example, *убива* (kills), should be described by its dependence on the verb's non-transitive construction *умира* (dies) (i.e. *почнува да не живее* (begins not to live)) from the abstract verb *предизвикува* (cause). By replacing the complex predicated (meaning *почнува да не живее* (begins not to live)) with the verb *умира* (dies), concurrently, we replace the construction 'X causes Y to die' with the construction 'X causes – Y dies' in which 'causes – dies' is lexicalizes as 'kills'.[114]

Verbs of this type can also be found in the Macedonian language. For example, *го умира* (he is being died), as well as *го легне, го седне, го трча, ги лета, ги бега* (being put to sleep, to sit, to run, to fly, to escape), etc., which in certain syntactic and semantic conditions can secondarily perform as transitive verbs bearing causative meaning or being causative lexis, for example ...*детето трча* (the child is running) – *тој го трча детето* (he is running the child). These verbs are not included in any special morphologic or semantic group – on one hand, they can be verbs of motion – *бега, оди, лета, шета,* mental verbs – *мисли* (think), they can even denote meteorological phenomena *врне, стемни, раздени* (it rains, it is getting dark, it dawns), etc. On the other hand, they all have causative semantics.[115] Even though this phenomenon has already been noted in the Macedonian literature, it has not been fully studied, yet. Moreover, it was named using different terminology. Causative constructions are the primary topic of this discussion. For example, *Го легнав // седнав детето, го загинав клучот* (I laid // sat the child down, I lost the key). In addition, these terms have different functions: pseudo-causative use of verbs and secondary causativization or argumentation of intransitive verbs.[116]

The main purpose of the analysis is not to combine the abovementioned verbs in a particular group, for example, of secondary causatives, causatives, pseudo-causatives or verbs created by secondary transitivization. Syntactic-semantic mechanisms of causation in the Macedonian and the Polish language should receive more attention.

Here are some examples of such causative verbs together with their semantic explications and contexts:

---

114 J. Lyons, *Semantyka*, Vol. 2, p. 106.

115 Ibidem, p. 106–111.

116 Б. Корубин, *За дезаргументизацијата на транзитивните и аргументизацијата на интранзитивните глаголи*, "Studia Gramatyczne" 1982, V, p. 141–146.

Macedonian – Polish

бега – X causes someone to run – spowodować, że ktoś ucieka;
Дај двајцата, дружно да бегаме и да го добегаме уште малку што ми останало (КСМЈ[117]).
Let us both run together and finish running what little is left.

врне – (something) causes it to rain – spowodować, że pada deszcz, grad… itp.
Облаците да не врнат град (К).
Clouds should not rain hail.

зрее – X causes Y to ripen – spowodować, że coś dojrzewa;
Ги оставаа сливите, ги зреат (К).
They were leaving the plums unpicked, so they would ripen.

заспие // **заспива** – X causes someone to go to sleep – spowodować, że ktoś zaśnie, uśpić // usypiać (К);
Бабата Тода ги заспиваше сите девојчиња (К).
Granny Toda put all the girls to sleep.

игра – X causes the horses to dance – spowodować, że konie ćwiczą, trenować – o koniach (СМЈ);
Момчињата ги играат коњите.
The boys trained the horses.
Напред мургавиот алкар го играше вранецот (СМЈ).
The swarthy chain maker trained the black stallion.

лета – X causes someone to fly – spowodować, że X zacznie latać;
Тој ги лета гулабите (Inf).
He caused the pigeons to fly.

легне – X causes someone to lay – spowodować, że ktoś się położy;
…го легна (К);
to lay him down.
Треба на нешто да го легне царот, да го седне, да го најаде (КСМЈ).
He should lay the king down on something, to sit him down, to feed him.

---

[117] All examples come from the following sources: СМЈ – *Речник на македонскиот јазик: со српскохрватски толкувања*, т. 1–3, ed. by Б. Конески, Скопје 1961; (К) – Б. Конески, *Граматика на македонскиот литературен јазик*, Скопје 1976; (КЈМЈ) – index of The Dictionary of the Macedonian lanuage at The Institute for Macedonian Language K.P. Misirkov in Skopje; (inf) – informants from Skopje.

мисли – X causes someone to think of someone else – spowodować, że się myśli o kimś;
Кутрата, го мислат сега, не го знајт кај е (К).
Poor thing, she thinks of him, she doesn't know where he is.

најаде – X causes someone to give someone else a lot to eat, eat their fill – spowodować, że ktoś się naje, dawać komuś jeść;
Јас ќе те најадам и напијам (К).
I will feed you and give you something to drink.

наруча – X causes someone to have lunch – spowodować, że ktoś zje obiad, dawać komuś obiad;
...прво ги наруча децата, а после ги покани големите да ручаат (CJM).
...first she will feed (give lunch to) the children, then she will invite the elders to have lunch.

навечера – X causes someone to have dinner – spowodować, że ktoś zje kolację, dawać komuś kolację (К);

оди – X causes someone to go over something – spowodować, że ktoś przejdzie przez coś;
Го одам полево како ништо за еден сат!
I will go over the field in an hour! (К)

падне – X causes someone to fall down – spowodować, że coś spadnie, upadnie;
Студот го падна системот (Inf).
The cold knocked (caused to fall down) the system down.

почине – X causes someone to rest – spowodować, że ktoś odpocznie;
...почини го татко ти, многу работи.
...let your father rest, he works too much. Таму ќе ги починат коните; го починувам конјот (CJM).
They will rest the horses there; I rest the horse.

помине – X causes someone to cross over something – spowodować, że ktoś przejdzie przez coś;
...преку вода ќе те помине, капка вода не ти дава (CMJ); ...јавни ме ти и помини ме пред владиката (К).
...he will cross over the water and won't let me have a drop; ...put me up and take me across before the bishop.

поодрасте – X causes someone to grow up – spowodować, że ktoś podrośnie;
Фросина раѓаше деца и штом ќе ги поодрастеше умираа (СМЈ).
Frosina gave birth to children and as soon as she raised them (they grew) up a bit, they died.

пошета – X causes someone to walk – spowodować, że ktoś spaceruje;
...еве ги пошета децата (СМЈ).
...she walked the children.

попрошета – X causes someone to walk briefly – spowodować, że ktoś się przespaceruje // spaceruje;
...го попрошетавме стариот (СМЈ).
...he walked the old man briefly.

породи – X causes Y to give birth (deliver) – pomóc przy porodzie, spowodować, że X urodzi dziecko;
...еве ја бабицата што ме породила (СМЈ), Доктор, кој ме породи...
...here is the midwife who delivered me, the doctor who delivered me (Inf).

порасне – X causes someone to grow up – spowodować, że ktoś urośnie, dorośnie;
...ги изгледавме децата, ги пораснавме (SMJ); Ја порасна ли?
...we raised the children, we brought (grow) them up (K).
Од нас зависи да го пораснеме до возрасниот (Inf).
It is on us to bring (grow) him up to adulthood.

премине – X causes someone to get over something – spowodować, że ktoś przejdzie przez coś;
Како да ги премине децата преку река?
How to get the children over the river? (K)
Качи ми се на вратот и ќе те преминам преку река (СМЈ).
Pop up on my shoulders and I will get you over the river.

пукне – X causes something to break – spowodować, że coś pęknie, stłucze się;
...си играше со шишето додека не го пукна (СМЈ).
...he played with the bottle until he broke it.

радува – X causes someone to rejoice – spowodować, że ktoś się cieszy;
Госпо ќе те радува со машко дете (К).
God will bring you joy (rejoice you) with a baby boy.

расте – X causes someone to grow up (rosnąć) – spowodować, że ktoś, coś urośnie;
Сум ги растел на овие две раце (КСМЈ); А не помислуваш како јас сум го растел тоа дете (…)
I grew them up on these two hands; And you do not think of how I had raised (grown) that child up.
…баба Угра си ги растела, како две јаболка на гранка (КСМЈ).
…grandma Ugra was growing them as two apples on a branch.

раздени – X causes someone to dawn – spowodować, że kogoś zastał świt, dzień;
ме раздени… (К) го раздени во една планина (РМЈ).
The day dawned on me. (…The day dawned on him in one mountain.)

седне – X cause someone to sit – spowodować, że ktoś usiądzie;
…го повикал зета си, го седнал на стол (СМЈ); На престол ќе те седнам (…)
He call his brother-in-law and sat him on a chair; I will be sat on a throne.
Кога го седна на клупата беше блед (…) да ја доведе накај миндерот и ја седна (КСМЈ).
When he was sat on a bench, he was pale (…) to lead he to the settee and sat her down.

слезе – X causes someone to come down from somewhere – spowodować, że ktoś zejdzie skądś;
Едвај чека да ја слезе во дворот негов; …да го слезат на земјата; Слезе го сонцето, да си го земам.
He couldn't wait for her to come down in his yard; …to put (come) it down; Put (come) the sun down so that I can take it.
Не ќе ме слезат од височини…
I will not be put (come) down from the heights…(КСМЈ)

смее – X causes someone to laugh – spowodować, że ktoś się zaśmieje, doprowadzić do śmiechu;
…ги смееше децата (СМЈ);
…made the children laugh.

стане – X causes someone to stand up – spowodować, że ktoś wstanie;
…go stana (K);
…he was made to stand up.

шета – X causes someone to walk – spowodować, że ktoś spaceruje z kimś;
…ги шетав децата (СМЈ); …го шетале низ ливаѓето…(КСМЈ)
…I walked the children; …he was walked through the meadow…

трча – X causes soomeone to run – spowodować, że ktoś biegnie (zacznie biec);
...го трча детето (Inf).
...he runs the child.

умре – X causes someone to die – spowodować, że ktoś umrze // umiera, zabić kogoś;
Двапати умираш еден ист човек, тоа веќе не може да се прости (К).
She // he made the same man die twice, it cannot be forgiven.

Regarding the phenomenon of transitivity of the primarily intransitive verbs, B. Koneski in *Граматиката на литературниот македонски јазик* (*Grammar of the Macedonian Language*) wrote the following:

> It has been noted that in our contemporary language there are cases in which primarily intransitive verbs take an object, thus becoming transitive verbs.[118]

The author lists numerous cases in which transitivity is developed and broadened. According to the author, this phenomenon can be seen when:

> a) we have transitive and intransitive verbs which have an associated meaning" and only by a "certain derangement of meaning can a shade of transitivity be developed in the appropriate intransitive verb. Thus, for example, when we find such a case in M. Cepenkov: *Мајка ти ќе ти ја умрам; издумале еден марифет, за да ја умрат; неа ништо не ја умирало, (I will make your mother die; they thought of a trick to make her die; but nothing could make her die)* – then, the importance of transitivity development in this verb is undoubted, because it associates in meaning with the transitive verbs *отепа, убие, умртви, усмрти (slaughter, kill, slay, murder)* (ex. *умрен, отепан (dead, killed)* etc.), hence, when used as transitive, it becomes synonymous.
>
> b) some verbs can be differently used as transitive, but in other relations, in another sense – while in the given case there is more or less perceptible transit in the field of transitive verbs with a different meaning." The author explains this phenomenon by using the verb *приближи (approach)* as an example: "This verb is used as a transitive synonym to the

[118] Б. Конески, *Граматика...*, p. 354.

verb *доближи (get close)*: *приближи го прстот до уста – доближи го прстот до уста.*
approach your finger to your mouth – get your finger close to your mouth.
The intransitive verb is, in turn, used in these cases: *приближавме до селото, до градот.*
approach the village, the city (...) it is completely possible, although unusual, the verb to be considered as transitive in this case as well: *кога ќе го приближиш (волкот) до село, ќе излезам со сето село за да го пречекам (when you approach (the wolf) to the village, I will come out with all villagers and welcome it)*" (M. Cepenkov).

c) transitivity broadens and "from one prefixed verb it goes to another, formed by another prefix, primarily intransitive verb: *Бабата Тода ги заспиваше сите девојчиња (...).*
Granny Toda put all the girls to sleep. Here, transitivity is transferred from the verb *успива (некого) (put (someone) to sleep).*

d) transitivity corresponding to the meaning of the transitive form of a given verb. It is completely common to say *тој ги скара (he scolded them).* However, this expression has two meanings: 1. corresponding to the verb *скара (укори некого) (scold (reprimand someone)): тој ги скара да бидат мирни (He scolded them to be quiet)*; 2. corresponding to the verb *скара се (to quarrel): тој ги подбуцнуваше и најпосле ги скара еден со друг (he provoked them and at the end made them quarrel with each other)* (he made them quarrel).

e) there is a certain kind of broadening of transitivity i.e. with some verbs that are transitive, however, as such, they are rarely used and when used, it is in particular structures, broadening the possibilities for their transitivity by entering in simpler structures with other verbs that are otherwise closely associated with in meaning. Thus, the verbs *вели, зборува (say, speak),* though transitive, can be found in fewer verb-object relations than the verb *кажува (tell).* It is common to say, for example, *кажува прикаска (tell a tale),* but it is uncommon to say *вели, зборува прикаска (say, speak a tale)* (...) However, today these verbs enter the sphere of use of *кажува*, too, thus broadening their transitivity: *Сите го велеа местото, оти било лошо (Everybody says the place to be bad)*" (M. Cepenkov).

f) verbs in which the more common prefix form enters a certain object-verb relation instead of the one that can be also found without prefixation: M. Cepenkov. Here, it is more common for the prefixed form

> *израдува* to be used (...) Similarly, in the example: *се сетив да и пишам и нив (I remembered to write them, too)* (M. Cepenkov) *пишам (write)* is used instead of the prefixed verb *запишам (write down).*[119]

The last example (*пишам* (write): *запишам* (write down)) is very interesting because there is a shift of the semantic association of the Macedonian verb пише with its nominal supplements, which can only be characterized by sub-categorial marks: -ANIM, not +HUM.

At the end, the author lists a number of cases drawn from folk tales, contemporary literature and spoken language in which these shifts "go so far as to develop object-verb relationships with originally intransitive verbs":

1. EXAMPLES FROM FOLK TALES

- Ако можите планината да ја проодите, што је онде каршија, ќе ве простам.
  If you could go through the mountain, which is just across, I will forgive you.

- Во истото време ќе ја тропнеле камбаната.
  At the same time they would toll the bell.

- Да и пребегаш ониа три планиње.
  You should run over those three mountains.

- Облаците да не врнат град.
  Clouds should not rain hail.

- Јавни ме ти и помини ме пред владиката.
  Put me up and take me across before the bishop.

- Пес да те лајт, ќе се скараш со некого.
  I'd be barked by a dog, you will get in quarrel with someone (Marko K. Cepenkov).

- Како да ги премине децата преку река.
  How to get the children over the river (D. Matov).

- Најсетне го поминале преку река.
  At the end, they crossed him over thse river (E. Sprostranov).

---

119 Б. Конески, *Граматика...*, p. 354.

- Ќе го застанат; ќе го починат.
  He will be stopped; he will be rested.

- Јас ќе ми те најадам и напијам.
  I will feed you and water you.

- Го навечерала, со што и дал Госпо, леб и сол.
  What God has given her, she gave him for dinner: bread and salt.

- Како овчарите што и рипаат браздите.
  Just like the sheep jump over the grooves (M. Cepenkov).

- *Стемни се (It got dark) и стемнило (and nightfall)* (Marko K. Cepenkov); *ме стемни, ме раздени.*
  The night fell on me, the day dawned on me; ме здоболе, ме мачи; it hearts me, it nagging me.

2. EXAMPLES FROM CONTEMPORARY MACEDONIAN LITERATURE

- Продолжи диво молскајќи го со очите Кирета.
  She continued wildly throwing lightning from her eyes when looking at Kire (K. Chashule).

- Ме седна па една столица.
  I was sat on a chair.
  На престол ќе те седнам.
  I will sit you on a throne.
  Радоста не помалку го вивна срцето на Крстета.
  The joy skyrocketed Krste's heart (K. Chashule).

- Подигни очи – очи засвети.
  Raise your eyes – light up your eyes (K. Racin).

- Да подземе неколку сакои за да го „опули" нашиот огон.
  To take some сакои to "give sight" to our fire.
  Пламенот што го исфрлаа неговите очи го вцрви Настета.
  The flame casting from his eyes made Naste blush (V. Maleski).

- Двапати да умираш еден ист човек, тоа веќе не може да се прости.
  She // he made the same man die twice, it cannot be forgiven.
  Едвај чека да ја однесе дома, да ја слезе во дворот негов.
  I couldn't wait for him to bring her home, to let her down in his yard.

Ја порасна ли?
Did you raise her? (S. Popov)

3. EXAMPLE FROM THE SPOKEN LANGUAGE

According to B. Koneski, "it is very common to say, for example: го *легна, го стана, го падна (he was laid down, stood up, fallen down)*, so one can even hear structures like: *Ги оставаат сливите – ги зреат (They were leaving the plums unpicked, ripening them)* (i.e. leaving them to ripe)."

"All of this shows – concludes the author – (...) that this case of a live phenomenon that reaches deeply in the hereditary relation between transitive and intransitive verbs, vacillating the difference between them."[120]

All this exhaustive information and materials rich in examples concerning intransitive verbs shifting to transitive verbs, as well as the, sometimes, intuitive analysis, not once touch upon the problematic concerning the core of the causative semantics of verbs, not only in the classical sense of the notion causativum as a word-forming category (pol. *pić – poić*), but also as a syntactic – semantic category.

The category *causativum* in the Macedonian language can be treated within the framework of the syntactic – semantic process of transitivization of intransitive verbs on all levels of language communication – folklore, literary texts and spoken language.

In the Polish language, the development and extensive distribution of causation processes of intransitive verbs to the extent present in the Macedonian language are not observed. There are no parallel intransitive verbs in the Polish language for following the Macedonian transitive verbs: *бега, легне, лета, падне, шета, зрее, мисли* (run, lay, fly, fall, walk, ripe, think). Polish: *uciekać, położyć się, latać, upaść, spacerować, dojrzewać, myśleć. One cannot run someone else* in the Polish language *да го бегаме некого (*uciekać kogoś), да го летаме некого* (to fly someone else) (**latać kogoś), да го шетаме некого* (to walk someone else) (**spacerować kogoś), да го седнеме некого* (to sit someone else) (**usiąść kogoś), да го трчаме некого* (to run someone else) (**biegać kogoś), да го умираме некого* (to die someone else) (**umierać kogoś*).

Polish equivalents to the abovementioned Macedonian constructions are analytical constructions (periphrastic causatives) having incorporated component in their semantics (Mac.) 'предизвикува' (Pol.) 'powodować' – (Eng.) 'cause'.

---

[120] Ibidem, p. 358–359.

If we compare Macedonian causative constructions with their Polish equivalents, for example:

Јанко го пукна шишето (Janko broke the bottle) – Janek rozbił butelkę
Јанко го напи Петрета (Janko gave Petre to drink) – Janek dał pić Piotrowi
Јанко го седна детето (Janko sat the child down) – Janek posadził dziecko (na krześle)

we can see that semantic constructions in Macedonian and Polish sentences have an incorporated component + cause:

X + V + cause + Y

Јанко го седна детето (Janko sat the child down)

X causes + Y + Verbum
X (+cause) + Y + V

This pattern can be used with the following sentences:

(mac.) (pol.)

Јанко го пукна шишето (Janko broke the bottle) – Janek rozbił butelkę
(Јанко предизвикува шишето да пукне – Janko caused the bottle to break)
(Jan spowodował, że butelka pękła)

Јанко го падна Петрета (Janko fell Peter down)
Jan przewrócił Piotra
(Јанко предизвикува Петре да падне – Janko caused Peter to fall down)
(Jan spowodował, że Piotr upadł)

Јанко го седна детето (Janko sat the child down) – Jan posadził dziecko (na łóżku)
(Јанко предизвикува Петре да седне – Janko caused Peter to sit down)
(Jan spowodował, że dziecko usiadło)

In interpreting causative constructions we can distinguish two basic, but closely related chronological and formal processes: first – determining morphological and word-forming causation (today there are only traces in some Slavic languages) and second, a contemporary – related to syntactic – semantic causation and transitivization of originally intransitive verbs.

J: Lyons considers the phenomenon of causation based on the example with two (a pair) of English verbs: *die* – *kill* in the following sentences:

1. Bill died
2. John killed Bill

According to Lyons, the verb *kill* can be semantically defined *die* + *causa* and considers that sentences 1/ and 2/ are transformationally related with one another – transitive twofold construction *John killed Bill* derives from the intransitive single construction by means of a causative operation. The author writes:

> In such cases we can say that the relation of the causative transitive verb to the intransitive one is lexicalized. It is a matter of the lexical structure of English that we say *John killed Bill*, rather than **John died Bill.*[121]

According to Lyons' words, if we say that *Јанко го умира Петрета* (Janko died Peter), not necessarily meaning that *Јанко го уби Петрета* (Janko killed Peter), we are actually talking about the lexical structure of the Macedonian language.

In the Macedonian language, the functioning of causative constructions such as *Мајка ти ќе ти ја умрам* (I will die your mother) is closely connected to the process of transitivization of originally intransitive verbs i.e. to the process of transitive derivation.

intransitive veb ► transitive verb

In this regard, Jerzy Kuryłowicz wrote:

> Causativa is a morphological verb category representing the regulated transitivization of intransitive verbs.[122]

J. Kuryłowicz's thought was a starting point for the analysis of Slavic causative verbs made by Z. Gołąb in his article *The Grammar of Slavic Causatives*. This author also connects the phenomenon of causation with transitivization of intransitive verbs:

---

121 J. Lyons, *Wstęp do językoznawstwa*, transl. by K. Bogacki, Warszawa 1989, p. 262.

122 J. Kuryłowicz, *The Inflectional Categories of Indo-European*, Heidelberg 1964, p. 88.

Causative is derived from basic, relative to them, intransitive verbs (...) morphological structure of "causativization" is comprised of regulated transitivization of basic irregular verbs.[123]

The author illustrates this definition by the following two patterns:

a)

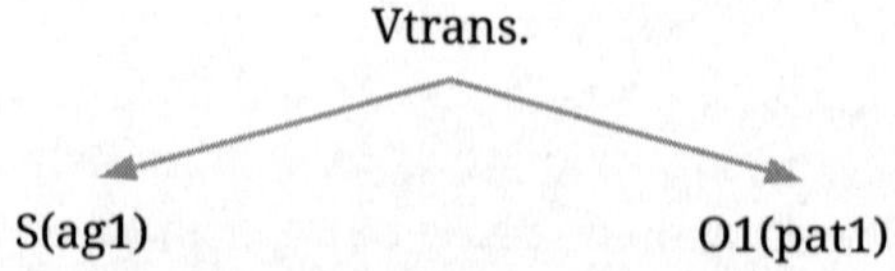

b)

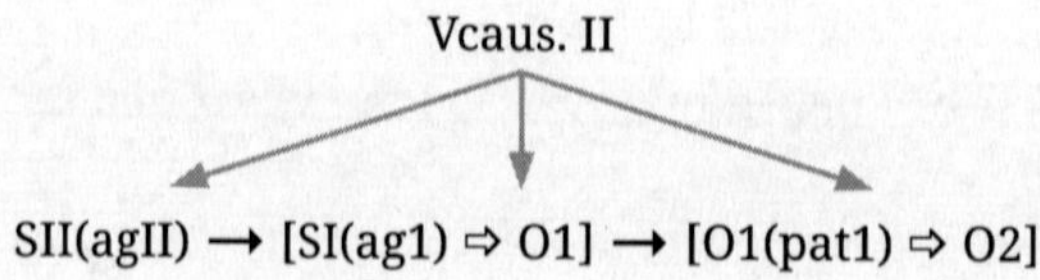

where: SI = first subject
SII = second subject
ag = agens
pat = patiens
O1 = object 1
O2 = object 2
⇨ = immediate transformation
→ = immediate syntactic relation between nominal sentence elements
 = immediate syntactic relation between verb and nominal sentence elements

In his article about the Slavic causative verbs, Z. Gołąb separated the following types of verbs, usually representatives of old Indo-European and Proto-Slavic *causative*. These types of verbs are separated based on the following formal indicators of causation:

1. suffixation + apophonic alterations (*ležati* → *ložiti*, *sěděti* → *saditi*, *tešti* → *točiti*);

---

[123] Z. Gołąb, *The Grammar of Slavic Causatives*, in: *American Contributions to the Sixth International Congress of Slavists*, Prague 1968, p. 74–76.

2. dereflectivization (*ženiti sę → ženiti, gněvati sę → gněviti*);
3. derivation of denominal and deadverbal verbs (*besъ → besiti, bogatъ → (o)bogatiti, xudъ → oxuditi, krotъkъ → (u)krotiti*);
4. "syntactic-contextual causativa" – characteristic of South Slavic languages (Serbo – Croatian and Macedonian in their contemporary state) – *On šeta konja, u večer me lijegaše, a jutru ustaje, Jovo konja trče, treba na nešto da go legne carot.*[124]

Old apophonic alterations (1) are represented in the Slavic languages by certain verbs. They are not much present in the two languages discussed here (Polish and Macedonian), for example (pol.): *mrzeć – morzyć, pić – poić, stygnąć – studzić, toczyć – ciec, wrzeć – warzyć*; (mac.): *čiti → kojiti – počine, gybnąti → gubiti – zagine,* ležati → *ložiti – legne*. Causative verbs of types 1/ and 2/ belong to the category which, to date, has been productive (alive) in Slavic languages (for example pol.: *dziwić się – dziwić kogoś, gniewać się – gniewać kogoś, złościć się – złościć kogoś,* as well as the adjectives: *brązowy – brązowić, cichy – uciszyć, czarny – czernić,* etc.) However, from the current point of view, the category of "syntactic – semantic" causatives is the most important. Here, the transitivization of originally intransitive verbs is an exclusive formal indicator of causation. This phenomenon is widely present throughout the Macedonian language (literary, spoken and folklore). Obviously, verbs which are extensions of the old Proto-Slavic formations can be found among Macedonian causatives, for example *orski || orstiti porasne, sěděti || sesji || saditi sedne, stati || stojati staviti – zastane, merti,moriti – umre.* However, the basic feature (mark) of the Macedonian causative verbs creation process is the transitivization of intransitive verbs, rather than apophonic alternations, dereflectivization or suffixation, which can only accompany this process.

The formation of causatives by means of semantic mechanisms is presented in a rather different manner. This primarily concerns the basic predicative – argumentative structures of Macedonian causative formations. In constructions with transitive causative verbs, as are *Јанко ја чита книгата* (Janko reads a book), semantic (predicative – argumentative) structure with two arguments can be distinguished, traditionally determined as *agens* and *patiens* (doer and recipient of the action), however, in constructions with causative verbs, such arguments can not be found at the right side of the predicate. A new predicative – argumentative structure, represented by a nominal element, noun – object, at the surface of the text, is hidden in patients' semantic position in sentences with a causative verb:

---

124 Ibidem, p. 90–92.

Тој ги лета гулабите.
(He causes the **pigeons** to fly.)

This can be seen if we compare two semantic structures of sentences, one with causative verb and the other one without it:

Semantic structure

pol. Jan czyta książkę –	Ag + V + Pat
mac. Јанко ја чита книгата (Janko reads a book) –	Ag + V + Pat

Causative construction

S1[Ag1 + V(+cause) + Pat]
pol. Jan przewrócił Piotra
mac. Јанко го падна Петрета (Janko fell Peter down (made Peter fall down))

S2 [Ag2 + V(-cause)]

Jan spowodował	Piotr upadł
Janko caused	Peter to fall down

The same situation arises in other constructions with syntactic – contextual causatives in the Macedonian as well as in the Polish language. We should add here that Agens2 (Ag2) has got to have a sub-categorical constraint: + *animal* (+Anim) или + *human* (+Hum).

1. On the Modal Verb *може // móc* in the Macedonian and the Polish Language

In linguistics, the term modality is used as a category expressing the correlation between the speaker and the expression's content and the described situation. Modal words serve to evaluate the truthfulness and possibility of events primarily in the sphere of epistemic and deontic modality. Some even serve to indicate alethic modality. Most often these are the auxiliary verbs and adverbial particles, for example, mac. *мора, може,* pol. *musieć, móc*; the particles, mac. *ќе, би,* pol. *choćby, jakoby, chyba,* and intonation.

The linguistic categorization of modality rests upon linguistic forms of its expression: grammatical – they belong to the category of manner of action, and linguistic – these are for example, functional or auxiliary verbs, as are: can, should, must, etc. Categorization of modality in linguistics is diverse, for example Bożena Bojar and Małgorzata Korytkowska distinguish three types of modality: alethic – concerning the truth, epistemic – concerning the meaning and deotic – concerning permission and order.[125]

Alexander W. Bondarko[126] speaks about six meanings of modality conferred with particular linguistic functions: lexical, grammatical and intonational:

1. sentence interpretation in terms of reality and unreality (realized through verb's category of manner or some particles),
2. interpretation of a described situation in terms of its feasibility,
3. interpretation of the degree of a speaker's certainty regarding the reality of presented information,
4. speaker's complete behavior: indicative, active or optative,
5. sentence interpretation in terms of truthfulness or falsehood,
6. emotional and qualitative interpretation of sentence content.

The very complicated problem of modality was a subject of description to Renata Grzegorczykowa in her book *Wstęp do semantyki językoznawczej* (*Introduction to Linguistic Semantics*).[127] The author mainly divides modality on: epistemic – in example, hypothetical modality, determining whether the fact in question is expected, postulated or desired; deontic – expressing duty, obligation; and analytic, informing on the objective possibility or necessity of facts and phenomena. The conclusion that the following sentence is ambiguous:

Jan może jechać w góry
Јанко може да патува во планините (Janko can travel in the mountains)

is interesting and it denotes:

- permission and possibility,
- an objective conclusion.

In the first case, the verb may belong in the sphere of modality, and in the second, it is treated as a "recognizable" part of the sentence, rather than as an expression with modal meaning.

---

125 B. Bojar, M. Korytkowska, *Problemy modelowania kategorii modalności a wykładniki leksykalne tej kategorii*, in: *Studia gramatyczne bułgarsko-polskie*, Vol. IV, *Modalność a inne kategorie językowe*, Warszawa 1991, p. 39–52.

126 А.В. Бондарко, *Модальность. Вступительные замечания. Теория функциональной грамматики: Темпоральность. Модальность*, ed. by А.В. Бондарко, "Наука" 1990, p. 59–67.

127 R. Grzegorczykowa, *Wstęp do semantyki językoznawczej*, Warszawa 1990, p. 134–163.

Modal information in the Macedonian and Polish language is presented by lexical means, primarily by modal verbs. These include Macedonian verbs: *може, смее, мора, треба* and Polish: *móc, śmieć, musieć, trzeba* (*potrafić, chcieć*). A basic characteristic of modal verbs is their sinsemantic character and inability to function independently. They may function as a verb (predicate) part of a sentence construction. See Ilija Chashule's article *Modal verbs in Macedonian language*[128] for the system of modal verbs and its semantic and formal traits in Macedonian language. However, this discussion is mainly dedicated to the verb *can* (*може*). According to the three-volume Dictionary of the Macedonian Language (1961–1966),[129] the verb *can* has three basic meanings:

1. Има сила да стори нешто (*Јас можам да го кутнам*).
Having the strength to do something (*I can knock him down.*)

2. Знае, умее (*Можам да читам многу*).
Knowing, having a skill (*I can read a lot.*)

3. Смее (*Можам ли да влезам*).
May (*May I come in?*)

4. Безлично (*Може да се вратил*).
Impersonality (*He*[130] *may have returned.*)

In the Macedonian language there is a regular use of congruent constructions as are for example *Јас можам да читам, Ти можеш да читаш* (I can read, You can read), etc. The situation in the Polish language is somewhat different: the modal verb *móc*, along the mechanism of rection, requires use of the infinitive instead of a verb in the personal form. Syntactically, in the Macedonian and the Polish languages, the modal (epistemic and deontic) verb is a constituent part of a complex predicate, the so-called modal predicate.

---

128 For the system of modal verbs and its semantic and formal characteristics in the Macedonian language see an article by I. Chashule titled *Модалните глаголи во македонскиот јазик*, Прилози МАНУ, X1V/2, Скопје 1989, p. 89–117.

129 *Речник на македонскиот јазик: со српскохрватски толкувања*, ed. by Б. Конески, т. I–III, Скопје 1961–1966.

130 In Macedonian language the pronoun is omitted being implicit in the verb infliction.

Ja mogę czytać, ty możesz czytać… (*mogę* as possibility, ability, order or permission) + OBJECT.

In both languages, the modal verb can connect to an autosemantic verb in accordance with the following models:

I.

Mac. The modal sinsemantic verb can be in a personal form + an autosemantic verb in a personal form with *да* (to), for example *да пишувам* = *Јас можам да пишувам* (to write – I can (to) write). The verbs have a congruence relationship: *Јас можам да пишувам, Ти можеш да пишуваш etc.* (I can write, You can write, etc.)

Јас можам + *да пишувам* (I can + (to) write) (congruence).

Pol. The modal sinsemantic verb *może* is in the personal form + autosemantic verb in infinitive = *Ja mogę pisać, ty możesz pisać…*

In this case, the auxiliary verb *może* orders (demands) that the verb pisać takes it infinitive form, hence we can talk about a form of rection.[131] *Może* takes only infinitive, no other form of the autosemantic verb, as an additional member.

Mogę pisać (rection or constellation).

Both constructions include an expression of modality conveying the meaning:

X jest w stanie coś zrobić, pisać, czytać…
Тој е во состојба да пишува, да чита + објект.
He is able to write, to read + object.

The English language counterpart is the modal verb *can*, the German is *können*, and the French is *pouvoir*. This is a regular construction that in both languages semantically expresses the alethic modality of ability.

Other uses of the modal sinsemantic verb *can* (*може*) and the autosemantic verbs, for example, *write, read,* do not include congruence. *Can* (*може*) operating in such sentences has the following model:

---

131 Rection – the determination of the form of one word by the presence of another word in a phrase or sentence.

II.

Може (*безлично*) + *да пишувам, да нишуваш, да пишува* (I can (impersonal) + (to) write, You can (to) write), etc.

Hence we can distinguish three modal meanings:

1. Meaning of permission or order,
2. Meaning of possibility,
3. Meaning of probability.

Олимписките игри може да почнат! (The Olympic Games can begin!) (is allowed)

Дали може да се залубите преку ИРЦ? (Can you fall in love through IRC?) (it is possible)

Каде може да преземете бесплатни апликации или шри за мојот на Apple iPhone? (Where can I download a free application or games for my Apple iPhone?) (it is possible)

Such constructions are beyond the linguistc norm in the Polish language. However, that does not mean that deontic modality is not real ized. In the Polish language the modal function is performed by other adverbs, for example *można, prawdopodobnie, chyba* (ang. can, probably, etc.).

For example, the last sentence in Polish would be:

Skąd można wziąć bezpłatne aplikacje lub gry na mojego iPhone'a?
Where can I download a free application or games for my Apple iPhone?

having the same modal epistemic meaning.

Such use of *can* in the Polish language can be compared only with Polish constructions expressing modality of probability, as for example: *może czytam, może czytasz, może czytamy, może przeczytam*, which are rare and they only convey the meaning of probability, where the second verb is a finite verb: *może przeczytam, może przeczytasz, może przeczyta*...

However, the biggest difference between the Polish and the Macedonian modal system of meanings expressed by *can* is in the use of the Macedonian modal verb *може* in its impersonal form and in the position of an adverbial particle. This is related to the 'Balkan' tendency to reduce sinsemantic verbs to a form of unalterable, petrified, adverbial particles. This phenomenon of evolution or reduction of the sinsemantic verb *може* to the form of a modal and adverbial particle (in the Polish language this function is performed by the adverbial *można*) leads to the very fact that in the informal Macedonian language, the form *може* is very often used (principally in questions, retorts and negations) in different communication situations (some refer to that kind of modality as a discursive or pragmatic modality), for example:

III.

A. *Сакаш кафе*? (Would you like some coffee?)
B. *Може.*
A. *А Coke.*
B. *Може.*
A. *Дај ми ја играчката* (Give me the toy.)
B. *Не може* (No.) *Моја* е (It's mine.)
A. *Вака веќе не може* (This is no longer possible.)

In all provided communication situations, the use of the Macedonian modal verb *може* requires verb a complement in its personal or impersonal form (Examples A, B) or appears independently (C). Thus, it aquires the function of a petrified adverbial particle with the meaning of alethic modality. In the Polish language, the predicative *може* has the same modality *można* – (мак.) *може* (it is possible) in the third group of examples.

2. On the Category: Verb Distribution (function of prefixes *po-, pos-, poz-* // *по-, поис-, поиз-* in the Polish and Macedonian languages)

Regarding the formation of distributive verbs (distributives), there are formal and semantic similarities and differences between the Polish and the Macedonian language. Two parallel tendencies (conformities) can be noticed in that process – the first – formally semantic and the second – relating to the development of that category. The first refers to the manners in which poly prefix formations of finite (perfect) verb stems are created using the prefix *no-*, while the second shows that the Polish and Macedonian poly prefix formations formed of prefix stems with the prefixes (Pol.) *pos-*, *poz-* and (Mac.) *поис-* // *поиз-* can be found in the same stage of development of distributive verbs. The functions of those prefixes can differ depending on the type of derivation – mutation, transposition, modification, and formal and semantic structure of back-formation – distributive, causative, inchoative, factitive, etc.

On this occasion, our subject of description are the poly prefix verbal derivatives with the prefix pol. *po-*, mak. *no-* (with its variations) on the initial position, i.e. formations in which the prefix *no-* is preceded by another prefix: (pol.) *poz-*, *powy-*, *pona-*, (mac.) *ноис-* // *ноиз-* *pozeszywać*, *powyginać*, *ponalewać*; (mac.) *ноиспиma*, *ноизгради*, *пoнacaди*. Lexical (morphological) derivatives and derivatives with one prefix, for example *porobić*, *pożenić*, will be left out of the analysis.

Prefixes relating to the verb stem can perform several functions. In the prefixation of non-finite verbs they can become finite, can have their type changed, and the prefixes can also change their meaning, however most usually, prefixes have both a grammatical (type) and a semantic function – they change the type and meaning of non-finite verb stems. In performing its grammatical function, the prefix does not change anything in the verb's basic meaning, but it only changes its type and has solely grammatical function. Prefixes which have semantic function change or only modify the semantics of the verb stem. When a prefix changes the verb's type and meaning, it fulfills a mixed function – grammatical and semantic. The latter is the most common function. If the manner of action can be linked to the given prefix, several different semantic groups and verb formations can be distinguished, for example determinative, perdurative, accumulative, limiting, completive, etc. Such groups include iteration[132] and distribution i.e. iterative distribution. The basic property of the distributive verb meaning is connotation of the subject and // or the object in plural. According to M. Kucała, the essence of distributiveness is the division (divisiveness) of the verbal action on several actions:

> Istotą znaczenia dystrybutywnego (...) jest nie wielość podmiotów, ale wielość czynności i to czynności nierównoczesnych // przynajmniej w języku polskim.[133]
> (The essence of distributive meaning (...) is not comprised of several subjects but of several actions including non-simultaneous actions // at least in the Polish language.)

---

[132] The problem of verb iterativity and distribution is completely different in the Polish language by M. Kucała, *Rozwój iteratiwów dokonanych w języku polskim*, Wrocław 1966.

[133] Ibidem, p. 26.

C. Piernikarski tends to neutraise those two stend points as follows:

> (...) odcień niejednoczesności realizacji poszczególnych aktów (...) nie jest koniecznym warunkiem użycia czasowników dystrybutywnych.[134] ((...) a nuance of non-simultaneity in the realization of single actions is not a necessary determinant for the use of distributive verbs.)

In the context of these definitions, the larger number of non-simultaneous actions can be accepted as a principle for an analysis of the category distributiveness. Poly prefix verbs having the prefix *no-* in the initial position, excerpted from several works of modern Macedonian literature[135] and the *Речник на македонскиот јазик* (*Dictionary of the Macedonian Language*) edited by B. Koneski,[136] were subdued to analysis. The analysis demonstrated that the number of verbs excerpted from the works of the Macedonian literature was smaller than their number in the *Речник на македонскиот јазик* (*Dictionary of the Macedonian Language*). Nearly three thousand pages of Macedonian literature contained just over 200 examples, while the *Dictionary* included only the number of formations as are: *поизбега, поискрши, поиспегла* amounting to much more than 200. Yet, there is still a huge number of verbs combined with prefixes as are: *подо-, поза-, поо-, пооб-, поод-, попо-, попре-, поприраз-* // *порас-, поу-, поиз-* // *поис-*,[137] etc. It is characteristic that in the dictionary these poly prefic verbs somehow automatically form a series.

When it comes to determining the function of poly prefix verbs, two viewpoints prevail – according to the first 'in Bulgarian and Macedonian language the prefixes *no-* and *cno-* arise even with the same verb stems bulg. *no + цупја, испо- цупја,* mac. *no + тера, испо + тера*',

---

134 C. Piernikarski, *Czasowniki z prefiksem po- w języku polskim i czeskim*, Warszawa 1975, p. 87.

135 Those are the following works: Ѓ. Абаџиев, *Пустина*, Скопје 1980, Т. Георгиески, *Црно семе*, Скопје 1980, Б. Ѓузел, *Куќа цел свет*, Скопје 1974, С. Дракул, *Белата долина*, Скопје 1980, В. Малески, *Разбој*, Скопје 1980, С. Јаневски, *Стебла*, Скопје 1976, В. Костов, *Нов ум*, Скопје 1980, Ј. Стрезовски, *Свето проклето*, Скопје 1980, М. Фотев, *Потомците на кат*, Скопје 1980, К. Чашуле, *Простум*, Скопје 1980, Ж. Чинго, *Големата вода*, Скопје 1980; *Пасквелија*, Скопје 1968, П. Ширилов, *Земја во дулбија*, Скопје 1977.

136 *Речник на македонскиот јазик: со српскохрватски толкувања...*

137 K. Koneski in the book *Зборообразувањето во современиот македонски јазик* (Скопје 1995) wrote: "The prefixes *po-* and *iz-* form a complex prefix *poiz-* that is, as a second prefix, primarily accompanied by verbs prefixed with the prefix *na-* (rarely with other prefixes) and convey the meaning 'completion of an action in greater, sufficient degree'": *поизнабоде се, поиизнавади, поизнавалка, поизнагледа се, мпоизнајаде се, поизнакине, поизопие, поизприкаже, поизрасипе* (p. 148).

according to the second – in the Macedonian and the Bulgarian literary languages, the prefix *по-* is not known as indicator of the category distributiveness. The primary indicator of distributiveness in these languages is the prefix *из-*.

For example *Сите селани се изнапиле.*[138] (All villagers drank as much as they could.)

Basic indicators of the category of distributivity in Polish and other Slavic languages – Bulgarian, Macedonian and Russian, are the prefixes *po-* (Polish) and *из-* // *ис-* (Macedonian and Bulgarian) that rival competitively and are added to poly prefix and mainly iterative verb stems. However, having different intensity, development of those prefixes in the Slavic languages was not equivalent and neither was the distribution of those prefixes. In these languages, the distributive function of the prefix **po-** developed relatively late.[139]

According to B. Koneski, in the Macedonian language the prefix *по-* fulfills the following functions:

1. Spatial: "*по-*. Spatial meaning of this prefix used on initial position in relation to the stem suggests an action on a given surface (...) *повие – завие, посоли – насоли, потури, постеле, покрие, посипе, покаже, погоди, посребри, позлати*";
2. Meaning of transition towards a new quality – *поцрвени, пожолти, потурчи, погрчи, попишмани*;
3. "*по-* indicates that the action is done to a small, limited extent: *постои, поседи, потопли се, почува, побега, посвири, повјаса, поскара, подржи, попрска, помрдне*".

And even at the end of the description of the functions of the prefix *по-*, the author notes that the meaning of the prefix *по-* can "concern more subjects, and therefore can also develop a meaning of enhanced action: *попаѓа, полегне*. More enhanced: *спопаѓа, исполегне.*"[140]

This description provides the possibility to list these verbs prefixed with *по-* or *испо-* in the group of distributive verbs. However, it seems that the main function of the prefix *по-* in the Macedonian language is semantic: performing an action on the surface or to a small, limited extent, and even with a third meaning, concerning more items.

In the Polish language the prefix *po-* has two primary functions: the first – semantic and the second – distributive. In relation to the semantic function there are no basic differences between the Polish and the

---

138 L.I. Rojzenzon, *Slawjanskaja glagolnaja poliprefiksacija*, Minsk 1970, p. 71.

139 M. Kucała, *Rozwój...*, p. 145; J. Němec, *O slovenské předponě po- slovesné*, Slavia XXIII, Praha 1954, p. 21.

140 Б. Конески, *Граматика...*, p. 399.

Macedonian languages, however, in relation to the distributive function, certain essential differences do exist.

In the Polish literary language, distributive verbs are formed by use of the prefix *po-* excluding the secondary imperfectives as are:

lać	–	wylać	–	**wylewać**	–	**powylewać**	**(lać – лее – bark)**
szyć	–	zeszyć	–	zeszywać	–	pozeszywać	(szyć – шие – sew)

Limitation may refer to the third degree of formation (derivation) when prefixes with an accumulative function are added to the verb stem, for example *na* – in the Polish language as an independent formation **napisywać* does not exist although it is very natural for the distributive iterativum – *po* + *na* + *pisywać* or prefix intensivum with double *na-* to take place: *na* + *po* + *na* + *pisywać*.[141]

However, the development of these formations cannot be with verbs in the perfective form (perfectives). In the Polish language, back-formation chains cannot arise without a third stage of derivation in the form of secondary imperfectivum most often with an iterative meaning: *zeszywać* // **pozeszyć*. Typically, in the Polish language the derivation chain is realized with an interchange of finite and nonfinite verbs:

ND[142]	–	DK	–	ND	–	DK
szyć		zeszyć		zeszywać		pozeszywać

However, in the Macedonian language and in other Slavic languages (Czech, Russian) the formation of poly prefix verbs with the prefix *no-* is possible as well as the distribution of finite verbs with an omission (elimination) of the third stage of derivation. However, a derivation chain with a characteristic interchange of grammatical pairs is also the most typical and widespread manner of distribution formation in the Slavic languages, which also governs the Polish language with the exception of some dialects. For example, in the northern Polish dialects – Bory Tucholskie, Kociewie – the formation of distributive verbs is possible by using the prefix ***po-***, which is part of the prefixed and finite stems. This phenomenon has already been observed by K. Nitsch. Here are several examples cited by an author from the territory of Kaszuby:

---

141 M. Kawka, *Intensiva prefiksalne (na materiale gwarowym)*, "Poradnik Językowy" 1973, 3, p. 139–143.

142 ND – niedokonany, DK – dokonany (ND – non-finite, DK – finite).

> *bulvi povigniju, bo voda je pozalała; povižući, povikopał, porozdrućić, pozab'jili, poumarl'i, pozagris*[143]

or isolated examples of the territory of Malopolska: *chytrzy ludzie ponastali.*

This phenomenon is associated with the development of aspectual-lexical (grammatical) relations within dialectal poly prefix formations under the influence of the expansive nature of the prefix ***no-***.[144]

Two types of derivation chains can be postulated for the Macedonian language and some Polish northern dialects (kashube), the example the verb ***влече*** (pull):

I.	влече	завлече	завлекува	позавлекува
	---------	------------	----------------	--------------------
	ND	DK	ND	NK (distributivum)
II.	влече	завлече	∅	позавлече
	---------	------------	---	---------------
	NK	DK	∅	DK (prefix intensivum + distributivum)

The basic contrast between the Polish and Macedonian literary languages when it comes to the realization of the various functions of the prefix *no- // po-* is that, besides the many similarities when fulfilling the semantic functions, this prefix in the Macedonian language does not fulfill the distribution function to the same extent as it does in Polish language. Besides the strong expansion of the prefix *no-* in fulfilling its distribution function in the Polish and other Slavic languages, in the Macedonian language this function is not fully developed and is preserved in the stage of expression of various semantic relations.

In a way, B. Koneski shaded light on this problem when he wrote:

> The merger of two, and sometimes even more prefixes, is a phenomenon common in our language, and not in addition, a lively way of nuance of verbal meanings.Thus, the prefixes can maintain their meaning: *пре-рас-каже* (re-tell) (also: *пре-пре-рас-каже*) (re-re-tell), or may serve as enhancers or limiters of an action, which, indeed, arises from their own

---

143 K. Nitsch, *Wybór pism polonistycznych*, Vol. 3, *Pisma pomorzoznawcze*, Wrocław 1954, p. 141, 336, 403.

144 M. Kawka, *Czasowniki typu „pozrabiać, naponapisywać" w polskich gwarach*, "Zeszyty Naukowe UJ. Prace Językoznawcze" 1974, 14, p. 163–179.

meaning: *из-на-спие, по-на-чека*, and there are instances when they enter into a closer connection, forming a certain unity: *испо-тепа, испо-краде*.[145]

So I confirm that there are very strong relations between an intense tendency and poly prefix derivation and, on this basis, the creation of new combinations of verb meanings, which hinders the possibility for complete development of the category of distributivity in the Macedonian language.

A similar phenomenon of poly–prefixation can be observed in another group of Macedonian verbs, for example: *поизнатепа, поизнашета, поизнагледа*. These verbs comprise one categorical group not only from a formal aspect (morphological – same morphological category), but also from a semantic one. In the Dictionary of the Macedonian Language, there are around 60 such verbs serially formed by use of the prefix *поиз- // поис-*. They are contrary to the poly prefix formations, for example: *по-застане, по-завлече, по-избриши* which mean that the action is performed to a limited extent with a numeric element – 'малку', 'донекаде' ('little', 'to an extent'). The prefixes *по-*, *ис-*, *поис- // поиз-* intensify the action, and their function gets closer to the accumulative function, which is mainly introduced by the initial prefix *на-*. Formations such as *по-из-на-тепа* have total,[146] complete or full function, upon which the verb gets the distributive meaning later.

Here, general developing tendencies noticed in the language (Kashubian dialects in Poland), in which the condition is represented by dialectal formation, show the strong competition between expansive *по-* and distributive *ис- // из-* verbs in the Macedonian language. For example: *поизнашета, поизнатепа-* attest to the very early stage

[145] "Спој од два, па понекогаш и од повеќе префикси, е една појава обична во нашиот јазик, и не само тоа, ами еден жив начин на нијансирање на глаголските значења. Притоа префиксите можат да го чуваат своето значење: пре-рас-каже (може и: пре-пре-рас-каже), можат да служат за усилување или ограничување на дејството, што произлегува впрочем пак од нивното значење: из-на-спие, по-на-чека, а има случаи кога тие стапуваат во потесна врска, чинејќи извесна целост: испо-тепа, испо-краде". (The blend of two or, sometimes, more prefixes is not only a common feature of our language, but also a vivid manner of shading verb meanings. Thereto, prefixes can keep their meaning: *пре-рас-каже* (also: *пре-пре-рас-каже*); can serve to emphasis or constraint the action, a feature deriving from their meaning, in turn: *из-на-спие, по-на-чека*; and there are also cases when they enter a closer connection creating a certain compound *испо-тепа, испо-краде*.) Б. Конески, *Граматика* ..., p. 393.

[146] According to N.B. Thelin, the creation and development of the category of distributivity should be connected to the development of total meanings. Only later, the total meaning turns into a distributive meaning. N.B., Thelin, *Towards a Theory of Aspect, Tense and Actionality in Slavic*, "Acta Universitatis Upsaliensis, Studia Slavica Upsaliensia" 1978, 18.

of creation and development of the distributive function of the verbal prefix *no-* in this language and the Polish dialects.

3. Peter Draganov Danilovich as a Linguist – In Light of the Text on Nasal Vowels in Modern Macedonian Slavic and Bulgarian Dialects[147]

> Serbians, and especially Bulgarians, despise this dialect. They don't know that the literature of authentic Macedonian dialect, however meager, is a fact in any case… In my views on the Macedonian dialect, I do not suffer from the Serbo-Bulgarian political dizziness, and my philological work is characterized by scientific sobriety.
>
> From P.D. Draganov letter to V.I. Lamansky

Peter Danilovich Draganov[148] was born in 1857, probably on the 1 or 13 February in the city of Komrat (in Bessarabia, currently Moldova). He was a bibliographer, philologist, ethnografist, and a historian. He worked as a librarian and a teacher. He came from a poor family of Bulgarian colonists. He completed high school in Komrat, Kishiniev and Kharkiv. In the period between 1880–1882, he studied philology and history in Kharkiv and in Sankt Petersburg from 1882 to 1885 where he graduated with a post-doctoral degree. In Kharkiv he attended lectures in the field of slavistics by M.S. Drinow and also worked under V.I. Lamanskij, a renowned historian and slavophile – author of a text pertaining to the assimilation of the Slavs in Spain.

In the period between 1885–1887 he was employed as a teacher in world history, Bulgarian language and literature, and Latin language and geography, in the gymnasium in Thessaloniki. In the years between 1887–1895 he taught Russian language and literature in the gymnasium in Komrat, Sevastopol and Kishiniev. For eight years (1896–1904) he was employed as an assistant librarian in the department of Slavic manuscripts in St. Petersburg. He also performed many administrative functions such as: inspector or director in schools or the high school in Astrakhan, in the cities: Kagul, Komrat, and in Belgrade in the years

[147] П. Драганов, *Носовые гласные звуки въ современных македонско-славянскихъ и болгарскихъ говорахъ*, "Ruskii filologiceskii vestnik" 1888, XIX, g. 10, Varsava, p. 2.

[148] Б. Ристовски, *Бугаринот Петар Драганов за посебноста на македонската нација, историја, јазик, и култура*, in: *Сознајби за јазикот, литературата и нацијата*, Скопје 2001, p. 283–302.

from 1904 to 1926. He had a variable education, knew many western languages, almost all the Slavic languages, in addition to Romanian, Greek and Latin. Under the influence of Lamanskij and his lectures, he got interested in the work of Sts. Cyril and Methodius. Moreover, his three-year stay in Thessaloniki and thanks to his knowledge of many regions in the Balkan peninsula, allowed him to aquire a vast linguistic, historical and ethnological or ethnographic material pertaining to the local population. The results of his research were published in scientific and socio-political magazines.

Draganov is the author of over 30 scientific papers, some of which relate to a narrower language issue. Particulary, he worked on the language of the population of certain regions in Macedonia, where he stayed and about which he wrote. Unfortunately, those notes have no special scientific character (linguistic) and are only one part of the historical and ethnographic description of different Slavic ethnic groups and their language.

In this regard, we can particulary distinguish his work titled *Носовые гласные звуки въ современныхъ македонско-славянскихъ и болгарскихъ говорахъ*. Published in Warsaw in 1888, the work tries to prove the thesis that the remains of nasal sounds in the dialect from the surrounding region of Thessaloniki testify to the ties of this dialect, with the Old Church Slavonic language.

The work is comprised of 27 pages and is devided in two parts, theoretical and empirical. In the first part, Draganov refers to A.H. Vostokov, author of the first historic – comparative phonetics of Slavic languages in 1820. According to Vostokov, in "Ostromir's Gospel," a monument of the old Russian literacy of the XI century.

> In the Old Church Slavonic language, **ѫ** and **ѧ** appear where **ą** and **ę** (...) appear in the Polish language. In this monument of literacy, he also comes across a similar difference in the use of the letters: **ѭ** and **ѩ**. The first is seen in the use of **ją** and **ję** by the Polish people.

We shall omit the interpretation of the meaning of the words "by Polish people," when it comes to the letters in the old-Russian monument, this comparison should also be the Polish monument of literacy from the XI century, not so generally about the Polish people.

In a further part of this work, the author proves the existence of nasal sounds in Proto-Slavic and Old Church Slavonic, while citing scientific authorities. Thereto he emphasizes the thesis by the Slovenian linguist Jernej Kopitar saying: Kopitar was unfortunate to justify the nonexistence of the mentioned nasal sounds in the Old Church Slavonic language.

According to Draganov, the Slovenian linguist was angry with his great teacher Dobrovski because he, as well as Vostokov, considered the origin of Old Church Slavonic language to be related to Macedonian or Bulgarian-Macedonian-Serbian, not the language of Krajina, Moravian or Panonian language.

From today's point of view, there is no doubt that there were two nasal sounds in the Proto-Slavonic language. We find the oldest testemonials from the XI century in the Old Church Slavonic language – we can read about them in the *Gramatyka historyczna języka polskiego* (*Historical Grammar of the Polish Language*) by Z. Klemensiewicz, S. Urbańczyk, T. Lehr-Spławiński.[149]

Was this question worthy of scientific discussion at the end of the XIX century in the time of Draganov, if at the same time many European scientists did not object to the existence of nasal sounds in the Proto-Slavonic and Old Church Slavonic language?

This part of the introduction was most probably necessary to the author for a logical presentation of his work's content. The reflective logic in the text seems simple – consisting of two hypotheses and a conclusion.

1 hypothesis: Nasal sounds existed in the Old Church Slavonic language – evidenced by the opinions of the scientists.

2 hypothesis: Their remnants can be found in the dialects spoken in the surrounding areas of Thessaloniki. Empirical dialectal materials serve as evidence for this.

Conclusion: If nasal sounds existed, and their remnants have been kept in the dialects spoken in the surrounding areas of Thessaloniki, then the Macedonian dialect spoken in the surrounding areas of Thessaloniki was foundation of the Old Church Slavonic language.

According to Draganov's version, this is how the thesis about the "Macedonian origin of the Old Church Slavonic language" was proven. It is obvious that Draganov is wrong, in this case, when he uses the word "origin" since this word indicates a historical process that does not actually exist as a genetic process. Instead, this is about an "elaboration," or as used in methaphorical terminology by modern Macedonian linguists, "the first codification of the Macedonian literary language."

Yet, it is worth while considering the logical structure of this linguistic work in detail. Further on Draganov wrote,

---

149 "The oldest attested continuants of *ą and *ę from the IX c. can be found in the Old Church Slavonic language." See: Z. Klemensiewicz, S. Urbańczyk, T. Lehr-Spławiński, *Gramatyka historyczna języka polskiego*, Warszawa 1964, p. 102.

> (...) but this is not all that can be said in favor of the nasal pronunciation of yuses in the Old Church Slavonic language, in addition to Vostokov's evidence regarding the Macedonian origin of this language. Describing the many Slavic dialects in poly-tribal and poly-cultural Macedonia, where I stayed for about three years as a teacher in the Bulgarian high school "Sts. Cyril and Methodius" in Thessaloniki, from where I have recently returned and got interested in the origin of the Old Church Slavonic language, the problem that has so far not been unbundled in Slavic philology, I was lucky to come across a myriad of words with preserved nasalism. These, incredibly numerous, nasalisms, which I came across in the land of Cyril and Methodius, are present in the dialects of: Thessaloniki, Kastoria-Gorchani, Meglen Voden, partly in Ohrid, Bitola and Demir Hisar.[150]

This part of Draganov's work is the most voluminous since almost 14 pages (from page 14 to 27) contain language material. As the author writes,

> I present a complete list of evidence for the existence of "rhinesm,"

he uses a term very rarely used today, which according to him means the nasal pronunciation of vowels in the Old Church Slavonic language. Proof of this would be that words containing half-sounds with the consonants n and m supposed to signify the pronunciation of ancient **ѧ** = **ън** and **ѫ** = **ъм**.

Words such as for example:

> available in the region of Visoka – in Polish "węzeł"
> *гъмба* = *гыба* – Thessaloniki and Kostur
> *рънка* = *рука*, Old Church Slavonic – *ржка*. Found as *ronka* in dialects.

There are total of about 120 expressions of this type *ен*, *ем* = ѧ.

For example: *bratočend*, *ventr*, *devent*, *kolenda*, *grenda*, etc.

All these examples of preserved nasalisms come from Thessaloniki and the surroundings of Thessaloniki, which is mainly the territory of Macedonia where Draganov resided. And their abundance in this area should testify to the close relationship of the Old Church Slavonic language with the Macedonian dialects from the surroundings of Thessaloniki.

---

150 П. Драганов, *Носовые гласные*..., p. 14–15.

Apart from this, the author opposes the Macedonian condition regarding nasal sounds when compared to Bulgarian dialects when he writes: "in contemporary Bulgaria we find only scarce remnants of 'rhinesms'" and he lists about 12 examples from the surroundings of Tarnovo, Zagorsk and Kazanlik.

To a large extent, however, this incomplete information provided by Dragan regarding nasal sounds in the dialects in the surroundings of Thessaloniki confirms the subsequent researches. To mention only Mieczysław Małecki's work.[151] However, today this obvious thesis on the familiarity of the dialect of the surroundings of Thessaloniki with the Old Church Slavonic language could not allow Draganov to conclude that:

> If these numerous 'rhinesms' have been kept in such a large number to date, then we can only think what was the case in the past. There is no doubt that at the time of Cyril and Methodius they were used everywhere in Macedonia and that argument, along with others, testifies to the Macedonian origin of the Church-Slavonic language.[152]

In this case we can only speak of one hypothesis by Draganov according to which at the time of Cyril and Methodius nasal sounds in the territory of Macedonia were in general use, as well as we can hypothetically say that nasal sounds at the time of Cyril and Methodius were not so wide spread because in the dialectal material, there is not enough evidence to support either the first or the second thesis. Contrary to the author's expectations, today, nasal sounds are almost absent from Macedonia and Bulgaria, and we can only speak of some remnants in the south-western part of Macedonia.

In modern trends, Slavic languages are dominated by processes of denasalization and diphthongization of nasal sounds. The Polish language (where nasal sounds are almost completely gone) and certain regions where the Macedonian and Bulgarian languages are used are exceptions. In most Slavic languages nasal sounds do not exist. Yet, despite these numerous remains of the nasal sounds in the Polish language, nobody has formulated a thesis or a hypothesis that the Polish language is the basis of the Old Church Slavonic language. It confirms the position of Frantisek Maresh who wrote:

> It is obvious that the Old Church Slavonic language was originally conceived as a common Slavic (intraslavonic) literary language that as a literary

---

151 M. Małecki, *Dwie gwary macedońskie (Suche i Wysoka w soluńskiem)*, Kraków 1934.

152 Р. Драганов, *Носовые гласные...*, p. 3.

language had not been inextricably bound to a particular language area (specific dialect). However, this does not fully negate Draganov's opinion on the Macedonian origin of the Old Church Slavonic language, but only confirms the genius of its authors, Cyril and Methodius.[153]

4. Some Questions on the Sintactic – Semantic Dictionary of Verbs in the Polish and the Macedonian Language

Introductory Remarks

The basic methodological commitment of every syntactic and semantic description of a particular language is usually the postulate of separation and classification of text elements. Previous syntactic descriptions of natural languages do not always realize this postulate. However, the semantic description of a sentence in the field of theoretical propositions as well as its implementation, still remains a distant vision.

It is also proven that structural descriptions of syntax, consisting of a distributive analysis and classification of sintactic units, have led to many simplifications. This arose from the fact, that an essential feature of structural analysis was the splitting of syntactic properties of sentence units from their semantic markers.

And this is exactly the reason why today the basic task and postulate of a syntactic description of natural languages is to consider, preferably to the broadest extent, semantic information. In accordance with the full description of the specified language sintax, it should contain:

a) Classification and distribution of syntactic elements;
b) Rule of syntactic blend of sentences;
c) Classification of semantic elements that are relevant to syntax (semantic contours of the sentence);
d) Rules of the semantic fusion of text elements (semantic constraints);
e) Rules of sentence order of syntactic-semantic structures.

It seems that the best method for implementation of the majority of the above postulates will be a dictionary of verbs known as lexicographic description of their sintactic and semantic features.

From this point of view, a comparison of the syntactic-semantic structures of the Polish language with analogous structures in other

---

[153] F.V. Mareš, *Makedonská gramatika...*, p. 12.

Slavic languages would be very interesting. The Macedonian language was chosen for this purpose.This language has a specific grammatical structure and therefore the confrontation of the Polish and the Macedonian language, regarding the volume of sintactic-semantic constructions, should result in interesting conclusions.

From a methodological point of view, the realization of thus understood confrontation of syntactic-semantic structures within the scope of the Slavic languages can be a confrontative syntactic-semantic dictionary of verbs in the Polish and Macedonian language.

Such dictionary would fulfill a dual role:

a) would show structural and semantic differences or similarities between the two Slavic languages;

b) this dictionary will assist students who study one of the two Slavic languages – Polish or Macedonian.

The attention of this paper will be mainly devoted to the principles of construction in the said dictionary. Some phenomena in the field of semantic syntax will also be discussed. They will be the following: issues of semantic roles, theory of semantic roles, nominalization constraints and problems, reduction of syntactic-semantic structures, examined from semantic point of view.

SEMANTIC SINTAX

General Remarks

Recently, the main issue of the language syntactic-semantic description is postulation of the existence of syntactic-semantic structures ascribed to corresponding fragments of reality, the objects, their attributes and events. The assignment of linguistic expressions that correspond to the ontological categories leads to the construction of so-called predicate-argumentative structures. Usually, the verb occurs as a predicate (but not only the verb) – as an argument – noun (expression of corresponding reference). In this paper, the subject of interest are the underlying structures that, in logical terminology, could be characterized as linking of the predicate with the argument, which has an object reference – object argument.

The concept of predicate-argumentative structures largely depend on the logical theories of language.[154]

---

[154] For example, *Logika i język. Studia z semiotyki logicznej*, ed. by J. Pelc, Warszawa 1967. Besides the logical ones, there are also other theories connecting sentence elements to different relations by means of connotation. (Z. Gołąb, *Próba syntaktycznej klasyfikacji czasowników polskich (na zasadzie konotacji)*, "Biuletyn PTJ" 1967, XXV, p. 1–43,

Such logical concepts appear as basis for construction of certain types of grammars, called generative semantic grammars.

Syntactic-semantic theory that relies on the existence of predicate-argumentative structures came to the fore in the works of the American linguists: Ch. Fillmore, G. Lakoff, J.D. McCawley and others.[155] Lately, papers on predicate-argumentativnite structures of the Polish language also began to appear in Polish linguistics: A. Bogusławski, M. Grochowski and others.[156]

For this study, from a structural view point of the confrontative dictionary, the formulation of rules of syntactic-semantic description of selected constraintsand semantic roles, which are attributed to corresponding verbs, will be the most important.

The verb (predicate), as a constituent part of the sentence, and its nominal argumentations (subject and prepositional arguments) i.e. predicates linking subject arguments and predicates linking prepositional arguments, and will be the subject of description.

Verbs, generally fulfilling the function of predicates, as constituent members of the sentence and their nominal supplements (subject and object arguments) will be a subject of the description.

The description contains:

sintactic information

- on the Polish language
  a) number of sintactic supplements formally related to the verb,
  b) obligatory and facultative supplements,
  c) morphological factors of sintactic determination;
- on the Macedonian language

valency (L. Tesniére, *Éléments de syntaxe structurale,* Paris 1959) or intention.) In Polish linguistics, it should be noted that a good reference is *Słownik syntaktyczno-generatywny czasowników polskich,* ed. by K. Polański, Vol. 1–5, Wrocław 1980. The term *intention* is used more often in the Czech and Slovak linguistics (*intencie slovesného deja*) introduced by E. Pauliny, *Štruktúra slovenského slovesa; štúdia lexikálno-syntaktická,* Bratislava 1943. In addition, the term 'intentional' functions in Macedonian linguistics, for example: *Интенцијално-синтаксички речник на македонските глаголи,* Vol. 1–6, Институт за македонски јазик „Крсте Мисирков", Скопје, 1992–2001.

155 Ch. Fillmore, *The Case for Case,* in: *Universals in Linguistic Theory,* ed. by E. Bach, R.T. Harms, New York 1968. G. Lakoff, *Irregularity in Syntax,* New York 1970. J.D. McCawley, *The Role of Semantics in Grammar,* in: *Universals...,* p. 124–169.

156 A. Bogusławski, *Preliminaries for Semantic-Syntactic Descriptions of Basic Predicatives Expressions with Special Reference to Polish Verbs,* in: *O predykacji,* Wrocław 1974, p. 39–57. M. Grochowski, *Środek czynności w strukturze zdania. Narzędzie, substancja, materiał,* Warszawa 1975.

a) number of nominal supplements of the verb in the sentence,
b) obligatory and facultative supplements,
c) morphological factors of syntactic determination – prepositions;

semantic information on the Polish and the Macedonian language
a) determining the semantic constraints of every verb,
b) determining the semantic relation between the verb and noun (predicate and argument),
c) assignment of certain composition of semantic roles to the verb,
d) semantic obligatory and facultative roles and on the surface of the text.

THEORY OF SEMANTIC CONSTRAINTS

The theory of semantic constraits was firs formulated by N. Chomsky[157] in accordance with the conception of phonological markers.

According to Chomsky's theory of selection constraints on verbs (frighten) (scare), it could be said that he allows subjects with abstract meaning and objects determined by the signs

+ Anime, + Hum, and hence the above mentioned rule does not provide a reverse situation:
– Anime, – Hum.

W.L. Chafe presents the selection constraints problematic in a similar manner.[158] He considers the core of semantic constraints by giving sentence examples:

a) I frightened the dog
b) I assembled the table

Selection constraints (+Anime) for *dog* and (– Anime) for *table* are the reason why these elements cannot be transferred from one into another sentence. In discovering the semantic constraints, Chafe uses text of opposition (compare: phonological oppositions). The following sentences are not correct:

a. # I assembled the dog
b. # I frightened the dog

---

157 N. Chomsky, *Aspects of the Theory of Syntax*, Cambridge, Mass.: M.I.T. Press 1965.
158 W.L. Chafe, *The Meaning and Structure of Language*, Chicago and London 1971.

Unfortunately, Chafe does not write about the semantic values allowed by the verb frighten in regards to the subject.We are familiar that N. Chomsky uses abstract subject (+Anime) for the same verb.

Chomsky's conclusions on the topic of semantic constraints, and specifically the opposition of his concept, became the grounds for A.Wierzbicka to formulate her own theory on semantic constraints:

> Zjawisko ograniczeń selekcyjnych w języku naturalnym nie jest fikcją – i z pewnością zasługuje na dokładny opis – ale nie ma ono nic wspólnego ze „szczerością, która przeraża chłopca" (znany przykład Chomsky'ego) (...) „Przestraszyć" znaczy „spowodować, żeby się bano". Co może być przyczyną czegokolwiek? Tylko jakieś zdarzenia. Dlatego słowo „przestraszyć" otwiera w zdaniu miejsce dla wyrażenia oznaczającego zdarzenie. Nie znaczy to, żeby zdarzenie (np. przejaw czyjejś szczerości) było głębokim podmiotem „przerażenia". Zdarzenie nadaje się na treść zdania, nigdy na jego podmiot (...). Na mocy bardzo ogólnej transformacji zdanie mówiące o przyczynie jakiegoś zdarzenia może być skrócone do samego podmiotu lub predykatu.[159]
> (The phenomenon of selective constraints in natural languages is not fiction – and it certainly deserves an accurate description – however, it has nothing in common with "sincerity that scares the boy" (a known example by N. Chomsky) (...) "scare someone" denotes that "someone causes someone else to be afraid." What could be the cause for anything? Only an event. That's why the word "scare" opens a place in the sentence for an expression denoting the event (...) This does not mean that the event (for example the appearance of one's sincerity) can be a subject of deep "fear". The event may be the content of the sentence, but it will never be its subject (...) By the power of a very general transformation, the sentence talking about the reason for some event can be shortened to the very subject or predicate.)

In addition, the author distinguishes between two types of semantic constraints:

> Istnieją przypadkowe, zależne od danego języka ograniczenia selekcyjne i istnieją ograniczenia selekcyjne motywowane semantycznie.[160]
> (There are cases dependent on selective constraints of a given language and there are semantically motivated constraints.)

---

159 A. Wierzbicka, *Dociekania semantyczne*, Warszawa 1970, p. 28.

160 Ibidem, p. 29.

As an example, for the constraints which cannot be predicted based on their meaning, the author gives us the word use constraints: *blonde, strew*.

A. Wierzbicka explains semantically motivated constrains by the examples in the following sentences:

> Adam uśmiechnął się do Ewy. (Adam smiled at Eve.)
>
> 'Adam uśmiechnął się po to, aby Ewa wiedziała, co Adam myśli.' (Adam smiled at Eve so that Eve could know what Adam was thinking.)
>
> Adam mrugnął do Ewy. (Adam winked at Eve.)
>
> 'Adam mrugnął do Ewy po to, żeby Ewa wiedziała, co on myśli.' (Adam winked at Eve so that Eve could know what Adam was thinking.)
>
> Adam mówił do Ewy. (Adam talked to Eve.)
>
> 'Adam mówił do Ewy po to, żeby Ewa wiedziała, co on myśli.' (Adam talked to Eve so that Eve could know what Adam was thinking.)

In these sentences, the preposition (pol.) "do" (ang.) "to" functions as an abbreviation of a very complex semantic structure containing the elements "chce" (want) and "myśli" (think)" and thus it requires a human subject.[161]

Semantic constraints are differently defined in the work of I. Bellert and Z. Saloni. For the semantic description of the verb in the Polish language, the project's authors define selective constrains as follows:

> (...) zbiory wartości, które mogą przyjmować zmienne występujące w danej funkcji zdaniowej.[162]
> ((...) sets of values, which can take the propositional variables occurring in a given sentence function.)
>
> (x – obszar (space)) x„ leżeć (lay) y_{loc} – (y – obszar (space)); x„ rozważyć (think) *ya* – x – osoba (person); x_n wyjechać (leave) z *yg* – (x – osoba (person)) lub pojazd (vehicle) (y – obszar (space)).

---

161 Ibidem, p. 40.

162 I. Bellert, Z. Saloni, *O opisie semantycznym haseł czasownikowych*, in: *Semantyka i słownik*, Wrocław 1972, p. 221.

In this work, semantic constrains are generally understood as defined by N. Chomsky and W. Chafe. For each verb, they will be formulated in the form of distinctive symbols of semantic features. For example ± Animate, ± Human, ± Abstract, ± Count, ± Male, ± Adult... etc. In some cases, collections of semantic values for specific verbs will be determined.This part of the semantic information in majority of the cases can be found in the definitive part of the expression or in the noun symbol.

For example (Polish lang.) *lać się* (o wodzie: *cieknąć*), N (płyn), N (-anim)

(woda)
Macedonian lang (leak) pour:
For water N (liquid) N (-anim)
(water)

Concepts of Semantic Roles

The verb feature is immensely significant and an important part of the description of the sentence semantics given the semantic relation that exists between the verb and the noun.The same applies to the relation: predicate – argument. The results of the semantic analysis should provide the content, list of semantic roles, i.e. the so-called "deep cases" for each verb. The autor of the grammatical cases writes:

> The case notions comprise a set of universals, presumably innate concepts which identify certain types of judgments human being are capable of making about the events that are going on around them, judgments about such matters as who did it, who happened to, and what got changed.[163]

It should be said that this concept is as highly universal as is often modified by its author. This work presents all semantic roles described by scientists who are dealing with this problem. Some of those semantic roles will be used in the glossary.

---

[163] Ch. Fillmore, *The Case...*, p. 29.

Semantic roles compiled by Ch. Fillmore, W. Chafe and J.T. Platt are given below:

Ch. Fillmore (1968)	Ch. Fillmore (1971)
Agentive	Agent
Instrumental	Couter-Agent
Dative	Object
Factitive	Result (Factitive 1968)
Locative	Instrument
Objective	Source
	Goal
	Experiencer (Dative 1968)

W. Chafe (1971)	J.T. Platt (1971)
Agent	Affective
Patient	Agentive
Experiencer	Benefactive (inner, outer, far-outer)
Beneficiary	Factitive
Instrument	Instrumental
Complement	Locative (inner, outer, far-outer)
Location	Neutral
	Participative
	Purposive

The issue of the place of action binds the question of timing and the manner of its execution.There is finity in the determination of this type of semantic roles determined in accordance with the verb. They would include *Manner* (Mann) of execution of the action and *Temporal* (Temp) determination of the time of execution of the action.These roles appear in the description only when they are semantically implicit through finite verb.

Semantic roles used in this confrontative glossary of verbs (definitions)

Agens (Ag)	Executor, initiator of the action (man, animal, natural occurrences, disasters, mechanical devices)
Patient (Pat)	Object which is subject to the action of the agent, state or object which is subject to the process (does not cover mental states and processes)
Experiens (Exp)	Living being subject to mental, intellectual and sensational states

Beneficiens (Ben)	Living being in whose benefit the action is executed or that benefits from the steady state
Instrument (Iństr)	Instrument, substance, material, body part
Substance (Sub) Material (Mat)	Auxiliary, which serve to perform the action
Result (Res)	Product, result of the action
Locative	Object, which marks the place of the action process, which is subject to the the given sentence and indicates the spatial relations of the activities, processes and conditions expressed by a finite verb
Manner (Mann)	Manner of execution of the action, performance of the processes and states
Temporal (Temp)	Determination of the point in time of execution of the action, the duration of the event, processes and conditions expressed by a finite verb
Natural Force (For)	Disasters, natural phenomena that act in function of an agent
Body Part (BPart)	Patients body parts that are subject to the agent's action
Object (Obj) Extent (Ext)	Least neutral objects that more closely precise the verb meaning
Comitative (Comit)	"Accompaniment" of the action, state, process expressed by a finite verb

Notes for nominalisation in the polish and the macedonian language

The basic method for qualification and determination of concepts are: Ag, Pat, Exp, Ben, etc., was subordinated, in most general terms, to ontological categories of syntactic-semantic categories and relations (such procedure is considered as linguistic competence). However, qualification of the referent relations in the frame of expressions of the given language and, as a result, the semantic language description caused researchers a great problem.

It seems that the description of referential relations regarding expressions in the given language is equally possible. These must be univocal expressions and expressions that do not have the same intension.

Minimal sentences in the Macedonian and the Polish language represent the attempt to construct this type of expressions contained in this comparative dictionary. These are syntactic-semantic expressions where the semantic sufficiency is independent from context and constitution.

The difference existing between the reflected logical-semantic structures, which also represent models of ontological structures and formal-functioning structures, most often is established during the description of referential and semantic relations in the natural language.

Complete absence of subordination between logical-semantic structures (so called deep structures) and formal-functional structures (surface structures) is often claimed. Is appears that this phenomenon is the most pronounced representation resulting from the process of nominalization (condensation, substantivisation).

Here are some examples:

Cieszę się z twego przyjścia – Cieszę się (z tego), że przyszedłeś.
I am glad you came – I am glad that you came.

Martwi mnie wyjazd Janka – Martwi mnie to, że Janek wyjeżdża.
I am worried about Janek's trip – I am worried because Janek is traveling.

It seems that in the process of nominalization, apart from the condition for non-disturbance of entering predicative-argumentative structure, a an equally important, and maybe even more important condition is the type of logical-semantic structure (predicative-argumentative) of the matrix sentence. From the conducted analysis it follows that the verb that expresses a mental state (psychological predicate) is most often the predicate of matrix sentence. Moreover, it could be said that the majority of psychological predicates, determine the subject's semantic position, the semantic role of Exp. The experiential meanings of a matrix sentence predicate the cause, the reason for the psychological state of the subject – Exp to be exclusively a case that at the surface of the text is realized as an object – semantic subject of the copulative sentence. The above mentioned statement can be used with all logical-semantic structures that comprise the semantic role of Exp and can be recorded as a pattern:

$$\text{Exp} + \text{V} \left(+ \frac{\text{NOM}}{\text{S}}\right)$$
$$(\text{Ag}, \text{Pat}\ldots + \text{V})$$

Polish language	Macedonian language
Jan dziwi się Piotrowi // postępowaniu Piotra Jan wierzy Marii Jan interesuje się Marią	Јанко му се чуди на Петре // од постапката на Петре Јанко и верува на Марија Јанко се интересира за Марија

or

$(^{NOM}_{S})$ + V + Exp
(Ag, Pat...+ V)

Jan martwi Piotra Postępowanie Piotra martwi Jana Jan lekceważy Piotra Jan wyśmiewa się z Marii	Јанко го загрижува Петре Постапката на Јанко го загрижува Петрета Јанко го омаловажува Петрета Јанко ја исмева Марија

In the above sentences, the nominalization is conditioned and provides the matrix sentence with a logical-semantic type of structure. However, the morphological and derivative category of nominalized structures is of a lesser importance. It is certain that the claim of synchronic origin cannot exclusively be the nominalization agent in the field of verb – designation of the action (verbal noun), designation of the doer of the action. The phenomenon of syntactic, surface structure of verbal nouns has little meaning with the nominal processes. Verbal nouns (nomina actionis) can appear only after mental verbs or in the middle of psychological predicates. Their appearance largely depends on the meaning of the matrix sentence – not on the morphological character of the verbal derivate. However, the change in the logical-semantic structure described above generally does not prevent the existence of nominalization processes.

Another very important factor in the process of nominalization is the phenomenon of ellipsis and truncation of sentence structure. Prepositions and prepositional expressions are the most common formal agent so such nominalization processes, for example *Maria marzy o wyjeździe – Марија мечтае за заминување* (Maria dreams to leave); *Jan czeka na Marię – Јанко ја чека Марија* (Janko waits for Maria); *Jan się martwi o Piotra – Јанко се грижи за Петрета* (Janko takes care of Peter). Obviously, psychological predicates are also dominant here.

The phenomenon of nominalization in the Polish and Macedonian languages is noted only in this instance. This was dictated in the field of issue relating to the description of logical-semantic structures characterized in more detail with the rise of subject reference (subject arguments).

The problem of nominalization, related to the description of prepositional arguments, awaits a correct and detailed elaboration.

Principals for the construction of confrontative dictionaries

Subject of description

The subject of description is the verb as a constitutional part of the sentence acting in the minimal sentence in non-derivative form and used in its defined meaning. Verbs with a different meaning are ascribed certain compositions of minimum sentence to which formalized syntactic and semantic structures with lexical markers, i.e. selective constraints, belong.

Verbs contained in this dictionary have been selected from the following lexicographic works: *Słownik języka polskiego* (*Dictionary of the Polish Language)* edited by W. Doroszewski[164] and *Речник на македонскиот јазик* (*Dictionary of the Macedonian Language*) edited by B. Koneski.[165]

Verbs used in the above sentences were subject to selection. The following verbs were excluded from the analysis:

a) rarely used and stylistically depicting verbs rich in qualificators (Polish language: dialekt. augm. fraz., etc.; Macedonian language: dialect. augm. phrase. liter. med. vulg., etc.); b) rarely used verbs without qualificators: (Polish lang.) *niebieszczeć, impregnować, śrubować*, etc., (Macedonian lang.) *руменее* (blush), *шпарта* (scarf), *жонглира* (joggle), *кркори* (seethe), etc.; c) verbs with a metaphoric meaning – metaphors; d) prefixal verbs.

Structure of sentence units

Syntactic-semantic description of the verb will be shown in four degrees:

I. Sentence units – (Polish language) verb in form of infinitive (Macedonian language) verb in third person singular present tense. Definition of meaning (The concept of significant explications used in the works of A. Wierzbicka and M. Grochowski et al. was not used for the purpose of defining the meaning.) Explications were used only in the work on semantic analysis of sentences and the particular verbs. However, out of practical reasons, these cannot be found in the definitive

164 *Słownik języka polskiego*, ed. by W. Doroszewski, Vol. 1–11, Warszawa 1958–1969.

165 *Речник на македонскиот јазик: со српскохрватски...*

part of the expression's basic meaning. In defining meaning, synonym determinants were used for the less complex contents, which is on a more elementary scale than is the basic expression. The concept of selective constraints was used in the construction of definitions.

II. Types of syntactic supplements of verb.
III. Types of semantic roles: Ag, Pat, Exp, Ben... (obligatory and optional roles)
IV. Examples of syntactic and semantic uses of verb supplements – minimal sentence is given for every supplement. Certain semantic constrains have been prescribed to the syntactic categories – in form of distinctive semantic markups or in form of content compositions.

In addition, in the II and III degree of verb description, information on the topic: obligatory and optional verb supplements is prescribed.[166] This contrastive question so far has not been adequately described. In determining which supplements are obligatory of optional, sentence clarity played the decisive role, its semantic and formal sufficiency independently of the context and constitution. At the end, intuition and language competence of the author had a decisive meaning.

EXPLANATION OF SIGNS AND ABBREVIATIONS

N	–		noun
nom	–		nominative
gen	–		genitive
acc	–		accusative
instr	–		instrumental
loc	–		locative
± animate	–	animate	living being

+ huma	human
+ abstr	abstract
b. o.	without constraints
Ag	Agent
Pat	Patient
Exp	Experiencer
Instr	Instrument
BPart	Body Part
Obj	Object

166 D. Buttler, *Innowacje składniowe współczesnej polszczyzny*, Warszawa 1977.

Comit	Comitative
$(\frac{NOM}{S})$	Nominalization Reduction
p	Proposition
/ /	Optional sentence part
[ ]	Obligatory sentence part from the possible semantic verb
W1, W2…	Variations
//	Alternative

EXAMPLES

bać się	*плаши се*
I. *bać się* II. 2 III. 1	(W1 = o człowieku i zwierzętach, odczuwać lęk, strach) $N_{nom} – N_{gen}$ Exp – $(\frac{NOM}{S})$
IV. $N_{nom\ (+\ hum)}$ *(+ anim)* $N_{gen\ (b.\ o.)}$	– Exp (*Jan* boi się ciemności. *Kot* boi się psa) – $(\frac{NOM}{S})$ (Jan boi się *ciemności, psa, złodzieja*)
I. *плаши се* II. 2 III. 1	(В1 – за човекот и животните: чувствува страв) $N_1 – N_2$ Exp – $(\frac{NOM}{S})$
IV. $N_{nom\ (+\ hum)}$ *(+anim)* $N_{gen\ (b.\ o.)}$	– Exp (*Јанко* се плаши од темнината. *Мачка* се плаши од куче) – $(\frac{NOM}{S})$ (Јанко се плаши *од темнина, од куче, од крадец*)
I. *bać się* II. 2 III. 1	(W2 = o człowieku: troszczyć się, niepokoić) $N_{nom} – pN_{acc}$ Exp – $(\frac{NOM}{S})$
IV. $N_{nom\ (+\ hum)}$ p = o $pN_{acc\ (b.\ o.)}$	– Exp (*Jan* boi się o zdrowie dzieci) – $(\frac{NOM}{S})$ (Jan boi się *o zdrowie, o dzieci, o psa, o samochód, o przyszłość*)
I. плаши се II. 2 III. 1	(В2 – за човекот: се грижи, се беспокои) $N_1 – N_2$ Exp – $(\frac{NOM}{S})$
IV. $N_{(+\ hum)}$ p = за $N_{(b.\ o.)}$	Exp (*Јанко* се плаши за здравјето на децата) – $(\frac{NOM}{S})$ (Јанко се плаши *за здравјето, за децата, за кучето, за колата, за иднината*)

bić	*тепа*
I. *bić* II. 2/3/ III. 2/2	 N_{nom} – N_{acc} [N_{instr} pN_{loc} pN_{acc}] Ag – Pat [Instr BPart $\frac{\text{NOM}}{\text{S}}$]
IV. $N_{nom\,(+\,hum)}$ $N_{acc\,(+\,hum)}$ *(+anim)* $N_{instr\,(-anim)}$ p = *po* $pN_{loc\,(-anim)}$ p = *za* $pN_{acc\,(+abstr)}$	– Ag (*Jan* bije dziecko) – Pat (Jan bije *dziecko, psa*) – Instr (Jan bije psa *kijem, paskiem*) – BPart (Jan bije psa *po grzbiecie*) – $\frac{\text{NOM}}{\text{S}}$ (Jan bije Piotra *za kradzież*)
I. *тепа* II. 2/3/ III. 2/2/	(B1 = за човекот: удира, задава болка) N_1 – N_2 [pN_3 pN_4 pN_5] Ag – Pat [Instr Bpart ($\frac{\text{NOM}}{\text{S}}$)]
IV. $N_{nom\,(+\,hum)}$ $N_{acc\,(+\,hum)}$ *(+anim)* p = *co* $pN_{(-anim)}$ p = *по* $pN_{(-anim)}$ p = *за* $pN_{(+abstr)}$	Ag (*Јанко* тепа дете) Pat (Јанко тепа *дете, куче*) – Instr (Јанко тепа куче *со стап, со ремен*) – BPart (Јанко тепа куче *по грбот*) – $\frac{\text{NOM}}{\text{S}}$ (Јанко го тепа Петре *за кражба*)

czekać	*чека*
I. czekać II. 2/3/ III. 2/2 IV. $N_{nom\,(+\,hum)}$ p = na $pN_{acc\,(b.\,o.)}$	 N_{nom} – pN_{acc} Ag – $\frac{\text{NOM}}{\text{S}}$ – Ag (*Jan* czeka na Piotra) – $\frac{\text{NOM}}{\text{S}}$ (Jan czeka *na Piotra, na list, na pociąg*)
I.чека II. 2 III. 1	 N_1 – N_2 Ag – $\frac{\text{NOM}}{\text{S}}$
IV. $N_{(+\,hum)}$ $N_{(b.\,o.)}$	Ag (*Јанко* го чека Петрета) – $\frac{\text{NOM}}{\text{S}}$ (Јанко чека *воз, писмо,* го чека *Петрета*)

gniewać się	*лути се*
I. gniewać się II. 2/1/ III. 1	 N_{nom} – [pN_{acc} pN_{acc}] Exp – $\frac{\text{NOM}}{\text{S}}$, – $\frac{\text{NOM}}{\text{S}}$„
IV. $N_{nom\ (+\ hum)}$ p = na $pN_{acc\ (+\ hum)}$ p = o, za $pN_{acc\ (+\ abstr)\ (-\ anim)}$	– Exp (*Jan* gniewa się na Piotra) – $\frac{\text{NOM}}{\text{S}}$, (Jan gniewa się *na Piotra, na Marię*) – $\frac{\text{NOM}}{\text{S}}$„ (Jan gniewa się na Piotra *o książkę, za spóźnienie*)
I. лути се II. 2/1/ III.	 N_1 – [pN_2 pN_3] Exp – $\frac{\text{NOM}}{\text{S}}$, $\frac{\text{NOM}}{(\ \text{S}")}$
IV. $N_{(+\ hum)}$ p = *на* $pN_{(+\ hum)}$ p = за, поради *pN*$_{(+\ abstr)}$	– Exp (*Јанко* се лути на Петрета) – $\frac{\text{NOM}}{\text{S}}$, (Јанко се лути *на Петрета, на Марија*) – $\frac{\text{NOM}}{\text{S}}$„ (Јанко се лути на Петрета *за поради закаснување*)

grać	*igra, sviri*
I. grać II. 2/1/ III. 2/1/ IV. $N_{nom\ (+\ hum)}$ p = *w* $pN_{acc\ (-anim)}$ p = *z* $pN_{instr\ (+hum)}$	(W1 = o człowieku: brać udział w grach sportowych, towarzyskich, hazardowych) N_{nom} – pN_{acc} (pN_{instr}) Ag – Instr (Comit) – Ag (*Jan* gra w karty, w piłkę) – Instr (Jan gra *w karty, w piłkę*) – Comit (Jan gra w karty *z Piotrem*)
I. grać II. 2/1/ *N*$_{nom}$ III. 2/1/ *Ag* IV. $N_{nom\ (+\ hum)}$ N_{acc} P = na $pN_{loc\ (-anim)}$	(W2 = o człowieku: wykonywać utwory muzyczne) – [N_{acc} pN_{loc}] – [Obj Instr] – Ag (*Jan* gra na skrzypcach) – Obj (Jan gra *serenadę, sonatę, uwerturę*) – Instr (Jan gra *na skrzypcach, na pianinie*)
I. игра II. 2/1/ III. 2/1/ IV. $N_{(+hum)}$ p = *co* N // $pN_{(-anim)}$ $pN_{(+hum)}$	(B_1 = за човекот: зема учество во спортски, хазардни игри) N_1 – N_2 // pN_2 (pN_3) Ag – Instr (Comit) – Ag (*Јанко* игра карти) – Instr (Јанко игра *со топка, карти*) – Comit (Јанко игра карти *со Петре*)

I. свири	(B2 = за човекот: исполнува *музички творби*)
II. 2/1/	N_1 – [N_2 pN_3]
III. 2/1/	Ag – [Obj Instr]
IV. $N_{(+hum)}$	– Ag (*Јанко* свири на виолина)
N	– Obj (Јанко свири серенада, *соната, увертира*)
p = *на*	
$pN_{(-anim)}$	– Instr (Јанко свири *на клавир*)

C. LITERATURE.
TEXT IN THE DISCOURSE

I. Text in the Discourse

1. Basic Connection Indicators in the Macedonian Language – Anaphoric Function of the Article

Text linguistics is considered to be a modern area of study in the science of language in which the research subject is not only the text understood and treated as multi-level structure and completely organized multi-dimensionalmacrosign,[167] but also involves its analysis as a linguistic unit,[168] not only as a construction or folding structure, but also its role in the context (the text in the context). It is easy to arrive to the notion of discourse if text is analyzed, as a process and an event, in context.

The most important problems in text linguistics include:

1. Linearization;
2. Multiple sentence structures;
3. Cohesion and coherence;
4. Subjectivity;
5. Communicability;
6. Dialogicality;
7. Text pragmatics.

Research in this discipline is concentrated on the following topics:

1. Communicational character of text conditioning its organization, its semantics and above all, its pragmatics;
2. Creation of text as a multiple sentence unit (a single whole) requiring other non-exclusively linguistic or grammatical categories of description, primarily, processes of acquisition and unification (synthesis) of information that include its linear character (anaphoric and cataphoric relations);

---

167 T.A. van Dijk, *Textwissenschaft. Eine interdisziplinäre Einführung*, Tübingen 1960; T.A. van Dijk, *Badania nad dyskursem*...

168 J. Bartmiński, S. Niebrzegowska-Bartmińska, *Tekstologia*, Warszawa 2014.

3. Functional sentence perspective;
4. Indirect (immediate) information with implications and presuppositions;
5. Problem of text cohesion and coherence;
6. Typology texts and their genres, types and style variants;
7. Text composition (passages, chapters, paragraphs).

The question of connectivity or conjunction of language elements in a text rises as the main problem in linguistic textology, in addition to the role of text-context in and of the paralinguistic elements – prosody and intonation, and nonverbal elements – kinesics, proxemy, haptics, chronemics in text and discourse construction. Accordingly, two kinds of such connectivity can be distinguished: cohesion and coherence.

- Cohesion[169] is considered to be a relation between two successive sentence elements or larger text fragments (paragraphs, chapters, larger narrative fragments). We can single out, for example, cohesion in one simple or complex clause. It has superficial indicators (for example conjunctions and metaoperators) and is verbalized as opposite to implications and presuppositions, which are contextually conditioned or derived from the speakers and listeners common knowledge.
- Coherence is considered a property of multi-clausal text consistent of marked and united logical, content and thematic relations, which are semantically homogenous.

According to one most commonly repeated but also most questionable definitions of cohesion (for example, if we consider the relations: question – answer or dialogue (polylogue) analysis), cohesive text relies on three unities – one author, one listener, one topic:

1. Only a text created by one person – dealing with uniformity of all modal frameworks of text;
2. It is a text meant for a recipient or a listener. Here, it is not only about one person, but maybe a group of people, one generation, whole nation or two or three nations (international communication);
3. Text must be constructed so that its content, i.e. the content of all sentences, results in a description of a subject, narration (recounting of one subject, case, opinion) proving a single topic.[170]

---

[169] It seems that the terms: Macedonian – *спојност* and Polish – *spójność* (Eng. Connectivity // Cohesion) correspond and most importantly, they are needed as superimposed terms to cohesion and coherence. This means that "текст споен" or "spójny" (connected text) remain to be terms that are immanently incorporated within the definition of text, since the adjectives "споен" or "неспоен" (connected/unconnected) do not change anything in the meaning of the noun "text." "Текст неспоен" or "niespójny" or "unconnected" is simply no text, since the word text incorporates the valorization "споен."

[170] M.R. Mayenowa, *Spójność tekstu a postawa odbiorcy*, in: *O spójności tekstu*, ed. by M.R. Mayenowa, Wrocław 1971, p. 189–205.

Most characteristic indicators of cohesion are considered to be:
1. Morphological mechanisms (for example homogeneity of verbal suffixes, noun inflexion, and connotation).
2. Use of personal pronouns in anaphoric and cataphoric function;
3. Use of verbal suffixes in anaphoric function (so called zero anaphora);
4. Syntactic indicators of continuity and permanence (function of conjunctions);
5. Syntactic parallels and other textual mechanisms (for example repetition), which organize the formal structure of expression;
6. Paralingual mechanisms – prosody (in verbal text variation) and graphy (in written text variation).

The following are indicators of coherence:
1. Lexical-semantic mechanisms – repetition, paraphrases, metaphors;
2. Syntactic structures – sentences with negation, contradictions, antonyms, etc.;
3. Structures pertaining to: question – response, for example dialogue, conversation;
4. Matatextual structures, which connect thematic part of the text;
5. Narrative structures pertaining to: associations, collections, metonymic connections;
6. Conclusions, points, logical conclusions;
7. Function of modality in the text;
8. Anaphoric and cataphoric function of articles (in the Macedonian text).

The indicators of text conjunction provided above are universal and not connected to any particular genre of expression, however, some of them can be more frequently present in certain languages. In the Macedonian language this especially applies to the function of the definite article *-ot* (and the other two articles: *-ov* and *-on*) in the text building and especially in its thematisation – the article is one of the most important ways of building linear cohesion in the Macedonian language. A sentence, which is part of a text – as it is well known – can be functionally divided on theme and rheme. Themes of the following sentences (partially or completely) repeat the information already incorporated in the previous sentences. It can be information incorporated in the theme or the rheme, in the whole sentence or in multiple sentences. It can be repeated information found in the immediate vicinity, for example information incorporated in the rhema of the previous sentence or information which is distant.

All indicator of text cohesion and coherence in the abovementioned frame can be found in one fragment of Zhivko Chingo's *The Great Water*.

Во **домот** имаше повеќе непријатни **места**, такви **места** кои, ако можете, поубаво би било да ги заобиколите. Но **подрумот** беше нешто друго, **подрумот** никој не знаеше што беше, никој не знаеше што се крие во **подрумот**. Никој дотогаш немаше ѕирнато во **тој дел од домот**, **ѕвонарот** беше целосен и единствен господар на **подрумот**. **Клучот** му висеше околу гуша како крст. А **тоа** веќе беше доволно за да **го почувствувате стравот во сета своја тежина. Другарот Анески беше** роден **за тоа, беше работилница за страв**. Проклет да бидам, Кејтен така го викаше, **работилница за страв. Можеби поради тоа татенцето, и не само татенцето, туку целата управа, толку многу полагаше на ѕвонарот при воспоставувањето на редот. Во тој поглед ѕвонарот** беше господ. Се колнам, господ. **Лудаци.** Проклети **лудаци, со ѕид во очите. Слепи.**

Еден ден, сепак, **тоа будалиште** беше добар. **Прогледа.** Проклет да бидам, прогледа. Беше добар како јагне. Тоа беше **негов ден**. Празнуваше, **полуде од среќа**.

А имаше и **причина**, вистинска **причина**. Тоа што тој успеа да го постигне во однос на редот беше на таков степен што предизвикуваше **општо одушевување**. Тоа што векови ги мачело умните, длабоки луѓе, – **самосвеста, човечноста, една таква дисциплина**, нашиот **ѕвонар** успеа да го постигне во текот на една година, Проклет да бидам, **слепи.**

Денот беше многу **бурен. Саноќ** дуваше силен, **дождлив ветар**. Од брегот доаѓаа ужасни, претсмртни **крикови на птици**. Не разбудија тие вознемирени, страшни **гласови**. Никој во **спалните** не спиеше. Се чинеше божем **бурата** влегла во **домот**. Кејтен, кој сигурно пред сите ја чул **бурата**, уште со првиот **звук**, веќе беше излезен од **спалната**. **Креветчето** му беше празно.

(There were many unpleasant **places** in the **home**, **places** which, if possible, would be better to be avoided. But the **basement** was something else, nobody knew what the **basement** was, nobody knew what the **basement** was hiding. Nobody has ever looked at **this part of the basement**; **the bell ringer** was full and sole master of **the basement**. **The key** hung around his neck as a cross. And **this** was already enough for you **to feel the fear in all its gravity. Comrade Aneski was** born **for that, he was a fear workshop.** I'll be damned, Kejten called him so, **fear workshop**. **Maybe this is why daddy, and not only daddy, but the whole government, relied so much on the bell ringer for establishing order**. **In this regard, the bell ringer** was a god. I swear, a god. **Nut jobs. Damn nuts, with a wall in their eyes. Blind.**

One day, yet, **that fool** was good. **He regained his sight**. I'll be **danmed**, he regained his sight. He was as good as a lamb. This was **his day**. He celebrated, **went insane with joy**.

And he had a **reason**, too, a real **reason**. What he managed to accomplish in regards to order was of such a degree that caused **general exaltation**. What tortured wise, deep people for centuries – **self-awareness, humanity, such a discipline**, and our **bell ringer** managed to accomplish in a year. I'll be damned, **blind**.

The day was very **stormy**. **Last night** the wind was blowing, a **rainy wind**. From the shore came a dreadful, mortal **bird screeching**. Those disturbed, horrifying **voices** woke us up. In the **bedrooms**, nobody was sleeping. It seemed as if the **storm** had entered our **home**. Kejten, who certainly must have heard the **storm** before anyone else, even the first **sound**, was already out of his **bedroom**. **His little bed** was empty.)

In building of the above text, repetitions with equivalent or partial reference are used: *домот, ден, подрумот, места, татенцето, причина, ѕвонарот, лудаци* (the home, day, basement, places, daddy, reason, bell ringer, nut jobs); repetitions as semantic derivatives – *бурата – бурен* (– the storm – stormy), partially synonymic repetitions: *звук – крикови – гласови; самосвеста, човечноста, дисциплина* (sound – screeching – voices; self-awareness, humanity, discipline). In addition, the text contains expression which reform anaphoric and cataphoric function; in general, these are the demonstrative pronouns: *тој, тоа*:

> **Клучот му висеше околу гуша како крст**. А **тоа** веќе беше доволно за да го почувствувате стравот во сета своја тежина. **Тоа** што **тој** успеа да го постигне во однос на редот беше на таков степен што предизвикуваше општо одушевување. **Тоа** што векови ги мачело умните, длабоки луѓе, – **самосвеста, човечноста, една таква дисциплина**, нашиот ѕвонар успеа да го постигне во текот на една година.
> (**The key hung around his neck as a cross.** And this was already enough for you to feel the fear in all its gravity. **(That) what he** managed to accomplish in regards to order was of such a degree that caused general exaltation. **(That) what** tortured wise, deep people for centuries – **self-awareness, humanity, such a discipline**, our bell ringer managed to accomplish in a year.)

Moreover, this brief fragment is built on three semantic fields of the main themes: **the home, the bell ringer, the day**, denoting that for the narrative to be coherent it must be thematically organized including the three elements: **place – person – time**. Thematisation of these three fields is developed not only by use of semantic relations which exist between them, but also by use of non-linguistic implications and presuppositions partially determined by the knowledge of the author and the reader. For example **the home** – the basement, **the bedroom** – the little bed, **the bell ringer** – the key.

All these relations, textually building Chingo's prose, are relevant for the Polish translation of *Големата вода* (*The Great Water*). However, in the Macedonian original, the article plays a very important function in text building, whereas in the Polish translation, this function is performed by demonstrative pronouns in anaphoric service.

The fact that in the Macedonian language the article is almost completely grammaticalised concurrently denotes that it is deprived of any semantic function and can perform another function – an anaphoric function which is directly connected to the text, but not directly indicating the objects in reality, which according to K. Bűhler is known as the *deixis ad oculos*. Hence, it can determine the identification of objects concerned in the text, can define them, but in another manner – textually by an indication of the objects concerned in the text, not those which exist in reality – and this would be the anaphoric or inner deixis.

Here, for the author and the reader (or speaker and listener) the article referentially identifies only those objects which are represented by suitable expressions in the text or expressions with which we suppose that the author is familiar. The article's anaphoric function in the Macedonian standard language determines those words indicating the objects which are discussed or have already been mentioned in the text by the author. The article's anaphoric function in the Macedonian modern language is one of the most important indicators of cohesion.

2. Zhivko Chingo, *Спроти Макавеите – од Макавејските празници*[171] *On the Eve of the Maccabees* – within the Circle of Biblical Transpositions

For centuries, the Bible has been a source of inspiration for all artistic fields. The Scripture takes an important place in the European culture and the European identity – it is a treasury of symbols, archetypes and literary *topoi*.

In wider cultural-civilizational context, the biblical together with the Jewish theme in literature is universal, especially for Western civilization, primarily because of the fact that

[171] Ж. Чинго, *Спроти Макавеите – од Макавејските празници*, in: *Пасквелија*. Скопје 1968, p. 157-164.

> (...) the Bible, as the best work of the Hebrew culture and literature with its spiritual wealth, exceeds the boundaries of its confessional importance and belongs to all mankind.[172]

Moreover, according to Eftim Kletnikov and Mirce Tomovski in the preface of the book *Искушенијата на Давидовата ѕвезда* (*Temptations of David's Star*)

> (...) the Jewish theme is inspiring for Macedonian creativity. It is especially close to Macedonian authors (...) because of the similar fate of their respective peoples – Macedonian and Jewish.[173]

The Bible is one of the most important sources of European culture, as is of religious and moral doctrines (for people who believe that the Bible is a holy book of revealed truths and commands, teaching one how to live), as well as in the field of artistic inspiration (it is a source of motivation for sculptors, painters, authors, and composers, to this day). It represents a treasury of personal motives and stanzas, stories, anecdotes and themes, motives, symbols and allegories, phraseology and style. The artistry of painting, music, literature, philosophy could not be possible without an invocation to the Bible. It is present in different areas of our lives, even in language. It is filled with words and text – examples including such phrases as "forbidden fruit," "Horns of Jericho," and "Lot's wife." Very often, these themes are set out by contemporary apocalypses, when faith prevails in the wake of inevitable death, which can cause crisis in values and in the philosophical, moral or external factors and implies impending destruction and fall of the world and the eternal struggle between good and evil. The presence of biblical motives in the treasury of Macedonian literature, film, theatre, folklore is great. Essentially, Macedonian literature can bear the atribute – biblical. Such are, for example, the characteristic poetic examples of literary prayers in modern Macedonian poetry, in the poem *Prayer* by Blaze Koneski, in the poem *Psaltirion* by Mihail Rendjov, in *Poetic Word* by Katica Kjulavkova, also in the verse by Aco Shopov, Slavko Janevski, Ante Popovski, Svetlana Hristova Jocic, Todor Chalovski, Slave Dimitrov... Or in the poetic creations by younger Macedonian poets: Metodija Zlatanov, Tihomir Jancevski, Lidija Dimkovska, Nikola Madjirov, Vladimir Martinovski, Janko Ninov (*Father David*), Zvonko Taneski, etc. In the

---

172 *Искушенијата на Давидовата ѕвезда*, ed. by М. Томовски, Е. Клетников, Скопје 2002, p. 5.

173 Ibidem, p. 26.

novel *Црно семе* (*Black Seed*) by Tashko Georgievski, one of the characters is named Christ. Biblical quotations are characteristic of the modern heroes' expressions, as for example, in the novel *Пирej* (*Pirej*) by Petre M. Andreevski, in *Фрески и гротески* (*Frescoes and Grotesques*) by Venko Andonovski, and in plays, the use of Christian prayers, call upon holy people by theatric heroes, for example, in the play *Диво месо* (*Wild Meat*) by Goran Stefanovski, etc.

These Biblical motives and topoi also include events related to the Maccabean Revolt, allegorically used in the short story by Zh. Chingo. In other words, in building of the story, Maccabean topos, plays the most important role that the author transposed in the context of the Macedonian reality after the war.

In his short story *On the Eve of the Maccabees*,[174] at least two biblical motives (topoi) take place. The first is wider, regarding the Maccabean Revolt described in the 1st and the 2nd Book of the Maccabees, and the second – being a sub-motive immersed in the composition of the first – regarding the seven brothers, martyrs of the Maccabean line who suffered a martyr's death. The first topos is related to the revolt led by Mattathias and his sons proceeded by Judah, who encouraged the armed rebellion against the Greeks from Syria and their collaborators. The name of this family was Maccabee originating from the nickname Makkaba (Hebrew – hammer), attributed to Judah. Mattathias put obedience to God before obedience to the King. He set an example – a man of God, zealous, brave, determined, ready to make sacrifice. Judah Maccabeus was a brave leader of the nation, hero in the fight for the righteous cause.

The second, shorter part than the first one, is related to the seven brothers, martyrs from the Maccabean line who are described in the Old Testament of the Holy Scripture (the Bible). The Bible does not include their names, but they are remembered by means of the church tradition and they are: Habim, Antonin, Guriah, Eleazar, Eusebon, Hadim (Halim), and Marcellus. Together with their mother Solomonia and their father, the priest Eleazar as well as other followers of the Moses' laws, suffered a martyr's death on the order of the Syrian Emperor Antiochus. But some he was called the enlightener, but others, insane. Because they defended their faith bravely, the emperor, before their mother's eyes, tortured them one by one, flayed their skin and then threw them into fire. When he did this to her last, three-year old son, the mother jumped into the fire, thus surrendering her soul to her only God. This happened 180 years before Christ.

---

174 All quotations are from Zh. Chingo, *On the Eve of the Maccabees*, in: Zh. Chingo, *Paskvelija*, Skopje 1968, p. 157–164.

Zhivko Chingo took over (transposed) this motive of the Maccabee brothers in a broad manner, in the form of a story of the situation in Macedonia at the time of the beginnings of communist rule. His narrative is focused on a village in which the inhabitants rebelled against the communist rule. In an atmosphere of apocalypse, Chingo pictures the protest and the revolt against totalitarianism and communism in an allegorical manner. The author used the Bible as a source of fiction and artistic inspiration to build the story of the Maccabean holidays in a Macedonian village.

The story *On the Eve of the Maccabees* begins in indefinite time:

> No one knew which year it was, whether it was day of night. It was winter, on the very day of St. Nicolas, an unseen storm engulfed and covered the land with thick snow (...) Lightning was striking from St. Naum (...) Joseph and Mary appeared there. Mary Elshanska gave birth there. Plague rushed in Koshishta and wasted everything.[175]

It begins with an evil that people face. Alekso Stepanoski urged people against the communists who "disrespect God" and this will cause them great misfortune. In an apocalyptic atmosphere revolt, treason and evil and death take place. After the events that transpired in the village, only one apocalypse can take place.

The title *On the Eve of the Maccabees* denotes something that will happen before the Maccabean holidays, however, the very word Maccabee is not defined, and yet, the title suggests that the events occur at the time of the Maccabean holidays, according to which weather conditions in Macedonia were forecasted. This is suggested by the second line of the title – *From the Maccabean Holidays*. However, the time is relativized – "No one knew which year it was" – the author states this in the first sentence of the story as well as in the last one – "It was in the eve of the Maccabean holidays. No one knew what the Maccabees would bring."

The Maccabean holidays themselves were strongly related to the biblical motive concerning the seven martyr brothers: Habim, Antonin, Guriah, Eleazar, Eusebon, Hadim (Halim), and Marcellus.

The Maccabean days have a very important place in religion and Macedonian folklore. Among the people, the holiday of the Maccabees is regarded as a strict holiday, however, in some places it is considered that these holidays last for six days, and in others for twelve. In Macedonia, depending on the weather conditions during these days, the

175 Zh. Chingo, *On the Eve...*, s. 157.

weather for the following six months (winter period) or for the whole year was forecasted. The holiday in honor of the seven Maccabee brothers begins with a feast on the day of the Assumption of the Blessed Virgin Mary on 1 August according to the old calendar or on 14 August according to the new one. In the Veles region, people did not work on the 1st of August, so that the women's fingers would not be worn (not to be gnawn), while spinning, and from the first to the sixth day of the month they could forecast the weather in the months from October to March. In Ohrid, the 12 days of August were known as Maccabean and this is when women did not wash cloth and did not do hard work. Here, as well, according to the Maccabees, the weather was forecast for the whole year given that a day coresponded to a month of the following year. In the words of the Miladinov brothers, we find the date that these 12 days were called the "Morinki" in Kilkis.

> The first twelve days of August are known as Morinki. During this days, the women do not work, nor wash cloths, neither bathe their children. These days speak about the good or the bad times during the whole year; if, for example, the first day of August is hot, Kolozhek (January) would be cold and the opposite; if the second day the weather is good, in Sechko (February) it will be bad; and so on.[176]

In Radovish, 1 August was considered to be a very strict holiday and it then when the elders held a strict fast and did not work at all. There was a belief that on this day the weather turned towards winter and that on this day the storks and the swallows began their migration to the warmer regions.

Such beliefs related to the Maccabees were also noted by M. Cepenkov. He testifies that on the first three days of August it was not good to wash or bathe, which means that water was not to be touched except for drinking. M. Cepenkov also noted that cloths washed on these days tore apart immediately.

> The mother of my daughter-in-law, Mary, 15–16 years ago bleached silk during the first three days of August and miraculously, the silk was torn apart piece by piece. So, you do not have to believe daddy – my daughter-in-law said – but I have seen it with my own eyes in my own home.[177]

---

[176] *Зборник на народни песни*, ред. Х. Поленаковиќ, Т. Димитровски, Скопје 1983, p. 496.

[177] М.К. Цепенков, *Македонско народно творештво во десет тома. Материјали, литературни творби*, ed. by Б. Ристовски, Vol. 10, p. 122.

In Porech, the Maccabees lasted for twelve days, but only the first days were considered a holiday.

> We celebrate them only for two days. We do not work – we do not do male or female work. For ages, since the days of old – to prevent snow, protect our livestock, our prosperity. So the Maccabee days show me what the winter would be like. If the weather is clear and windy, it will be cold, icy, we would not be able to go outside. If it is cloudy, the weather will be mild, rainy and the grass will flourish. There are as many months as there are Maccabean days.[178]

The first analogies are related to the martyr's death of the seven Maccabees brothers and the death of the Macedonians in the village, killed because their rebellion against the communist rule. But those who killed the Macedonians are not known. This is what the author says about the killers:

> It was evening when **armed** men arrived in the field... **comrade Alekso Stepanoski** gave the signalled the order for the death of those who rebelled the most... they were all **killed by the Bulgarian policemen**... **killed, my kin**... The old man rose from the ground again (...) as a black tree trunk he stood tall again before those **with the riffles**... It seems that this is not important in the apocalyptic visions, because only punishment for the evil deed is important: only after, only after the grasshoppers showed up, and desolated everything in the Paskvelian valley and fields (p. 164).

Analogies between biblical topoi and the contemporary situation in Macedonia at the time of the rise of the communism should not be sought for directly, but it can be said that the author himself suggests it even in the title – *On the Eve of the Maccabees*. What happened on the eve of the Maccabees? On the eve of the Maccabees it was winter, on the very day of Saint Nicolas; an unseen storm engulfed and covered the land with thick snow. Yet, it seems as if the Maccabean holidays have just arrived, because they fall on the 1 or 14 August. The events in the story happened in the winter before the Maccabees: "It happened before the Maccabean days. No one knew what the Maccabees would bring" – these are the words with which the author ends his story.

---

178 М. Китевски, *Денеска се Свети седум маченици Макавејски, Богородични поклади;* http: // sitel.com.mk/deneska-se-sveti-sedum-machenici-makavejski-bogorodichni-pokladi (accessed on: 7 April 2015).

But we already know what happened because Zhivko Chingo has just told us.

I. ONE SMALL REBELLION

1. The people raised a small rebellion and killed all agitators. **A man from the committee named Alekso Stepanoski prodded the people** by saying: – Blind men, we'll drop dead as mice, the agitators will take your land and your vineyards and will take all your fruit for themselves (...) Thus, this man Alekso Stepanski urged the people.

II. THE EVIL

2. There was no peace left among the people. Misery pushed them in the hands of evil. They took hold of the agitators and crushed them to pieces. And the comrade Ajdinkov, himself from the regional office, the most respectable of them all, like some dishonest woman was mounted on a donkey to be seen by all living creatures on earth, and to discourage the nonbelievers before the strength and punishment of God.

III. THE MAN

3. Then, the man named Alekso Stepanoski, he himself being part of the committee, who most vigorously inflamed the people with his own words, as if he was the most righteous of them all, came to the local office and told the authorities details about everything that he had seen and heard in the Paskvelian valley and fields. The famous agitators were killed, and comrade Ajdinkov as the most prominent among all, was carried on an old donkey to be seen and presented.

IV. THE AUTHORITIES

4. The authorities believed this man's tears (...) And they granted him the authority to bring order to the Paskvelian valley and fields. He joyfully girdled his belt and rifle, and did not forget to remind the authorities to enter all of it in his biography. The authorities did it with great praise for this man. And there, God willing, we created the collective. It was evening when armed men arrived in the field.

V. THE KILLING

5. (...) comrade Alekso Stepanoski, yet, again signaled to order the death of those who rebelled most fiercely.

   Thirteen were killed. Thirteen were killed. One of them was Blaze Pucoski (...) and then fell the nephew, Blaze Zengoski. He was even younger and most sadly, the last of his damned line of Zengoski (...) And there were more left in the field: Gligor Lovinoski, Dimko Shokaroski, Iljo Chuleski,

Josif Puleski, Risto Chifligaroski, Klime Bashuleski, Kole Lupeski and Lambe Mitreski. They all died in the Paskvelian field.

VI. THE APOCALYPSE

6. At that hour, the sun died and darkness set everywhere around. Neither man nor land could be seen, nor the bright eye of the lake, nor the golden cross of St. Kliment Ohrisdki. Nothing could be seen or known. Women and children and all those who were healthy and those who were sick again fell to the ground praying to God and His spirit. They were calling:

– Show yourself, our Savior, take us in your lap, here, the time you professed has come, the word of your Son came to be. The people prayed to be taken by God for three days and three nights.

And there at last, God willing, we created the collective. **We elected comrade Alekso Stepanoski to be the President.**

This is how Chingo pictures the manner in which, in totalitarian systems, the indecent man, by destroying (killing) many people, by means of treachery, can become their president and leader. The author emphasizes these events by the transposing of biblical motives related to the Maccabees in the narrative, connecting them to the events in the Macedonian village at the time of the rise of communism.

II. Functions of the Expression *проклет да бидам* (I'll be damned) in the novel *Големата вода* (*The Great Water)* by Zhivko Chingo

1. "Foreign Speach" in the Novel *Големата вода* (*The Great Water*) by Zhivko Chingo

The problem with "foreign speech" in this text structure, and especially in a narrative text, primarily relates to the use of foreign words from foreign languages. But not only that. "Foreign speech" is also "imported speech" where the replica content is preserved and is grammatically integrated in the narrator's text. "Foreign speech" may be "paraphrased speech" in which none of the elements of the speech act itself are preserved except for their content. However, those speeches can be mixed and representatives of foreign speech may equally exist. These are usually graphically emphasized by quotation marks in the narrative text. However, that does not apply to foreign words. As quotes from a foreign language code, they are not enclosed in quotation marks and in this case, the hallmark of the "foreign word" is exclusively, its foreign linguistic form or foreign pronunciation.

In a literal sense, "foreign speech" is a word that originates from another, nonnative language, for example, English, French, Russian, etc. However, "foreign speech" is not just a foreign word. A text written in a native language but from another author can have a role of foreign speech. It can be a separate word or an entire construction spoken by a character in a novel, by the author or the narrator. An example of "foreign speech," in its widest sense, also includes such constructions that originate from another plain of the text, which is distinguished from the main text, from the rest of the style, from the language region, from the other personal manner of expression[179] and at the end, from another language, completely different from the native one – that is, a foreign language. The problem of the foreign in contrast to the native narration refers to the relation: the author's text (original): translation text, narrator's expression: character's expression with all variations of the retold text as foreign in the language of the raconteur (author or narrator).[180] And, essentially, they are the intertextual[181] metatextual[182] and metalinguistic relations.[183]

Very often, the narrator or the character, in different forms, shows their own attitude towards the text and especially towards the foreign text. The narrator comments the character's language or the foreign text by means of the text that is graphically represented. This is usually when expressions are enclosed in quotation marks or whe words are spaced. In Chingo's text, such examples of foreign speech representation, by use of quotation marks, which usually have a function in the text, do not occur.

However, in the novel *Големата вода* (*The Great Water*), this function is performed by three means – two graphic and one lexical. First – foreign speech is placed in brackets, second – it is signalized by spacing and third – lexical, when this function is performed by the phrase: *проклет да бидам* (I'll be damned) – always in the same petrified form.

In the text of *The Great Water*, narration and, in a very modest proportion, dialogues prevail; the characters speak in direct style. A character's speech insertion in the text is predominantly in the form of indirect speech. Most often, as a signal for the use of a foreign language, the author uses repetition of an expression, some sort of exclamation, a phrase that is known from the informal (it would seem that the primary function of the magic cast by the use of words – a curse – has been lost), everyday language: *проклет да бидам.* I'll be damned.

Here are some examples from the very beginning of the text (page numbers are enclosed in brackets):[184]

---

179 M. Bachtin, *Estetyka twórczości słownej*, transl. by E. Ulicka, Warszawa 1986; W.N. Wołoszynow, *Z historii form wypowiedzi w konstrukcjach języka*, in: *Rosyjska szkoła stylistyki*, chosen and edited by M.R. Mayenowa, Z. Saloni, Warszawa 1970.

180 P. Michałowski, *Moje, cudze, wspólne, niczyje*, in: *Ja, autor. Sytuacja podmiotu w polskiej literaturze współczesnej*, ed. by D. Śnieżka, Warszawa 1996, p. 89–98.

181 M. Riffaterre, *Semiotyka intertekstualna: interpretant*, "Pamiętnik Literacki" 1988, LXXIX, l, p. 297–314.

182 A. Wierzbicka, *Metatekst w tekście*, in: *O spójności tekstu*, ed. by M.R. Mayenowa, Wrocław 1971, p. 105–121; M. Kawka, *Metatekst w tekście narracyjnym na przykładzie współczesnych utworów literatury dla dzieci*, Kraków 1990.

183 R. Jakobson, *Metajęzyk jako problem językoznawczy*, in: *W poszukiwaniu istoty języka*, ed. by M.R. Mayenowa, Vol. 1, Warszawa 1989, p. 382–390.

184 Ж. Чинго, *Големата вода*, Скопје 1974. (All quotes are from this edition.)

1. *Ми го одредија за другар во стројот.*
   I have been assigned a friend in the ranks. ***Проклет** да бидам*, другар од стројот.
   I'll be **damned**, a friend in the ranks. *Ме, задолжија со него, ми го натоварија на врат (9). I was tasked with him, they put him on my back (9).*

2. *Секој примерен беше задолжен со по еден таков лош другар во стројот. Each* exemplary person *was tasked with one such foul friend in the rank. Реков* примерен, **проклет ди бидам**, *заради* тој збор, *малку да го замрзнам целиот свет. I said* exemplary, **I'll be damned**, *because of* this word *I almost became hateful of the whole world* (9).

3. *Што да се прави, мило, мораш да појдеш во таа зандана.* ***Проклет да бидам**, така рече – з а н д а н а. Сигурно јас уште не можев да знам што значи тој збор, воопшто бев многу прост и неук. На своите дванаесет години се потпишував со ЕМ, бидејќи никако не сакав да ја запомнам буквата Л, зашто таа на нешто многу лошо ме иотсекаваше. (11)*
   There's nothing to be done, darling, you have to go to that dungeon. **I'll be damned**, that's what she said – d u n g e o n. Surely, I couldn't have known what that word meant at all, I was basically ignorant and uneducated. I was twelve years old when I still signed my name with EM since I did not want to memorize the letter L as it reminded me of something very bad. (11)

In only three of the above examples, the phrase *проклет да бидам!* (I'll be damned!) assumes three different functions. In the first case, the formula does not only fulfill a conative function. Its absence cannot lead to a lack of text cohesion. The repetition of the words *другар во стројот* (friend in the rank) without the previous phrase *проклет да бидам* (I'll be damned), does not change the text meaning in any way and it also does not bring about any incoherence to the text, which could exist without the phrase *проклет да бидам* (I'll be damned). However, this applies only to an informal language style, which is not the case here, in its literary style. In an informal language style, without the phrase *проклет да бидам* (I'll be damned), a special intonation or another phatic or conative signal would have to be used for the text to be coherent, and to fulfill its intended esthetic function. However, in written, literary language style, such a possibility does not exist.

This phrase (utterance), which is characteristic to *Големата вода* (*The Great Water*) – *проклет да бидам* (I'll be damned) – is repeated several times on every page of the text. Readers get the impression that the narrator does this without any visible and semantically (content) justified reason. This repetition affects neither communication, nor the text to any degree. In addition, this phenomenon is directly related to sentence semantics. Syntactic constructions made by use of the phrase *I'll be damned* and without it, have the same semantic value. It means that this redundant phrase can be easily erased (left out) from the text of *The Great Water*. However, if so, one should ask why this formula is so often used in the narrative structure of *The Great Water*. Why does the narrator use so often such highly stereotypical linguistic means, and what does he want to achieve with a repetition of the phrase: "I'll be damned"? In answering this question, first of all, it can be said that the author wants to signalize the informal character of the narrative. This phenomenon of repetition of some words, expressions and other constructions is characteristic of everyday communication. Very often, in our replicas, we repeat what we have heard only a moment ago. The same applies to situations when we want to be sure that we have really heard what was previously said. By repetition of replicas, the narrator realizes the language phatic function, as well as its impressive function, which Jakobson calls the "conative function." Unfortunately, this does not apply to the analyzed phrase that is really constantly repeated but never acts as a replica. Still, this is directly related to the text or its selected fragments acting in accordance with the formula that creates a very tight, logical and grammatical link to what is said. And that is not all – by repetition of the phrase *I'll be damned* + repeated replica, the narrator supports the narrative, and renews and reactivates the contact between the author and the reader. Moreover, and importantly, the phrase appears in the narrative only when spoken by the narrator, never in a direct expression of other characters. It is only his distinctive mark and a narrative feature in the form of a spoken prosthesis, serving to fill in an empty space in speech. In addition, the narrative dominates the text of *The Great Water* and other characters speak in very small proportions, predominantly in direct speech. The insertion of a character's speech in the text is predominantly in the form of indirect speech. However, it should be mentioned, that only the narrator uses the words *I'll be damned* and it is a distinct and characteristic utterance meant to be spoken only by him. So, when someone, somewhere, hears the words *I'll be damned*, it is highly likely that he will associate them with (identify) the narrator from *The Great Water* by Zhivko Chingo. This means that, even in the text itself, the function of these words is to signalize the narrator. Such is example 2, in which the narrator quotes his own words, the ones he previously uttered:

> Секој примерен беше задолжен со по еден таков лош другар во стројот. Реков примерен, **проклет да бидам**, заради тој збор за малку да го замрзам целиот свет.
> (Each exemplary person was tasked with one such foul friend in the ranks. **I'll be damned**, I said exemplarily, because of that word I almost became hateful of the whole world.)

Besides quoting (repeating in an unaltered form) his own words *секој примерен...*(each exemplary person...), the narrator uses verbum dicendi: *реков* (*примерен*) (I said (exemplary)) and then he uses the utterance *I'll be damned*, to manifest his own relation to the quoted words:

> (...) заради тој збор за малку да го замрзам целиот свет. Примерен другар, примерен пионер, примерен скоевец, примерен градител. Примерен, што уште не, **проклет да бидам**, примерен серко. Но таков беше редот, се колнам.
> (...) because of that word I almost became hateful of the whole world. Exemplary friend, exemplary pioneer, exemplary member of the party, exemplary builder. Exemplary what not, **I'll be damned**, exemplary asshole. But that was the custom, I swear.) (9)

The narrator speaks about the world, which, according to him, is primarily built of words. Words spoken by him and the other characters in the novel, build and organize the fictional world of the text. Even more so, in all excerpts from Chingo's text, the same mechanism is employed in the text organization by using the phrase, *I'll be damned*, which metatextually "sews up" the text. However, the narrator's attitude towards the words he repeats is negative.[185] The same situation occurs in example 3. The only difference is that the narrator acts negatively towards foreign speech, which is signalized by the phrase *така рече* (that's what he // she said). However, in both examples, the attitude towards the text is also negative, regardless of whether it is about Chingo's own text – in which case, by using the phrase *I'll be damned*

---

[185] This attitude towards words, and the manner of communication can be compared to the Orwellian "newspeak". See: G. Orwell, *Rok 1984*. In Polish literature there is a similar term: *nowomowa* – more on this from: M. Głowiński, *Nowomowa po polsku*, Warszawa 1991.

the author distances himself from the text, or he quotes someone – in which case it is explicitly about someone else's text.

However, are we always talking about the same thing, when in all situations the expression:

ПРОКЛЕТ ДА БИДАМ (I'LL BE DAMNED) + EPIPHORA (repetition of the last element from the previous text)

Се искачивме дури на **највисоката** карпа. **Проклет да бидам, највисоката.**
(We even climbed the highest rock. I'll be damned, the highest.)

is used in the text – a negative attitude towards the text in a much broader sense – semantic and formal? And what if the function of those words can be described as metatextual? And one more question: What did the author want to accomplish with such narrative rhetoric? Before giving the answers to the above questions, let's consider more material including examples with the phrase *проклет да бидам* (I'll be damned) + a repetition of the last element of the previous text functioning as rhetorical epiphora:

1. Јас уште ја гледам таа вода. Кејтеновиот сон, нашиот сон. **Проклет да бидам**, сиот наш сон (17).
   I can still see that water. Kejten's dream, our dream. **I'll be damned**, the dream of us all.

2. Се искачивме дури на највисоката карпа. Проклет да бидам (19).
   We even climbed the highest rock. I'll be damned.

3. ...колку толку затоплувајќи си ја душата. **Проклет да бидам**, душата (23).
   ...at least warming my soul. **I'll be damned**, my soul.

4. Особено тоа се забележуваше кај девојченцата. **Проклет да бидам**, нашите убави девојки! Истрижени, сакати, како грди момченца, стопени во општиот ред. **Проклет да бидам**, некој измислил општ ред за убавите девојчиња (24).
   This could especially be noticed with the little girls. **I'll be damned**, our beautiful girls! Sheared, crippled, like ugly little boys, melted in the general order. **I'll be damned**, someone made up a general order for beautiful girls.

5. Знаеш, ти си заграден со тој проклет ѕид. Немаш каде одделен си од другиот свет. **Проклет ди бидам**, од сите страпи си заграден (24).

You know, you are fenced with that damned wall. You have nowhere to go; you are separated from the rest of the world. **I'll be damned**, you are fenced in from all sides.

6. ...А секој оној што ќе се обидеше повторно да го мери беше најстрого казнуван. **Проклет да бидам**, најстрого (25).
...And anyone who tried to measure it again, was most severely punished. **I'll be damned**, most severely.

7. Тогаш пред нашите очи зашумуваше цело едно море. **Проклет да бидам**, море (26).
Then, an entire sea swished before our eyes. **I'll be damned**, a sea.

8. Тие во прво време на ништо не потсеќаа, беа излишни, големи црвени бубалки. **Проклет да бидам**, црвени бубалки (27).
At the beginning they did not remind one of anything, they were superfluous, big red bugs. **I'll be damned**, red bugs.

9. Сите прозорци од каде може да се гледа Големата вода беа ѕоѕидани. Се што гледаше кон таму беше ѕоѕидаио. **Проклет да бидам**, ѕоѕидано (27).
All the windows from which the Great Water could be seen were walled up. Everything that was facing it was walled up. **I'll be damned**, walled up.

10. Тоа не можеше повеќе да го гледа Кејтеновиот син, рече, јас морам да бегам. **Проклет да бидам**, го рече тој збор (31).
Kejtan's son could not look at that any more, he said, I have to run. **I'll be damned**, he said that word.

11. Не бевме сигурно толку чукнати, **проклет да бидам**, чукнати (32).
We certainly weren't that wacky, **I'll be damned**, wacky.

12. Јас заради вистината, **проклет да бидам**, заради вистината, – ќе почнам од почетокот како што е по ред... (33)
Because of the truth, **I'll be damned**, because of the truth, I'll start from the beginning and continue on...

13. ...а кога ќе запееше некоја борбена песна, тогаш станувaше чудесен (...) **Проклет да бидам**, песна (37).
...and when he sang some war song, then he became miraculous (...) **I'll be damned**, a song.

14. – Стани малечок, рече, стани силен Леме, пристигнавме! **Проклет да бидам**, пристигнавме, се уште ми беше темница в очи... (40)
– Get up little one, he said, get up strong Lem, we have arrived! **(I'll be damned**, we have arrived, it was still dark before my eyes...

15. ...Слушајте, таа иде, се колнам. **Проклеш да бидам**, пријателе, таа иде (41).
...Listen up, she is coming, I swear. **I'll be damned, my friend**, she is coming.

16. **Проклет да бидам**, циркус. Поети, артисти, оперски пејачи, балети, свирачи, кросисти, таленти (45).
I'll be damned, a circus. Poets, artists, opera singers, ballet dancers, players, cross-country skiers, talents.

17. Таквите работи се правеа во празничен ден. **Проклет да бидам**, празничен (45).
Such things were for the holidays. **I'll be damned**, the holidays.

18. Сигурно за да бидеме подготвени за дочек на музата. **Проклет да бидам**, муза (45).
Making sure we were ready for welcoming the muse. **I'll be damned**, a muse.

19. Пожари. **Проклет да бидам**, пожари (47).
Fires. **I'll be damned**, fires.

20. Немаше дете што не посака овој миг да потрае вечно, засекогаш. **Проклет да бидам**, вечно (49).
There was no child that didn't want this moment to last forever, always. **I'll be damned**, forever.

21. Повторно ја слушав Големата вода, стоев на највисоката карпа, повторно се јави оној ненознат глас, таа жена, мајка. **Проклет да бидам**, мајка (49–50).
I heard the Great Water again. I was standing on the highest rock when that unknown voice was heard again, that woman, a mother. **I'll be damned**, a mother.

22. Се колнам тој час неа и по вода да ја пуштевме – ќе одеше, водата ќе ја држеше. **Проклет да бидам**, би одела (51).

I can swear to you, at that moment, if we had let her walk on the water – she would have walked, the water would have held her. **I'll be damned**, she would have walked.

23. Можеше да е и вечер, полноќ, седно, за него беше само добро утро. **Проклет да бидам**, утро (53).
It could have been evening, midnight, whenever, for him, it was only a good morning. **I'll be damned**, a morning.

24. Тогаш Оливера Срезоска прв и последен пат ја видовме во блуска, слободна, откопчапа. **Проклет да бидам**, о т к о п ч а п а (54).
It was the first and the last time we saw Olivera Srezoska in a blouse, loose, unbuttoned. **I'll be damned**, unbuttoned.

25. Уште беше поделикатно со кандидатките за балет, (...) **Проклет да бидам**, балет (55).
It was even more delicate with ballet candidates (...) **I'll be damned**, ballet.

26. Иако бевме одделени, тој го видел мојот сон, знаеше каде лета моето срце, што бара тоа низ ѕидот. **Проклет да бидам**, видел (61).
Even though we were separated, he had seen my dream, he knew where my heart was flying, what it was looking for through the wall. **I'll be damned**, he had seen.

27. ...една многу грда женска работа, удри и штипни, в срце да те изгори. **Проклет да бидам**, в срце да те изгори (63).
...a very ugly female thing, hit and pinch, burns the heart out of you. **I'll be damned**, burns the heart out of you.

28. Во слободното време составуваше песни за деца. **Проклет да бидам**, песни (64).
In his free time, he wrote children's songs. **I'll be damned**, songs.

29. ...во часот помислив да не е нешто опфатен од д у х о в и т е. **Проклет да бидам**, д у х о в и т е (64).
...at the moment I thought he might be possessed by ghosts. **I'll be damned**, ghosts.

30. Пред моите очи како во најубав сон се откриваше целата површина на езеро. Големата вода. **Проклет да бидам**. Тоа беше Големата вода (66).
The whole surface of the lake was opening before my eyes, as in a most wonderful dream. The Great Water. **I'll be damned**. It was the Great Water.

31. Тој како да ми беше близнак, цел живот како да сме биле заедно. **Проклет да бидам**, цел живот (66).
It was as if he was my twin, as if we have been together our entire lives. **I'll be damned**, our entire lives.

32. ...повторно можев да мислам на Сентерлевиот рид, на оној рид од каде се раѓа сонцето. **Проклет да бидам**, тоа беше радост (68).
I could think of Senterlev Hill again, of the hill from where the sun is born. **I'll be damned**, it was a joy.

33. ...беше вљубен во својот позив и камбанчето. **Проклет да бидам**, камбанчето (72).
...he was in love with his call and the little church bell. **I'll be damned**, the little church bell.

34. Зар тоа не е најсвирепо, најстрашно самоубиство, о, на час кога би му се избистрила малку главата. **Проклет да бидам**, какво ужасно слепило, каква незамислива казна (73).
Isn't it the most ferocious, the most dreadful suicide, oh, if only he could have his head cleared for a moment. **I'll be damned**, what a horrible blindness, what an unimaginable punishment.

35. Така и беше, тој се плашеше од сонот. **Проклет да бидам**, се плашеше (73).
And so it was, he was afraid of the dream. **I'll be damned**, he was afraid.

36. Лудакот не оти ќе те праша, потегнуваше со железото и што ти пишал господ. **Проклет да бидам**, што ти пишал господ (74).
It is not as if the madman would ask me, he jerked with the iron and the rest was your destiny written by God. **I'll be damned**, your destiny written by God.

37. Еден ден, сепак, тоа будалиште беше добар. Прогледа. **Проклет да бидам**, прогледа (75).
One day, still, this fool was good. He recovered his sight. **I'll be damned**, recovered his sight.

38. ...пак тоа лице стана грдо, неубаво. Туѓо, **Проклет да бидам**. Туѓо (75).
...again, that face became ugly, not beautiful. Strange, **I'll be damned**. Strange.

39. Се колнам, господ. Лудаци. Проклети лудаци, со ѕид во очите. Слепи (...) **Проклет да бидам**, слепи (74).
I swear to God. Madmen. Damn madmen with a wall in their eyes. Blind (...) **I'll be damned**, blind.

40. Беше се искачил на бината во дворот, го ловеше дождот. **Проклет да бидам**, го ловеше дождот. Тоа беше прекрасен, пролетен дожд. Светол (76).
He had climbed the stage in the yard, hunting the rain. **I'll be damned**, hunting the rain. It was a wonderful springtime rain. Light.

41. Почпа да трча од одделение до одделение, да душка како загар, **проклет да бидам**, како загар, да се загледува во секое лице (...) (76)
He started running from one department to another, sniffing like a hound, **I'll be damned**, like a hound, staring in each and every face (...)

42. ...направивме еден митннг во чест на другарот Анески, нашиот ѕвонар. **Проклет да бидам**, митинг (78).
...we had a meeting in honor of comrade Aneski, our bell ringer. **I'll be damned**, a meeting.

43. ...од глава до петици бевме полни со вошки. Не јадеа и преку ден и преку ноќ. **Проклет да бидам**, непрестајно. Се изгуби секаков сон во домот (83).
...head to toe, we were full of lice. They were eating use day and night. **I'll be damned**, incessantly. All sleep was lost in the home.

44. Првпат се случи и храна да ни престане. Бевме сити. **Проклет да бидам**, сити (83).
For the first time, we had food to spare. We were satiated. **I'll be damned**, satiated.

45. Се чинеше божем тука поминала чумата и се усмртила. Гроб. **Проклет да бидам**, г р о б (84).
It seemed as if the plague had passed by here and killed everything. A grave. **I'll be damned**, a grave.

46. Небото над Големата вода беше црвено. **Проклет да бидам**, во пламен (84).
The sky above the Great Water was red. **I'll be damned**, in flames.

47. О, боже, се ќе се стопи, гледаш. Прав. **Проклет да бидам**, п р а в (85).
Oh, God, everything will melt, you see. Dust. **I'll be damned**, dust.

48. **Проклет да бидам**, сè, сè се претвора во прав, во н и ш т о (85).
I'll be damned, everything, everything turns into dust, into nothingness.

49. Ме легна в креветче за да спијам. **Проклет да бидам**, да с п и ј а м (86).
He put me in bed to sleep. **I'll be damned**, to sleep.

50. Без команда се оддели од своето одделение и летна кон мене. **Проклет да бидам**, л е т н а (88).
Without any command, he dashed off from his class and flew towards me. **I'll be damned**, he flew.

51. Какви луѓе можеа тие да бидат, какво е нивното поведение? **Проклет да бидам**, п о в е д е н и е (94).
What kind of people could they be, what was their conduct? **I'll be damned**, conduct.

52. ...му велеа, – речи ни старче Лентеноски, речи ни што барал тој човек? По неколку векови и тоа го дознавме. Човекот ги барал своето семејство, својата куќа, своите деца, мајката на своите деца. **Проклет да бидам**, тоа барал човекот (97).
...they said to him – tell us old man Lentenoski, tell us what was the man looking for? After several centuries, we found that out, too. The man was looking for his family, his house, his children, the mother of his children. **I'll be damned**, that is what the man was looking for.

53. Сигурно им било студено на децата, живееле во некоја колипка на крај село. **Проклет да бидам**, сигурно многу им било студено на децата... (99)
The children must have been cold, they lived in some cottage at the end of the village. **I'll be damned**, the children must have been very cold...

54. ...греело сонцето. **Проклет да бидам**, с о н ц е (99).
...the sun was shining. **I'll be damned**, the sun.

55. Ја пеевме химната. **Проклет да бидам**, х и м н а т а (10).
We sang the anthem. **I'll be damned**, the anthem.

56. Секој ден гледавме како сонцето умира. **Проклет да бидам**, сонцето у м и р а ш е (103).
Every day we could see the sun die. **I'll be damned**, the sun was dying.

57. Сѐ на светов има мајка, ни рече мајка Верна Јаковлеска, и сонцето има мајка. Сигурно, **проклет да бидам**, сѐ има мајка (103).
Everything in this world has a mother, told us mother Verna Jakovleska, and the sun has a mother, too. Certainly, **I'll be damned**, everything has a mother.

58. ...знаеш со светците сме начисто. **Проклет да бидам**, начисто (103).
...you know we are all clear with the saints. **I'll be damned**, all clear.

59. Сигурно затоа владееше толкава глупост, се плашевме. **Проклет да бидам**, сигурно тоа беше с т р а в (103).
That must have been why such folly reigned, we were afraid. **I'll be damned**, it must have been fear.

60. ...да реализира акции. **Проклет да бидам**, токму тоа – а к ц и и (105).
...to put through actions. **I'll be damned**, exactly – actions.

61. Девојките пред неа се тресеа како лист на гранка. **Проклет да бидам**, како лист на гранка (105).
The girls shivered in front of her as leaves on a branch. **I'll be damned**, as leaves on a branch.

62. ...Таа искрено се внесуваше по сета своја душа. **Проклет да бидам**, веруваше (106).
...She was honestly dedicated, with all her soul. **I'll be damned**, she believed.

63. ...гаќичките ѝ беа нешто најсвето во пејзиниот живот. **Проклет да бидам**, најсвето (106).
...her panties were the most sacred thing in her life. **I'll be damned**, the most sacred.

64. ...Оливера Срезоска остана без своите најмили гаќички. **Проклет да бидам**, без своите црвени гаќи (106).
...Olivera Srezoska was left without her dearest panties. **I'll be damned**, without her red panties.

65. Гаќи, можеби ќе речете, но за пего тоа беше живот. **Проклет да бидам**, живот (107).
Pants, you might say, but for someone they were their life. **I'll be damned**, life.

66. Сплеткани, неми веднаш застанаа во строј. **Проклет да бидам**, н е м и (108).

Confused, speechless, they immediately stood in line. **I'll be damned**, speechless.

67. Девојки молчеа како китови, залиени. **Проклет да бидам**, залиени (108).
The girls kept to themselves as statues, foundered. **I'll be damned**, foundered.

68. Претресот траеше неколку векови. **Проклет да бидам**, неколку векови (109).
The hearing lasted for several centuries. **I'll be damned**, several centuries.

69. Вториот случај беше нешто од п о о п ш т карактер и сета таа работа не се заврши само во внатрешни, домски мерки. **Проклет да бидам,** се прошири и на политички план. А во почетокот ни беше врашки смешно, весело. **Проклет да бидам**, весело (110).
The second case was of a more general character and all that matter was not closed only by internal, household measures. **I'll be damned**, it also expanded politically. And at the beginning it was hellishly funny, joyful. **I'll be damned**, joyful.

70. Не, не беше во прашање само еден млад човечки живот – самото д е л о, **проклет да бидам**, самото дело беше тешко над триста тони (111).
No, it wasn't the question of only one young human life – the act itself, **I'll be damned**, the act itself was over three hundred tons heavy.

71. ...ја будеа и кутрите девојки со солзи во очите, о, **проклет да бидам**, тие вистински се раслакаа (111).
...she was woken up by the poor girls with tears in their eyes, oh, **I'll be damned**, they were really smudged all over.

72. ...како вкопан, се загледував во сонцето што заоѓа. **Проклет да бидам**, како вкопан (112).
...as if I were stuck in, I stared at the setting sun. **I'll be damned**, as if I were stuck in.

73. Со тоа што ѝ беше во раце го нападна, со перодршката со која ги бележеше нашите одговори. **Проклет да бидам**, со перодршката. По лице, по очи (114).
She attacked him with the thing she had in her hands, with the penholder with which she wrote down our answers. **I'll be damned**, with the penholder. To his face, his eyes.

74. Кејтен е под клуч. **Проклет да бидам**, под к л у ч (119).
Kejten is locked up. **I'll be damned**, locked up.

75. Постоеше само една желба, да му се врати слободата. **Проклет да бидам**, с л о б о д а т а (119).
There was only one desire, to help him, to restore his freedom. **I'll be damned**, freedom.

76. Послушав, тоа беше гласот на Големата вода. **Проклет да бидам**, по толку века се јави гласот на Големата вода (119).
I obeyed, it was the voice of the Great Water. **I'll be damned**, after so many centuries the voice of the Great Water called out.

77. ...одеднаш стана роб на нешто страшно. **Проклет да бидам**, р о б (120).
...suddenly he became a slave to something horrific. **I'll be damned**, a slave.

78. – Ами камо му книга, – прашува детето, – зар, така, само по ветар! **Проклет да бидам**, по в е т а р (121).
– Well, where is his book – asks the child – he can't go just like that, just in the wind! **I'll be damned**, in the wind.

79. ...тој час беше со нив, чекореше. **Проклет да бидам**, ч е к о р е ш е (121).
...he was with them at that moment, pacing. **I'll be damned**, pacing.

80. ...сакав да му ја откријам својата голема тајна. Своето срце. **Проклет да бидам**, сето срце (121).
...I wanted to reveal him my big secret. My heart. **I'll be damned**, all my heart.

81. Се погледнавме пламено в очи. **Проклет да бидам**, п л а м е н о (124).
We looked at each other's eyes passionately. **I'll be damned**, passionately.

82. Бесцелно е тоа, Леме, нема никаква цел. (**Проклет да бидам**, ц е л) (124).
It is useless, Lem, it has no purpose. (**I'll be damned**, purpose.)

83. ...мала болка, само за еден човек, безначајно, еден човек. **Проклет да бидам**, токму така само за е д е н човек (125).
...mild pain, only for one man, meaningless, one man. **I'll be damned**, exactly, only for one man.

84. Неговата болест беше сонот. **Проклет да бидам**, сонот (129).
    His disease was his dream. **I'll be damned**, his dream.

85. Сакаше да го остават таму, на глувците. **Проклет да бидам**, на глувците (129).
    He wanted to be left there, for the mice. **I'll be damned**, for the mice.

86. Веднаш штом го допре виделото, тој како покосен падна наземи. **Проклет да бидам**, беше мртов (129).
    As soon as he touched the light, he fell to the ground as if swept away. **I'll be damned**, he was dead.

Words that can be found closest to the phrase *проклет да бидам* (I'll be damned) are most often repeated. The repetitive expressions can be found somewhat further away from the phrase, however, it is always related to the immediate and previous context. The choice of words from the previous context seems to be determined by the narrator's arbitrary decision and it does not depend on the meaning or the sense of the text, but it especially concerns the author, from different reasons often related to his autobiography. After a detailed analysis of the above listed examples, we can conclude that the reason for such frequent, yet loosely related to contextual meaning (rhetorical), use of the construction in the form of *проклет да бидам* (I'll be damned) is manifested by the narrator throughout the text for the purpose of emphasizing the foreign speech in the text and distancing himself from it. The narrator is saying that what the reader is reading and understanding is not the author's or the narrator's own words, but somebody else's words. Even when the narrator, after the formula *проклет да бидам* (I'll be damned), quotes his own, just uttered, words, he does this to ensure himself that they are his own, not somebody else's expressions. This means that the narrator is not completely certain in what he is saying, in his own narrative expression. He considers himself to be alienated within the expression (or maybe alienated by the expression) and by use of the words he wants to confirm the textual ownership that means textual truth. Throughout the text, the narrator struggles to prove what part of the text is his, what belongs to him, and what part of the text is not his, but is foreign.

The text of the *Great Water* is unremitting rivalry between what is native – from the narrator's (author's) point of view and what is foreign – from the aspect of the foreign narration of others – "некој така кажа" (somebody said so)[186] being literarily quoted in the text, in direct or indirect style, or as foreign speech. This means that with every appearance (in not such a voluminous novel, there are more than 150 examples with the same expressive formulas) in the text, the phrase:

Проклет да бидам (I'll be damned) + literarily repeated or modified word or syntactic expression from the previous text signalizes that what was said before the formula *проклет...* (...damned) is foreign or that the narrator does not identify himself with what he has said in the previous text, that he distances himself from the explicitly foreign (quoted) or implicit (his own) text. This continuously present process of such specific text organization can have very important, not only stylistic, but primarily semantic (ideological) consequences for the interpretation of the novel *The Great Water* by Zhivko Chingo, which have not been exhaustively and consistently described yet.

2. Formal and Dynamic Equivalence in the Polish Translation of *Големата вода* (*The Great Water*) by Zhivko Chingo

Eugene Nida,[187] first notices the advent of equivalence in theory of translation and divided it in formal and functional equivalence. Functional (or dynamic) equivalence conveys the main idea expressed in the source text. If necessary, this goal can be achieved on the account of literality of the original (what we have in the original as a form is conveyed by another form in literal sense) and also of the sentence word order, or the grammatical form of the source text. According to formal equivalence, the text of the original and the text of the translation are treated literally, "word for word" (*verbum pro verbum*).

According to Eugene Nida, there are two theories of translation: the theory of formal equivalence and the theory of dynamic (functional) equivalence. The main goal of the first is to express as precise as possible the whole power and meaning of every word and change of expression in the original text. The second – to create a text that doesn't resemble a translation at all, but acts as an equivalent of the source text. A good translator should never completely ignore either of these two theories. Formal and dynamic equivalence causes many controversies

---

186 M.R. Mayenowa, *Poetyka teoretyczna. Zagadnienia języka*, Wrocław 1974, p. 160–176.

187 E. Nida, *Zasady odpowiedniości*, transl. by A. Skucińska, in: *Współczesne teorie przekładu: Antologia*, ed. by P. Bukowski, M. Heydel, Kraków 2009.

even today, but at the same time, some believe this to be an obsolete question in the field of theory of translation.

R. Jakobson is considered to provide a landmark in the shaping of the bases of the theory of translation R. Jakobson. His essay titled *O językoznawczych aspektach przekładu* (*On Linguistic Aspects of Translation*) includes the following types of translation: intralingual – or paraphrasing of text, interlingual – between two languages and intersemiotic – between systems of signs and statements that

> (...) on the level of interlingual translation, there is ordinarily no full equivalence between code-units.[188]

However, over the course of these last 50 years, many other theories on translation equivalence have been elaborated. Still, the stance that texts with dynamic equivalence are more natural and more correct (accurate) than translations on which formal equivalence is used, prevails because the latter can be inaccurate in a decisive manner.

Some researchers oppose the theory of dynamic equivalence. U. Eco is among them. He, emphasizes that:

> (...) semantic equivalence can't be taken as a satisfactory criterion for a correct translation, (...) we cannot even accept the naïve idea that semantic equivalence is provided by synonyms, since it is commonly accepted that there are no complete synonyms in language. *Father* is not a synonym for *daddy*, daddy is not a synonym of *papà*, and *père* is not a synonym for *padre*.[189]

Eco further argues that

> (...) the translator does not translate a text on the basis of the dictionary, but rather on the basis of the whole history of two literatures. Therefore, translating is not only connected with linguistic competence, but also with intertextual, psychological and narrative competence. Thus, the translator is forced at all times to go beyond linguistic competence to the cultural spectrum. Consequently, translations do not constitute a comparison between two languages, but the interpretation of two texts in two different languages. In order for the translation to come to life, it must generate the same effect aimed at by the original.[190]

---

188 R. Jakobson, *O językoznawczych aspektach przekładu*, in: *W poszukiwaniu istoty...*, Vol. 1, p. 374.

189 U. Eco, *Experiences in Translation*, Toronto 2001, p. 5.

190 Ibidem, p. 14.

The theory of "dynamic equivalence" or "functional equivalence" was developed by Eugene Nida in his book *Theory and Practice of Translation.* Nida stressed the importance of communication, not only of grammatical form, as means for transferring meaning.

While remaining in the field of the theory of equivalence, it would be desirable to consider the Polish translation of *The Great Water*[191] as an example of a contemporary Macedonian novel, to analyze the relation of compliance regarding proverbs, curses and other expressions characterizing emotions, and at the same time fulfilling metatextual and intertextual functions, so as to see if formal equivalence is at all possible when translating emotional-colloquial lexis.

As Dragi Mihajlovski, the renowned Macedonian writer and translator of Shakespeare, emphasized in one interview:

> ....преведувачот не може без зборовите. Тие му се основно средство. Во нив е затворено значењето. Но преведувачот никогаш не преведува зборови, односно значење, туку задолжително се труди да преведува целини, реченици во кои има смисла. Преводот тргнува од значењето, но не го преведува, зашто тогаш ќе преведува буквално и ќе заврши во неразбирање, туку е во постојана потрага по смисла. Преводот има смисла само ако се стреми да преведува смисла. Оттука и најновите тенденции во сферата на теоријата на преведувањето (...) сè повеќе се говори за превод на култири, односно дека преведувачот преку својата сложена и исклучително противречна дејност не преведува само дела, туку култури.

> (...) the translator can't do without words. They are his essential tools. They have the meaning enclosed within. However, the translator never translates words or meaning, but must endeavor to translate whole units, sentences that make sense. Meaning is the translator's starting point, but he doesn't translate it, because thus he would be translating literally and cause misunderstanding; rather, he is always in pursuit of sense. The translation would have sense only if sense is being translated. Hence, the newest tendencies in the field of theory of translation (...) translation of cultures, is increasingly discussed i.e. the translator, through his // her extremely complex and contradictory activity, translates not only works, but cultures.[192]

---

191 Ж. Чинго, *Големата вода...*; *Wielka woda*, transl. by D. Cirlić-Straszyńska, Warszawa 1984.

192 Т. Огњанов, *Трпелива одбивност владее во културата*, "Dnevnik" 2009, 9 October, http: // www.dnevnik.com.mk/default.asp?ItemID=9D3E42AB6F5E0444AEB33639C8C12AEB

An interlingual equivalence of Macedonian and Polish expressions would be interesting to analyze in this context

(Mac.) проклет да бидам (original)
(Pol.) niech będę przeklęty (formal equivalence)
(Pol.) niech mnie diabli porwą (dynamic equivalence)

Expressive expressions as are (Mac.) *проклет да бидам*, (Pol.) *niech mnie diabli porwą* – the first used in the text of the Macedonian contemporary novel *The Great Water* by Zhivko Chingo; the second (with variants) – in its Polish translation – is part of a group of expressions, colloquialisms, phraseologisms, as a kind of colloquial-emotional lexis, an important register of the spoken language.

As does the first, so the second also belongs to the semantic category of curses, oaths, expressions and proverbs – expressions fulfilling a magical function in the text.

These also include the Macedonian expression: *проклет да бидам* as well as the Polish one: *niech będę przeklęty* (with variants – *niech to diabli, niech to diabli porwą, a niech to*). Use of such constructions in expressions (texts) is primarily related to individual language properties of the author since emotional colloquialisms allow the recipient to clearly identify the person who is speaking – the author of the text.

Moreover, given that they are mostly a characteristic feature of colloquial speech in his lexical layer, they belong to a marked register of his colloquial style, and for some, more or less, vulgar expressions, lexicographic descriptions can be found.

In the Polish translation of *The Great Water,* the Macedonian expression *проклет да бидам* (I'll be damned) found its equivalent in

1. niech mnie diabli porwą,
2. niech diabli porwą,
3. niech to diabli.

Literal translation of this expression should be the Polish variant: *niech będę przeklęty*. The translator, however, has chosen a different (dynamic) equivalent of the Macedonian expression and hid it in three formal versions. The stylistic point of view, perhaps, played a decisive role here, and the presumption that the Polish expression: *niech będę przeklęty* will not fulfill the same function in an appropriate manner, as does its Macedonian equivalent in the original text.

(accessed on: 12 September 2012).

Thanks to the use of the expression *проклет да бидам* (I'll be damned), in a special manner, the narrator curses his hitherto past life (cursing it only by speaking about it) and thus, the life and destiny of all post-war orphans who found themselves in the described Yugoslavian orphanage. It has an even more serious function, because through religious associations, it is connected to the pre-mortem, time and is meant to serve as a reminder of the events that had come to pass.

However, it is difficult to predict whether this presumption is true or not, because the literal variant never appeared in the text of the translation. Furthermore, this expression translated literally – *niech będę przeklęty* – cannot be found in the Polish language as an expression or spoken colloquialism as is the case with the Macedonian expression – *проклет да бидам.* It cannot be repeated for the purpose of obtaining valorization, and functioning as a text delimiter. This is where the general conclusion is derived from, that the conditions for the use of the Macedonian formula, and its literal equivalent in the Polish language, are different.

Because of the highly frequent use of the expression – *проклет да бидам* (I'll be damned) – in the novel as well as its petrified formal shape, it obtains a stylistic valorization. Moreover, the author does not use any formal variability, and throughout the text of *The Great Water* – *проклет да бидам* – is unchanged even when multiple times it is repeated on one page of the text.

Thus, this expression is deprived of its literal meaning in the original, and the curse's primary function is completely neutralized. A curse can be spoken only once; repeated several times, it looses its magical and enchanting properties.

Therefore, the frequent use of the expression *Проклет да бидам* should be treated as a purposeful stylistic tool containing a hyperbolization and individualization of the author's language. This consequence is not present in the text of the translation, and it is dominated by use of variants of the Polish equivalents to the Macedonian expression. There are three equivalent variants: *niech mnie diabli porwą, niech diabli porwą, niech to diabli,* which are synonymous in a certain manner. However, given the highly frequent use of the Macedonian expression in the original, the translation should respect this fact to a great extent.

III. On the Metaillocutionary Power of Negation in *Шеќерна приказна* (*Sugar Story)* by Slavko Janevski

The notion of negation can be considered from several aspects. In this case, three types of negation will be considered, of which two have an explicitly linguistic character. The first relates to the negation of expression. It is about the morphological and semantic conditionality of the connection of 'NO' with various expression, i.e. the thematic foundations of expressions. The participation of 'NO' is often expressed in relation to backformation processes – this manner of study of negation gives scarce information on its function in the text. However, placing morphological indicators of negation on a syntactic plain, also facilitates the explanation of negation function in text structure and the discourse from a methodological aspect. Sentence negation is the second aspect.

In addition to the involvement of negation constructions on a grammatical (syntactic) plain, attention should be paid to another, third sphere, to negation operations and to their indicators in the text. The functioning of negation in a literary text, and the problems related to illocution are in question here, and especially, the metaillocutory forces of speech, which act with negation in a literary text. This problem will be considered in the text of the children's tale, *Шеќерна приказна* (*Sugar Story*) by Slavko Janevski[193].

The illocutive character of literary works has been discussed many times, however, it is obvious that not all types of literary acts use illocution with the same degree and not all of them are endowed with the power of illocution.[194] Illocutive acts of speech are particularly often used in certain types of magical stories intended for children. These kind of works and special genres, enriched with fantasy, possess magical for-

193 С. Јаневски, *Шеќерна приказна*, Скопје 1980. (All quotes are from this edition.)

194 R. Ohmann, *Literatura jako akt*, in: *Studia z teorii literatury (Archiwum "Pamiętnika Literackiego")*, Wrocław 1988, p. 7–23.

mulae such as: magical words, curses, spells, messages, forbiddances, orders, etc., which if passed on, can harm (or help) the protagonist first of all, but in certain circumstances, supporting characters are not spared and can also fall under their influence. The delivering of magical formulae, for example, 'Open Sesame' (*Sezamie, otwórz się*) or 'Биди, арараио, камен, не-кјумур, не-мраз!' cause, thanks to the language magic, events that decisively or crucially change the further course of action.

In accordance with the concept of illocution by J.L. Austin[195] and his disciple J.R. Searle,[196] the illocutive power of speech should obligate the executor of this act, to certain convictions, intentions and acts. However, it is also possible, that the illocutive power of the speech act to not oblige (for example by use of negation) the executor to something which, at least up till now, hasn't received too much attention. In this regard, J. Lyons wrote:

> Speech act theory in its current state does not consider the non-obligatory acts (...) their perlocutive effect is not expressed as is the effect of statement. If by the non-obligatory act we denounce the acceptance of 'p', very often, in the listener's thoughts we incite a previously absent conviction that in reality 'p' could be true.[197]

Very often, statements of this type and magical formulae can be found in texts with a folklore content – for example in the collected works of M. Cepenkov[198] (in volume 8) and edition 5 of *Macedonian folklore* containing Macedonian bywords, riddles, proverbs, curses, etc., and may also be found in artistic texts intended for children. The latter may include magical speech act occurring in the sphere of fun and games, for example, it is said that children will 'not grow up' if they are stepped over, as well as in the sphere of chanting for the transfer of pain from a child to an animal, when the whole ritual is accompanied with the words "Up till now the nails were in Boris, now they are in the donkey" or within the frame of identification of elements in the relation – Word: object, for example magical words: 'Open Sesame'.

---

195 J. Austin, *How to Do Things with Words*, London 1971; *Expression and Meaning. Studies in the Theory of Speech Acts*, Cambridge 1979.

196 J. Searle, *Speech Acts. An Essay of the Philosophy of Language*, Cambridge 1969.

197 J. Lyons, *Semantyka*, p. 363.

198 М. Цепенков, *Пословици, поговорки, гатанки, клетви и благослови*, Скопје 1972; *Македонско народно творештво. Пословици и гатанки*, Скопје 1969; Д. и К. Миладиновци, *Зборник на народни песни*, Скопје 1983.

In Slavko Janevski's tale, the sphere of magical effect of expressions with negation, introduced in a form of 'NO' as a special morphological (particle) united or hidden in an antonym, is highly obvious. However, here we will discuss only some examples of structures with negation – those which have special meaning for text organization or for literary function building, and do not touch upon the problem, as it usually is the case, of truthfulness or falsehood, existence or nonexistence. Hence, the relation between negation and literary text (although it is its constituent element), in this case, has a metaillocutive character, since it does not refer to the truthfulness or the falsehood, but, among all else, builds the text by use of negated textual structures.

In magical (artistic and folklore) texts, especially those intended for children, relations between events in the text and factual events are conventional. This results from the fact that the relation between the sign and the designate, between truthfulness and falsehood, between assertion and negation is prearranged (it is fictional). In this context, it can be said that the prearrangement creates a new truth in the literary work – obviously determined by the occurrence of mimesis, new relation between the word and the object, realized here primarily thanks to the metaillocutive power of the negation act. And this is exactly why the artistic speech act could be considered to be a metalinguistic or metatextual phenomenon. Through use of, primarily, performative verbs bearing the strength to change either the truth or the text structure, the author or the narrator builds, creates a new truth in the text. Owing to the use of assertive judgment, it is so because 'p', or as a result of their negation – it is not so because 'p', and vary rarely owing to the use of modal sphere in the text – negation of modal operator, creation of artistic fiction can be generally discussed.

In artistic genres as are the children stories, tales or fables, the plain in which negation's illocutive act occurs is also important. There are only two possibilities here – narrative plane and dialogue plane. In the text of *Sugar Story* by Slavko Janevski, negation structures in speech acts occur on both of the abovementioned planes.

In this regard, the narrative introduction of the fable (story) is already characteristic.

> Пред сто, или уште толку и повеќе години, во градот Негобило живеел, а можеби и не живеел, слаткарот Марко... (p. 3)
> A hundred or more so and even more years ago, in the city Negobilo (Nowhereland) lived, or perhaps didn't live, the confectioner Marko... (p. 3)

The formula 'lived, or perhaps didn't live' is an alternative for the narrative modality – perhaps it is true, perhaps not; it may happen or maybe not. It is obvious that one of the wider modal framework elements of text is present here, which, in turn, is related to the narrator's appearance. The manner in which the abovementioned modal framework elements function in the text, that usually should follow, can be seen, possibly, after insertion of the metatextual verb "say" (which is implicitly already there) as in the following explication:

> – *I say, I narrate that* a hundred or more so and even more years ago... there lived or *I can also say that* didn't live the confectioner Marko;

> Explication:

> 'I can say so because I am the author and I would like the reader to know that I will speak about events that may happen, have happened or didn't happen.'

Prearrangement and conventionality of events in artistic text occur due to the negation that helps relativize the relation between truthfulness and falsehood, existence and nonexistence... it could be said that the author uses negation, absence of negation or shows indifference towards it, as a special means for text building.

On the narrative plane, negation can have one more role – it can also be connected to text creation, but it has a character of a language game:

> Градот Негобило не бил голем: триесет козји скокови на долж и два скока помалку на шир. А можеби и не бил град, туку село (p. 8).
> The city Negobilo wasn't big: Thirty goat jumps long and two jumps less width. And perhaps it wasn't a city, but a village (p. 8).

In addition to the above mentioned situation relating to the formula '...or perhaps didn't live' as well as '...or perhaps it wasn't a city', here supervenes the usage of negation – 'it wasn't big' – contradicting the city's name on the basis of paronomasia: 'Nowhereland' – 'was not big' ('Negobilo' – 'ne bil golem') and 'or perhaps it had not been at all'. From the examples can be seen that the text creates the text and there again occurs a metatextual relation. In view of this, as a result of the text operation, we can even speak about metaillocutive character of negation.

The fantasy related to the name of the city of Negobilo in the further text can be carved in a story by use of the language elements for negation: In the City of Nowhereland there was a judge who should have decided who the sugar child belonged to, however

> Граѓаните на градот Негобило веднаш виделе дека судијата не знае да суди, зашто не судел никогаш. А не судел, зашто во тој град никогаш не се судело... (p. 22)
>
> The citizens of Nowhereland immediately saw that the judge didn't know how to judge because he had never judged before. And he hadn't judged before because in this town nobody was ever tried... (p. 22)

The greatness of negation's creative power in the text is also witnessed by the names of two other settlements mentioned in the text:

> Волшебната ламба се скрши, мојата волшебна сила се изгуби. Дојдов овде во градот Ненајдам, а сега ќе одам во градот Неврат (p. 28).
> The magic lamp broke, my magic power is lost. I came here in the city of Nofind (Nenajdam), and now I will go to the city of Noreturn (Nevrat) (p. 28).

The presence of sentence negation in this text can be observed mostly in dialogues, however, language elements used by the characters or the author (narrator) in order to revoke someone's judgment on the truthfulness or falsehood are not in question here; it is, primarily, a confirmation of the creative function fulfilled by the negation indicators in the given artistic text. Here are the examples:

> Шеќерното дете, барајќи го начинот на ослободување на славејот од неволја од мечката, волкот и лисицата дојде до весела земја на бубалките и праша: „Знае ли некоја бубалка како да се совладаат мечката, волкот и лисицата?"
> The sugar child, looking for a way to free the nightingale from trouble with the bear, the wolf and the fox, landed at the merry land of the bugs and asked: 'Do any of you bugs know how to overcome the bear, the wolf and the fox?'
>
> These were their answers:
>
> – Јас знам да свирам на виолина – рекло штурчето. Друго не знам. Можеби знае пчелата.
> – I can play the violin – said the cricket. I do not know anything else. Perhaps the bee knows.
>
> – Јас знам да правам мед. Друго не знам. Можеби знае мравката.
> – I can make honey. I do not know anything else. Perhaps the ant knows.

– Јас знам да приготвувам зимовиште. Друго не знам. Можеби знае свилената бубалка.
– I can prepare a winter nest. I do not know anything else. Perhaps the silkworm knows.

– Јас знам да ткаам свила. Друго не знам. Можеби знае пајакот.
– I can weave silk. I do not know anything else. Perhaps the spider knows.

– Јас знам да плетам свилени мрежи. Друго не знам. Можеби знае бумбарот (p. 15–16).
– I can weave silk webs. I do not know anything else. Perhaps the bumble-bee knows (p. 15–16).

But it doesn't know either. The butterfly didn't know either, neither did the wasp, nor the grasshopper, the fish, the timid monkey goby, the frog, the crab or any other animals. The conclusion comprised of questions and answers is identical in all of the cases. When asked who can overcome the bear, the wolf and the fox nobody gave proper answers. All animals treated the speaker as if they didn't know what all was about and as if they didn't hear the second part of the question. Their answers corresponded with the question regarding what they could do best. At the same time, answers like 'I can play the violin', 'I can weave silk nets', etc., represent negative answers to the question asked, although there is no grammatical negation indicator present. The question here is not about giving an answer, but not giving one. Such a kind of NO answer could be named contextual negation.

This situation, in which hidden contextual negation is employed, is used for other purposes, other than reaching a decision, relating to realization of some didactic games in the text: assertion or negation, yes or no, true – false.

Again, it is about the employment of text negation in service of creation of suitable dialogue construction. Here is another example of thought exchange by use of negation:

– Знаете ли како да го спасам славејот?
– Do you know how I can save the nightingale?

– Ние не знаеме, ама секако ќе знаат играчките.
– No, we don't know, but the toys will certainly know.

– А каде живеат играчките?
– And where do the toys live?

> Ако се качиш на планинана и се поткренеш на прсти ќе ја видиш или нема да ја видиш нивната куќа (...) – Ако ние не знаеме, знаат снегулките.
> If you climb the mountain and rise up on your toes you will or will not see their house (...) – If we don't know, then the snowflakes know.

Indifference, neutrality in denying compared to the relation true – false should be put into consideration here.

> Ќе ја видиш или нема да ја видиш (нивната куќа).
> You will or will not see (their house) – as in the previous case 'lived, or perhaps not', 'The city (...) or perhaps it was no city'.

However, unlike in the previous fragment where assertion occurs first and is followed by negation – *Знам да свирам на виолина. Друго не знам* 'I can play the violin. I can't do anything else', here the situation is converse: *Ние не знаеме. Знаат снегулките...* 'We don't know. The snowflakes know...' The observed mutability of the type: assertion – negation in answers that have nothing to do with questions regarding the truth or falsehood is characteristic for Slavko Janevski's text and is in direct connection with the norms used in children's world of fun – in children's games. Such an example can be found in a further fragment of the story:

> Дај – не давам. Дај – не давам, и тие се скарале (p. 21).
> Give me – I'm not giving you. Give me – I'm not giving you, and they got into a fight (p. 21).

Negation in the text *Sugar Story*, besides having a denying function, determining or approaching the probability of the relationship between truth and falsehood, also has a conventional character. Precisely because of this, here, conventionality of the relations true – false, existence – nonexistence, is of particular meaning for the creation of the tale's fictional world. Creation of new order of objects and events – the new world – occurs in literary text not only due to interplay between truthfulness and falsehood, existence and nonexistence, yes and no, etc., but also as a result of author's demonstration of neutrality and indifference towards them and their purposeful coextending. Neutralization of opposition: assertion – negation, more firmly determines the illocutive strength of literary speech act that, given its creative relation to the text here, has a character of metaillocution.

IV. On Poetic Antonyms in the Poem *Огнот не знае, пепелта не знае* (*Fire Does Not Know, Ashes Does Not Know*) by Petre M. Andreevski

Antonyms indicate semantic opposition, contrast with another word, antonyms are expressions with opposite meaning, for example *hot–cold, smart–stupid, satiated–hungry.* Poetic antonimy used by P.M. Andreevski[199] in his poem *Огнот не знае, пепелта не знае* (*Fire Does Not Know, Ashes Does Not Know* belongs here: *ashes* instead of, for example: *fire : water*, athough this kind of juxtaposition is usualy found in sentence antonyms.

Antonyms take prominent place in structural descriptions of language lexis. Since the very beginning of structural linguistics development, its representatives emphasized the importance and the meaning of this relation for paradigmatic opposition in language (i.e. in the system).

Placed in lexicographic and word formation descriptions of meaning, the relationships between lexemes, as are the synonyms, antonyms and hyponyms, can established and organize the relations between words, but without any description of the way they function in text. The thesis that the language unites are not autonomous (depending on the context) allowed us to consider them in larger groups of words – semantic fields: paradigmatic (associative) and syntagmatic. Word formation theory also considers words and groups of words in isolation – isolated, i.e. outside of the text. This is especially true when it comes to structural methodology in language description.

Primary antonyms (these include adjectives and words included in the comparison system), for example nouns: *човек* (*почовек*, *најчовек*) – *нечовек* (*понечовек*, *најнечовек*) can be graded, for example young – old, younger – older, smart – smarter, stupid – more

---

199 П.М. Андреевски, *Огнот не знае, пепелта не знае*, in: *Тоа тогаш*, ед. А. Драговиќ, Скопје 2007, p. 155–157.

stupid, however, they do not indicate independent opposite qualities since they serve as lexical means for expression of gradation and comparison (for example tall – taller, old – older – oldest). Antonyms build the paradigm on the basis of their positive pair, and hence, the opposite word will appear in all forms, emphasizing the absence of the characteristic of the positive pair.) Pairs of complementary antonyms are words in which negation of one part carries information that represents anassertion: *тој е оженет – тој е неженет* (he is married – he is not married). These are lexemes which are mutually excludable and opposing, for example *ден и ноќ, жив и мртов* (day and night, alive and dead).

Antonyms also include converses – pairs of expression with opposite meaning, for example:

ang. *buy – sell* or mac. *омажи – ожени (merry).*

These types of antonyms can be pointed out, primarily, in structural language descriptions which do not describe their appearance in copious text or discourse. However, the term is no more precise than the opposition it represents. Sentences in certain languages define antonyms as pairs of lexemes connected to each other in different ways: *висок – мал, купува – продава, лево – десно, доаѓа – заминува, земја – небо, оган – вода; tall* and *short, buy* and *sell, left* and *right, come* and *go, earth* and *sky, fire* and *water*, etc. It should be mentioned that common trait of all these pairs is duality, meaning that there is no gradation, there have got to be two members with semantic opposition created by pairs of expressions.

Here, we will leave aside the question of whether the tendency to think by means of opposites, to express experiences in two-member pairs, is common human trait reflected in the language as secondary occurrence or it is indeed opposing: caught up in our mother tongue, large number of pairs of opposite lexemes dictates us to polarize our thoughts and experiences. In any case, according to J. Lyons "...the fact linguists must accept is that opposition consistent of two members is one of the most important principles corresponding to language structure. Most obvious phenomenon of this principle is antonymy."[200] How-ever, this stand point is correct only if structural language description is considered and language is seen as a system (or structure), not as a process of communication or language event that are taking place here and now (with determined time and space parameters) and are realized in specific speech acts. Hence, if defined, the so created new units of textual character, it

---

200 J. Lyons, *Semantyka*, Vol. 1, p. 34.

should also be considered how they will function in the new textual perspective. This predominantly refers to all current linguistic categories, beginning with phonological, morphological, syntactic categories and ending with the semantic category, or new text categories and discourse with completely different determinations and characteristics should be created. First attempts can be seen in Beaugrande's and Dressler's book *Wstęp do lingwistyki tekstu.*[201] Authors identify the following textual categories: 1) finity – infinity, 2) autonomy – nonautonomy, 3) text as a process and as a product, 4) subjectivity, 5) intertextuality.[202]

However, today we already know that at a time of turbulent development of text linguistics and the discourse itself, isolated and without context, semantic description of antonym pairs with opposite meaning cannot include more new information on antonyms and their lexical opposition if an analysis of their textual use is not conducted, and it is even arguable which of all two-member relations should be included in the term antonymy. Hereof arises the fundamental question of whether that which is recognizable in language structure as antonymy deserves to be also nominated in text and discourse or whether every antonymic relation determined in the lexical system, given it characteristics, has the same meaning in the text and the discourse. In addition, there are many lexemes with opposite meaning which, generally speaking, are not considered to be antonyms, for example *црвен* and *син*, *red* and *blue*, not including the countless pairs as *дрво – куче, квадратен – апстрактен*; *tree* and *dog, square* and *abstract.* These are not paired opposites."[203] If they were, the notion of opposite should be broadened and considered as a special and separate category or language description should be eliminated as nonfunctional. This raises the question of what is the antonyms' function in text and discourse: if it is about language (i.e. the system), then structuralism exclusively corresponds to semantic fields and lexical analysis, and this sphere may possibly also include processes of opposition in backformation. There haven't been any study analyses conducted in relation to antonyms and their function or other antonymic processes (for example creation and neutralization of antonymy) in wider (not only single-word) textual structure nor in the everyday discourse or the artistic literature.

---

201 R. de Beaugrande, W.U. Dressler, *Wstęp do lingwistyki tekstu…*, p. 20–25.

202 A. Wilkoń, *Spójność i struktura tekstu. Wstęp do lingwistyki tekstu*, Kraków 2002, p. 59.

203 Namely, when they are used with a negation (non-red – red): in the same stem antonymy, there are opposites to every color, and thus we enter the logic of defining opposite terms, when it comes to hypernymy, but antonymic pairs should be considered within the frame of hyponyms and hypernyms.

Every linguistic (stylistic) device must fulfill specific function in the building of poetic world vision in certain authors. This also concerns antonymy if considered as a stylistic device. Here, I would only like to emphasis the functions, not only grammatical, but also and above all, stylistic functions antonyms can have in a text when addressed not only as separate sentence or isolated pairs of antonyms placed in antonym dictionary or in semantic fields, but in text, especially when it comes to artistic style. It is about the antonyms in the poetry of Petre M. Andreevski. However, I would like to indicate some tendencies in poetic texts based on material borrowed from one poem. Namely, the poem named *Огнот не знае, пепелта не знае* (*Fire Does Not Know, Ashes Does Not Know*). I believe that the analysis of this poem could be representative of Petre M. Andreevski's similar tendencies to use poetic antonymic devices. It is known that antonyms together with synonyms, hoponyms and other lexemes of this type are fundamental devices insuring text cohesion. For this purpose, a broader category is created to include "contrastive-semantic models or systems" significantly enlarging the antonym category or in other words, excluding the notion antonymy from text description leaving it only as a description of lexis. This is especially important for poetic texts since, in addition to typical (structural) antonym pairs, as are bad – good, black – white, they incorporate broader textual antonymic models or compositions (systems) which guaranty not only text cohesion, but also organize the exclusive and unique, though somewhat antonymic and opposing, poetic world in the poem.

Petre M. Andreevski's *Огнот не знае, пепелта не знае* (*Fire Does Not Know, Ashes Does Not Know*) involves fundamental antonymic opposition: *fire* and *ashes* even though in Macedonian, Polish and lexis of other languages, the primary opposition is *fire* and *water*.

Yet, the goal is to realize, in more detail, how antonymic relations function in the poem by Petre M. Andreevski.

Mac.

Петре М. Андреевски
ОГНОТ НЕ ЗНАЕ,
ПЕПЕЛТА НЕ ЗНАЕ

(*Поплака на јагленарот*)

Огнот не знае како станува од **пепелта**,
Пепелта **не знае** што била пред огнот,
Како и година што **не знае**
Колку години е со мене,
Кому му е **лесна година**,
а кому – **тешка денгуба**.

Огнот **не знае** колкупати горел,
До кај било негово, до каде – од пепелта.
Огнот **не знае** кој во секого се **создава**,
Пепелта **не знае** кој во кого **изчезнува**.
Само јас **дознав** што ќе беше со огнот,
ако не **се сретневме,**
не знаејќи да **се разминеме**.
Зашто огнот **не знае** што му кажала пепелта,
А пепелта **не знае** што раскажала за огнот.
Огнот **не знае**
Кој ќе го изведеше од кременот,
ако задоцнев со раѓањето,
ако никогаш не се родев
и кој ќе го преведуваше низ мракот
низ горите и горењето,
кој ќе му дувнеше душа и височина
(топлина ќе беше уште неразбрана,
а **радоста** и **несреќата** сѐ уште непронајдени).
Огнот **не знае** што да прави со пепелта
пепелта **не знае** што направила со огнот,
само јас **дознав** кој со кого е во преписка,
кој во кого е и **кој без кого** е.
Огнот **не знае** кој би го спомнал без пепелта
пепелта **не знае** за спомени без огнот
ако јас не го **угаснам**, ако со мене не **догори**.
Зашто огнои **не знае** кој денизден го **краде**
и кој одново му **враќа украденото**.
Пепелта **не знае** што била без огнот,
кој ја води напред, што остава зад себеси.
И обата **не ќе знаеја**: кој на кого се потпира,
кој од кој е повидлив, кој-кого ќе надживее,
ако и јас крајот свој
во сјајот нивни не го видев.

Eng.

Petre M. Andreevski
FIRE DOES NOT KNOW,
ASHES DOES NOT KNOW

(*Complaint by the coal merchant*)

Fire does not know how it rises from the **ashes**,
So, the ashes **does not know** what was before the fire,
As the year **does not know**

How many years it has been with me,
To whom **the year** is **mild,**
and to whom – **severe waste of time**.
Fire **does not know** how many times it burned,
What it claimed, what the ashes owned.
Fire **does not know** who it **rises** in,
Ashes **does not know** within whom it **disappears**.
Only I **learnt** what will happen to the fire,
if we do not **meet,**
not knowing how to **pass by each other**.
Cause fire **does not know** what ashes has said,
And ashes **does not know** what story it told about the fire.
Fire **does not know**
Who would have started it with flint,
if I were late to be born,
if I were never born
and who would carry it through the dark
through the fields and the flaming,
who would breathe it soul and height
(warmth would still be senseless,
and **joy** and **misery** still undiscovered).
Fire **does not know** what it does with the ashes
ashes **does not know** what it did with the fire,
only I **learnt** who n correspondence with whom,
who is in whom and **who is without whom**.
Fire **does not know** who would mention it if it were not for the ashes
ashes **does not know** of memories without the fire
if I do not **put it out**, if it does not **burn away** with me.
Cause fire **does not know** who **plunders** it every day
and who in turn **gives the plunder back**.
Ashes **does not know** what it was without the fire,
who leads it forward, what it leaves behind.
And they both **would not have known**: who supports whom,
who is more respectable, who will outlive whom,
if I didn't see my end
in their blaze.

Poetic antonymy: here, *огнот* and *пепелта*: fire and ashes are fundamental devices creating text cohesion, besides numerous repetitions of the words fire and ashes, the connection is further strengthened by opposition: **know** – **does not know**.

Those which form some sort of chain of antonyms connected through antonymic pairs in parallel verses can be distinguished from the text of the poem:

знае : не знае – се создава : исчезнува
дознав : не знаејќи – се сретневме : се разминеме
мракот – горењето : радоста и несреќата
кој во кого е и кој без кого е
не го угаснам, ако со мене не догори
го краде : одново му враќа украденото

The poem ends with an allegorical image when the two contradictions (fire and ashes) cannot exist one without the other – only the unity of antonymity creates the glow at the end of a life, but it can no longer be seen:

ако и јас крајот свој
во сјајот нивни не го видев.

Hence, these antonymic devices play an important role in the very organization of the poet's poetic imagination. The creation of great number of poetic antonyms in the poetry of Petre M. Andreevski testifies for the dualistic conception of the world.[204]

---

204 According to conceptual philosophy, the world is created by two opposite components, for example, a spiritual and a material sphere, ideal and real – spirit and body (Plato).

V. Games in Text in *Расказ за тоа како се пишуваат раскази* (*Story about How Stories Are Written*) by Vlada Urošević

The Macedonian *Расказ за тоа како се пишуваат раскази* (*Story about How Stories Are Written*)[205] by Vlada Urošević should be listed in the world stream of autothematic and autocreative literature. The story, essentially, meets the principles of this writing strategy, and not just from that point of view but also from other aspects such as, for example: intertextual building and polyphonic narrative in all its narrative varieties and types of foreign speech. It should be stressed that it is very difficult to find so typical (for the abovementioned stream) work in Polish, and even in European literature. But some of the texts by K. Izhikovski, S. Vitkjevich, W. Gombrowicz, L. Buchkovski, K. Brandis and L. Gomulicki are highly representative of this narrative strategy.

Autothematism is a narrative strategy characteristic for the author of a literary work and consists of the fact that the text contains statements of the author, the narrator, the character (the description and other linguistic resources such as verbs of speaking – verba dicendi – can also fulfill this function), hence autocreativity becomes clearly visible in the structure of the text and has appropriate language indicators. There is no need of a particular analytic procedure for this to be revealed. A. Gide is considered to be a constructor and a representative of that stream and his works include: *The Counterfeiters* (*Smiths of Fake Money*) and *Swamp*. A. Gide attempted to fix similarities and analogies between the literary idea of the character and the work in which she // he has a part to play. The protagonist of *Swamp* writes

205 В. Урошевиќ, *Расказ за тоа како се пишуваат раскази*, in: *Ноќниот пајтон*, Скопје 1972, p. 7–15.

a book involving problematic that, essentially, approaches the problematic of the work.

Considered from the aspect of narrative structures description, this issue can be treated within the literary metatext. Antecedents of methodology for writing novels thus used should be sought in the new French novel and in the American metafictional novel, but terms such as autothematism as well as autothematic works, at the end of the XIX and the beginning of the XX century, were introduced in the literary practice by the Polish researcher and critic Artur Sandauer[206] with his three works: *Constructive Nihilism* (1947), *The Evolution of Narrative Experience in XX century* (1956) and the *Mitridat's Suicide* (1967), to indicate this new tactic of writing, which generally is most apparent in the novel of the XX century. According to the author, autothematism means confronting an already written work with the terms of its creation, and 'that, which is written, to be a logical conclusion of the writing.' On the question: 'What is written about?' the answer should be I accordance with the autothematic strategy, 'about nothing, about writing'.

Authothematic works should be considered as works that refer only to themselves, as works that are closed to them as in a closed circle. Hence, these are texts that can speak only about texts – nothing else, texts on texts, autotexts, autoparaphrasis, autotextual interventions, subject of which, from a formal point of view, is the language and the text of literary works, being a subject of creative activity, not a referential language that creates the fictional world of the novel as an entity. This is also a phenomenon which indicates the various instances of intertextual relations and concatenations. For example, it can be said that autoparaphrase occurs when an author's personal texts (autotexts) become a canon, a universe and a closed wholeness explicable by itself. Very often it is about the dependencies which are very diverse, as copies or clichés arising from the writer's unawareness, from the estate of his autobiography or creative biography, conventions, genres, etc.

Correct determination of the genesis of that type of literature will not be discussed here, neither will be its artistic values evaluated, but its structure will be described and analysis of the narrative structure of one of the three stories in the series *Writer's Craft will be made.*

The story by V. Urošević begins with a fragment in quotes which, at the same time, is part of the potential story construed by the narrator, being a compulsory condition for the writer to undertake a work on such problematics:

---

206 A. Sandauer, *Samobójstwo Mitrydatesa*, in: *Eseje*, Warszawa 1968.

1. Низ пустелијата одеше човек во бело кратко палто и со црна шапка. Ветрот ја разнесуваше песокта: песокта се селеше од еден до друг куп кожесто зеленило. Песокта се прпелкаше како некој од зад грмушките да мавта со бело шамиче, како да повикува. Краиштата од палтото на човекот се вееја. Човекот трчаше низ пустелијата. Беше сосема ситен. Беше неверојатно ситен. Како точкичка.
(A man dressed in white short coat and black hat walked through the waste land. The wind was blowing the sand: the sand moved from one to another pile of leathery greenery. The sandwallowed as if someone waving a handkerchief from behind the bushes, as if calling out. The edges of the man's coat were drifting. The man was running through the waste land. He was very tiny. He was incredibly tiny. As a little dot.)

That very vague and vapid (perhaps deliberate) content at the beginning of text is accompanied by metatextual clarification which starts or closes the fragment of text created in the text. This happens, in any case, when there is a simulated (in metacreative terms) fragment of the story, so those two texts receive a frame that separates them, but also builds them as texts. For example, after the above fragment follows a metatextual comment that evaluates the already written text:

Mac.

1a. Писателот беше задоволен. Тоа е добар почеток за расказ, помисли тој. Тој човек ветува изненадувања.
2. Небото беше големо и влеваше страв. По должината на стрмниот дол одеше ограда од боцкав тел: не се знаеше од каде почнува; се прекинуваше, исчезнуваше, почнуваше пак. Во далечината скиташе пес.
2a. Ова со песот е добро, рече тој. Се јавува како закана. Расказот би можел да се вика „Циганин и пес". Но од каде Циганин? Не го ставив во расказот.
3. Како би било да ставам и една жена во расказот, помисли. Кога дојде дома, тој запиша:
3a. Девојка береше булки крај оградата. Песот оттука не можеше да се види. Булките растеа мошне ретко, тек-тук, беа бледи и уште нерасцутени се ронеа.

Eng.

1a. The writer was satisfied. This is a good beginning of a story, he thought. This man promises surprises.

2. The sky was big and inspired fear. There was a barbed wire fence along the steep gully: one could not tell where it began; it was discontinued, disappeared, began again. There was a dog strolling in the distance.
2a. This thing with the dog is good, said Shoj. It appears as a threat. The story could be named 'A Gypsy and a Dog'. But how did the Gypsy show up? I didn't put him in the text.
3. How about I put a woman in the story, he thought. When he came back home, he wrote:
3a. A girl was gathering poppies beside the fence. The dog could not be seen from there. The poppies grew very scarcely, here and there. They were pale and crumbling even before they flourished.

The metatextual comment not only opens and closes the text of the created story, but can also directly refer to the writer's craft.

4. Ноќта писателот тешко спиеше. Му се присторуваше дека нема да може да го заврши расказот, дека некој му го украл, дека уредниците го тераат да го измени крајот.
5. Изутрината веднаш се фати за работа. По неколку пречкртани реченици конечно запиша...
4a. That night the writer didn't sleep well. He was afraid that he would not be able to finish the story, that someone stole the text, that editors would make him changes to end.
5a. In the morning, he got to work immediately. After several crossed-out sentences he finally wrote...

These are typical narrative tools for autothematism. Autothematic prose is its own subject of narration. It is autoreferential. The behavior of every statement that enters its composition, it becomes the statement. Obviously, in such case, it would be absolute autothematism, ideal and unrealistic. However, the story by Urošević is unreal and gets closer to that ideal in an ideal way. Simulated manner of writing not only imitates world tendencies in construing narration but also brings this strategy to the absurd in which the story generates itself or some similar text, thus, virtually, destroying the importance of the writer in the creative process, in the end leaving him with not much to say.

The beginning fragment, which is, thus, crucial to the narration, refers to:

A.
1) Пустелијата и песокта,
2) Ветрот, кој ја разнесуваше песокта.

B.
1) Човекот во бело палто и со црна шапка,
2) Човекот кој трчаше.

C.
1) Песокта се прпелкаше,
2) Некој (да) мавта со шамиче.

D.
1) Човекот и песокта,
2) Човекот ситен како точкичка.

A. 1) Waste land and sand, 2) The wind, which is blowing the sand.
B. 1) The man in white coat and black hat, 2) The man who runs.
C. 1) The sand wallowed, 2) Someone (to) wave with a handkerchief.
D. 1) The man and the sand, 2) The man tiny as a little dot.

This whole situation is written as an integral part of the story, although that is not in accordance with its surrealistic character. The described situation resembles Fata Morgana, a mirage or an illusion. A proof that the creative act is fulfilled is the following sentence:

> Не можеше да продолжи. Место човек со бело кратко палто и со црна шапка, низ пустелијата сега одеше Циганин.
> (He could not go on. Instead of a man with white short coat and a black hat, now a Gypsy walked through the waste land.)

The Gypsy, who earlier knocked at the writer's house door (meaning in his consciousness) goes through the waste land, yet, does not appear in the story (no one to buy old clothes from – at the moment, that solves his absence within the story's logical framework), but after a few sentences on, he becomes necessary to writer, only for the sake of the story's title, not because he is necessary to the content: The story could be named 'A Gipsy and a Dog'. But how did the Gypsy show up? I didn't put him in the text.

Thus, the author navigates the narrative to autodestruction. Was this really the purpose of the autothematic *Расказ за тоа како се пишуваат раскази* (*Story about How Stories Are Written*)? If we consider the author to be autoironic, then the answer would be: Yes.

VI. Instances of Deconstructivism in Zhivko Chingo's Short Story *Пасквелија* (*Paskvelia*)

Researches concerning the newest Macedonian literature consider postmodern metatextuality to its most important mark. Danilo Kocevski – literary critic and essayist wrote:

> We arrive at the most important properties of the newest prose = metatextuality and mannerism.[207]

It also points to its metaliterary basis and the creation of stories about the stories, the use of Bakhtin's "foreign speech,"[208] text in text, construction of narrative structures considering authentic persons beyond the fabula (foreign speech) and elements of irony and grotesque. This type of text is dominated by: fragmentation, minimization, incorporation of metatextual passages, creation of intertextual relations, usage of all levels and perspectives of the expression and invitation for the reader to take part in the creation of the text. Furthermore, in accordance with the theory of deconstruction, a text cannot have only one determined meaning, and the text's meaning is created during each reading. All these properties of postmodern and deconstruction literature are also characteristic of contemporary tendencies in most recent Macedonian prose.

Indeed, there is a very important difference between traditional treatment of literary text, in which the author tends to achieve an illusion of reality and that which literary canons related to the notion of "mimesis" impose on him, and the emergence of postmodern

---

207 Д. Коцевски, *Критиката како заблуда. Предизвиците на текстуалноста*, Скопје 1988, p. 156.

208 M. Bachtin, *Estetyka twórczości słownej…*; W.N. Wołoszynow, *Z historii form wypowiedzi w konstrukcjach języka*, in: *Rosyjska szkoła stylistyki…*, p. 413–477.

metatextuality, typical of most recent Macedonian literature. The author doesn't only show demonstrably that he is not interested in reality (as stylistic means), but rather than in creation of illusion of that reality, he is interested in its deconstruction. Moreover, deconstruction, even reality break-down and deformation of the literary image of the world, function in the name of language and utilization of its universal abilities for creation of text. Aspiration towards fictional deconstruction of reality or towards true reconstruction of the real world, which has already been deconstructed by deliberate action of every person (creator) with the assumption that the only available tool for recognition of reality is the text, led to partial elimination or complete lack of logical (causal) relations between individual sections of text content. This manner of treatment of the literary expression can be explained by some phenomenological theories related to authors as are: Theodor Adorno and Jacques Derrida. Very often in this context, researchers refer to the so-called American metafictional prose and (Donald Barthelme). His short story Eugenie Grandet as modern-style-parody of H. Balzac's novel *Eugenie Grandet* is a typical example of deconstructive prose. The work resembles a collage and the text includes photographies, quotations, repetitions, drawings and graphically separated fragments of text. At the same time, efforts are made for those tendencies to be treated as national phenomena and to be situated not only within the framework of Yugoslav literature, but primarily of the Macedonian literature. The following authors are treated as precursors of this type of Macedonian prose: Blaže Koneski, Dimitar Solev i Vlada Urošević. Koneski's influence over young Macedonian prose writers is seen in the course of his work that incudes short narrative forms intertwined with lyric and epic forms. In V. Urošević's prose, this would include works with fantasy in their content.

However, it seems that tendencies toward metatextuality and mannerism, which create postmodern course in most recent Macedonian prose, primarily take appear in the work of Zhivko Chingo, especially in his short stories in Paskvelia[209].

The topic of Zh. Chingo's narrative prose is related to a given historical moment. This is mainly a time of national liberation of the writer's homeland and the places where he was born and raised and can be easily identified in his novel *Paskvelia*. Chingo carefully followed historical changes, changes in the surroundings and his birth place, named Paskvelia in his novel.

---

209 Ж. Чинго, *Пасквелија*, Скопје 1968.

From the observations contained in the short stories, it turns out that liberation (revolution) is the reason for the breakdown of the previous world of values, and the people were forced to make decisions, which thus far they could not achieve, and were facing the necessity of implementing, for them, unexpected solutions.

In Zh. Chingo's prose, drama of freedom is replaced by drama of catastrophe and non-freedom of apocalyptic proportions. The revolution in Paskvelia's short stories is shown as incomprehensible fatum accompanied and announced by signs in the sky and on the earth: rain that falls continuously night and day, black snow, unusually cold wind from the lake, grasshoppers... etc. Chingo's revolution is suffering, famine, sickness, fire, death, flood, unusually cold winter...

Here are some example of the short story *On the Eve of the Maccabees* (the beginning and the end), overflowed with apocalyptic visions:

1. Не се знае која година беше тоа, дали беше ден или ноќ. Беше зима, сам ден Свети Никола, зафати невидена фортуна и целата земја ја покри дебел снег..., насекаде само волци и дивина.
   (No one knew which year it was, whether it was a day or night. It was winter, on the very day of Saint Nicolas, an unseen Fortuna engulfed and covered the land with thick snow..., only wolfs and wildlife all around.)

2. А од каде дојде и снегот и сè покри на земјата. Тежок и црн снег ја покри целата земја. Не се знае дали беше ден или ноќ... Потоа дури, потоа дури дојдоа скакулците и сè запустија во долината и полињата пасквелски.
   (And where did the snow come from to cover everything on the ground. Heavy black snow covered all the land. One could not tell if it was day or night... Only after, only after the grasshoppers showed up and desolated everything in the valley and the fields of Paskvelia.)

In this short story, encompassed in classical metatextual framework, evil and human injustice culminate in a genuine Maccabean manner. The image of the world in Paskvelia's short stories is not comprised of systemically arranged relations but rather, it is an image of antonymic (contradictory) relations and values, in an irrational manner, justifying the heroes actions in a logically and cognitively deconstructed reality. Deconstructivism as dismemberment, breakdown and fragmentation of the world is a testimony and a consequence of the absence of its textual convergence. Whereby, the language of Chingo's narration, which in its style and convention reminds us of the vernacular (rural or family chat), is unusually converged and coherent. The heroes (characters) are inhabitants of the village. However, they do not speak dialects, neither is their language stylized by dialect speech. However, thanks to the use of appropriate convention and the rules taken from the strategies of folk storytelling, *Paskvelia* reminds us of the original folk expression genially decanted into literary work.

Basic property of Chingo's narration is its connection with Macedonian folklore used to realize the stylistic manners shaped upon the cannons of folklore oral literature. There are three basic traits enabling all texts, including texts of Macedonian writers, to be included among those involving use of convention and stylistics of oral folk literature. Two of those, having formal character, decide on the possibility for the given text to be counted in the cannon of folklore; they are repetition and formulated expressions. The third is semantics of catastrophism and breakdown, semantics od apocalyptic visions filled with "creative and magical function of the formula"[210] included in the poetics of magical story.

The appearance of the abovementioned formula in the text of Zh. Chingo, according to J. Bartmiński – "raised up to the level of a main criterion for orality of a work even by Parry[211] and Lord"[212] – allow the work of an author to be situated within the framework of a literary movement in which conventional and compositional rules known from the folklore oral storytelling dominate – this primarily concerns the short stories and texts originating from Zhivko Chingo's homeland – the surroundings of Ohrid (Velgoshti).

Here are some examples of typical formula lexically related to the motive of rain from the short stories by Chingo:

1. А дождовите доаѓаа толку силни и поројни. Врнеше, врнеше (*Пожар*).
(And the rains come so strongly and stormy. It rained, it rained.) (*Fire*)

2. Веќе седум дена и седум ноќи непрестајно врне дожд (...) Седум дена и седум ноќи непрестајно врне... Потоп – викаа исплашени луѓе Потоп – избезумени пискаа жените (...) Потоп – пискаа и мажи и жени исправени на покривите од куките (*Ќерка*).
(It already rained unceasingly for seven days and seven nights. For seven days and seven nights it rained unceasingly (...) Then – scared people exclaimed Flood – the women screamed frantically (...) Then – men and women screamed standing on the roofs of their houses.) (*Daughter*)

210 J. Bartmiński, *Folklor – język – poetyka*, Wrocław 1990, p. 213.

211 A. Parry, *The Making of Homeric Verse: The Collected Papers of Milman Parry*, ed. by A. Parry, Oxford 1971.

212 A.B. Lord, *The Singer of Tales*, Cambridge 1960.

3. И врнеше непрестајно паѓаше тој ситен боцлив дожд (*Одродени*).
(And it rained continuously; that fine pricking rain was falling down.) (*Alienated*)

4. Веќе седум дена непрестајно паѓа снег: Другарот Димитрија Стенковски никако не можеше да си објасни од каде дојде тој тежок и црн снег (*Глувците на семоќниот бог*).
(It was snowing unceasingly for seven days: comrade Dimitrija Stenkovski could not understand where that heavy back snow came from.) (*The mice of the almighty God*)

5. Од некаде повторно дојдоа дождовите (...) Седум дена и седум ноќи непрестајно врне (...) (*Легенди за смртта на секретарот*)
(The rain came again from somewhere. The rain didn't stop for seven days and seven nights. Heavy waters crushed upon the Earth's unhealthy body days and nights.) (*Legend of the Secretary's Death*)

6. Веќе почнаа и првите дождови. Кога дојдоа оние непрестајни и тешки дождови, црни и матни (...) А дождовите непрестајно паѓаа целата таа пролет (*Љубовта на задружниот коњушар*).
(First rains have already begun. When those unceasing and heavy, black and misty rains, came (...) And rains fell unceasingly during that spring.) (*The Love of Collective Stableman*)

7. Дождовите почна да паѓаат оној момент кога го убивме Бершеровото магаре (...) Во ноќта настана вистинска поплава (*Ќерка*).
(Rains started to fall the moment we slaughtered Bersher's donkey. True flood occured during the night.) (*Daughter*)

The abovementioned formulas, and sometimes some expressions imitating the formulas, proceed or close narrative sequences that are expressly saturated with semantics of catastrophism and apocalyptic visions. For example: *Визија на потоп* (*Vision of flood*) (formula 2) *или на црн тежок снег* (or of a heavy black snow) (formula 4). This is related to the fact that the formula which is used in the literary text, and especially in texts stylized as are the folklore ones, could be treated broadly, not only as metric – lexical unit, i.e. "group of words regularly used in identical metrical conditions,"[213] but also as delimitating element, which is thematically (semantically) segmenting the

213 J. Bartmiński, *Folklor...*, p. 207.

text and is usually within the framework of the formal and semantically divided paragraphs. All these elements play a major role in creating the possibility for passing from the real world into the world dominated by apocalyptic events (cataclysms), which, as narrative formulas, appear rather often in Paskvelia, and their irrational credibility is confirmed by regular repetitions in form of petrified expressions and constructions. However, language connects the events in Paskvelia – their participants do not speak using local dialects, but use the convention characteristic for this type of creative works that must be stylized only on formal or similar level to the folklore storytelling and conversation.

All traits of Zh. Chingo's short stories listed here, together with the relation: JAC – ТИ (ME – YOU) between the narrator and the reader – allow the author's work to be situated upon formal basis within the frame of convention characteristic of oral communication.

Texts analyzed here are built upon antonymic (contradictory) basis. Formally cohesive language (based on convention), in a twisted fashion, is confronted by the degraded (deconstructed) world shown in the short stories. Chingo confronts the demonstrated continuous order and apocalyptic vision of the world with synthetic and cohesive language that realizes all conventions characteristic of folklore magic style. The confrontation of the acoustic (oral) and the semantic (written) level – in a very realistic and consistent (coherent) vernacular full of rules building the image of this irrational world by cataclysms and apocalyptic visions (fire, flood, black snow, fortuna, grasshoppers)... makes this unbelievable world become more realistic because it is constantly being reaffirmed by mechanisms of formular convention (by game of formulas). Thus, the formula of the narration and the text itself build the apocalypse in Paskvelia, rather than what happens there. The text with the formulas built in within is a source of fictional events, reality is constituted in a type of a short story through the text, with the text and in the text. These specific methods of text building cause the reader to start to believe in something that thus far was not credible, to see what is invisible, to experience the world from its irrational side even though, to the greatest extent, this world would be most believable. And as Jürgen Landwehr puts it:

> We do not speak, but we are spoken to, or discourses make us their subjects, subjects in the strictest sense of the word – liegemen. What can be said is never about what the thing is really about.[214]

---

214 J. Landwehr, *Poststrukturalistyczne wyzwanie. Próba dekonstrukcji*, transl. by M. Łukasiewicz, "Teksty Drugie" 1990, 2, p. 20.

According to the renowned theoretician of postmodernism, Jacques Derrida, there is only the text, textuality, and the reality is gone or it is only a specifica text and rule of discourses.[215]

Text and textuality dominate the short stories by the Macedonian writer – storyteller Z. Chingo, and thus explicit darkening of the ostensible border between text and reality appears. All notions and values, the whole reality presented in the text of this writer reaches extreme textual proportions, for example, in form of rhetorical amplification. Each phenomenon and even feeling – love, evil, hate, indifference – exist in the text only through it and can reach their apogee only in it, and only to be deconstructed and broken down a moment latter. Feelings and notions stop existing since the text itself creates them and deconstructs them.[216] However, the world of values disintegrates, rather than the language since extralinguistic and extratextual reality does not exist – there is only the text, the code, the language and textulity, and everything else is an illusion of reality and rule of discourses.

215 J. Derrida, *Pismo i telekomunikacja*, "Teksty" 1975, 3, p. 75–92.

216 The final consequence of this deconstruction is people's laughter and its forms – dark, gloomy humor: "онаа смеа од која сме повеќе тажни отколку весели (the laughter that makes us more sad than happy). With his short stories, Chingo has proved to be a concerned and committed author who observes life and thus manages uncompromisingly to reflect on what takes place before his curious gaze. And whenever the threads of the human and the reasonable crack in this life, whenever justice is lost, when the ideal is extinguished, when stupidity and ignorance come to reign, then that dark and gloomy humor becomes most evident." See: В. Мојсова-Чепишевска, *Современа македонска проза*, in: *Современа македонска литература*, I и II дел, Скопје 2004, p. 28.

VII. Variance in Translation (Ivo Andrić: *На Дрини ћуприја*, *Мостот на Дрина*, *Most na Drinie*, *The Bridge on the Drina*)[217]

The essence of translation theory can – generally – be treated as establishment or clarification of different relations between the language of the original and the language of the translation. Accordingly, language variance is related to the linguistic units which are formally different but function identically or, in turn, there is a different phonological, morphological, sintactic, phraseological and textual realization of one and the same unite.

Two analysis approaches derived from two types of variance can be distinguished in relation to the variance in translation theory. The first, interlinguistic – outside of the language, occurs within the borders of one language, and the second refers to the relations between the language of the original, source text, for example English, and the other languages in which the text is being translated, e.e. Polish or Macedonian. The immanent properties in theory of translation apply to the first approach, as well as the second one, and they can be accompanied by the phenomena of equivalence and adequacy.

The phenomenon of equivalence in the theory of translation was observed by E. Nida, who devived equivalence to formal and functional equivalence. Functional equivalence (or dynamic equivalence) conveys the main idea expressed in the source text. If necessary, that goal can be achieved at the expense of the literality of the original (what we have in the original as a form, transferred by another form in literal sense), as well as the word order in the sentence or the grammatical

---

217 И. Андрић, *На Дрини ћуприја*, Novi Sad 1971. Translation: (Pol.) *Most na Drinie*, transl. by H. Kalita, Warszawa 2007, (Mac.) *Мостот на Дрина*, transl. by B. Korubin, Skopje 1977, (Eng.) *The Bridge on the Drina*, transl. by L.F. Edwards, Chicago 1977.

form of the source text. According to the formal equivalence, the text of the original and the translation are treated literally, "word for word" (*verbum pro verbum*).

The difference between the variance of the translation and the equivalence – although the first and second appear at all levels of the original language (OL) and the translation (LT), yet, their scope is different: the first (variance) refers to, to several degrees, different equivalent (grammatical, lexical, stylistic) language versions of the translation. In case of the second, equivalence only basically connects the two languages – the language of the original and the language of the translation – and, yet, the connection is present on all language structure levels. In other words, equivalence does not allow variance, and yet within the framework of different text variations of one language (different translators and different editions) we can describe a phenomenon of equivalen between the language structure of the original and the translation.

On the following models, this is how differences appear:

I. EQUIVALENCE:
Structures of OL (1) ________________ Structures of LT (1a)

II. VARIANCE:

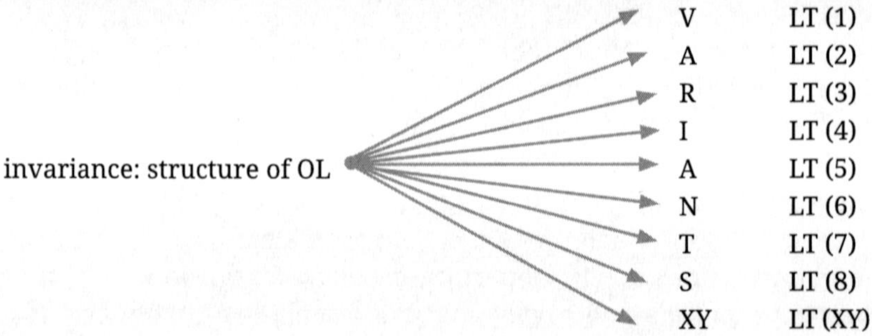

In theory of translation, variance can refer to the manner on which the original text is translated in other languages, at least two (not including the language of the original) – hence, the language of the original (LO) can be considered as invariant, however, all other texts of languages in which the original text is translated are considered as variants (LT 1, 2, 3, 4, 5... xy). The variance of translation can be realized within the frame of grammatical, lexical and stylistic (textual) form, for example calques, adaptations, neologisms, proper names, approximate translation, contextual translation, periphrases, type of text, etc.

Unfortunately, so far there are no complete descriptions of translation variance for any particular text (e.e. literary work) in several languages. Biblical texts were most commonly studied from this aspect, however, the description of different texts of the Bible is limited to lexical sphere and biblical concordancies and this only served the editorial and religious purposes. The study of variance in other texts (for example literary texts) will be of great importance to theory of translation and translation studies.

In translations of many languages, lexical variaties and target sentence structures have been most often observed and studied by comparing its translated equivalents[218] in the text of the foreign original.

Yet, those were lexems and sentences deprived of any context, isolated or completely drafted. Very ofren, if ever, broader textual structures implicated in liner or thematic-rhematic order (wording) were described.

If we accept the thesis that in translational science, the invariant indicates constant value, which will be preserved regardless of the row of expression transformations in the languages of translation, then the invariant can be considered as a linguistic construction appearing in the language of the original, however, all its variations realized in translations will be determined as variants. Hence, we can single out two types of variants.Using the phonological terminology, the first we will name individual variants – determined by the language of the translator, and the second, position variants – determined by the sintactic environment of the particular (translated) expression. This is also reflected in the language of the original and of the translation with particular wording with linear order regarded from two aspects: temporal – oral language and spatial – written language.

---

[218] M. Velevska describes ralations between variant realizations of French sentences using infinitives in the Macedonian translation. For example:

(5а) *Ги слушам како расправаат* (со начинска зависносложена реченица)

(5б) *Ги слушам дека расправаат* (со исказна реченица)

(5в) *Ја слушам нивната дискусија*

(5г) *Го слушам нивното аргументирање* (со именски форми, при што личноглаголската заменка е иреведена со посвојна придавска форма).

Je les écoute argumenter – equivalent translations would be as follows:

(5а) I can hear them arguing (with a complex sentence with dependent clause of manner)

(5б) I can hear that they are arguing (propositional sentence)

(5в) I can hear their discussion

(5г) I can hear their argument (nominal forms, where the personal pronoun is derived by possessive adjectival form). See: М. Велевска, *Преводни еквиваленти на некои конструкции со нелични глаголски форми од француски јазик на македонски,* XXXIII Научна конференција на XXXIX Меѓународен семинар за македонски јазик, литература и култура, Охрид 28–29 VIII 2006. Лингвистика, Скопје 2007, p. 7–10.

In languages in which the place of a term in the linear order depends on its semantic and syntactic properties, and all changes in the order are associated with the changes of semantic and syntactic relations – we find grammatical word order, and such a situation occurs in the following languages: English and French. However, languages in which such relations do not occur we call non-position languages, and the word order is free. These include most Slavic languages.This property of free word order languages allows us to create different functional order of the sentence, indicting a possibility to create specific functional sentence perspective. The actual breakdown is best viewed in isolated two-member sentences, single-sentence communicants without accentual emphasis, for example: *Peter left to Ohrid, Kristina lives in Skopje.*There are two parts in such sentences: the first is defined as 'point of expression exit' is called a theme, and the second refers to the first, informs of the expression's main goal and contains new information, unknown to the receiver – it is called rheme.

Word order functions simultaneously on two planes of the expression: first is the syntactic structure of the sentence and the second plane represents the actual sentence stratification (actual sentence perspective), whereas the first function is subordinate to the second and the following relations between the linear order of the text and its actual breakdown occur:

1. Variants of actual sentence stratification may be recognized thanks to the variety of word order.
2. Word order may serve the actual sentence stratification of the expression.
3. Between word order and actual sentence stratification occurs the same relation as between form and function.The given breakdown is usually expressed with the same word order.

There is a possibility for an actual breakdown to realize itself in the both variants of word order, but also an identical word order may allow for two variants of the actual breakdown. In order for us to follow the process as it takes place in practice, we chose examples of Polish and Macedonian translation variants from the novel *The Bridge on the Drina* by Ivo Andrić. In this instance, prosody does not impact the determination of the actual sentence stratification since the text is in written form (written language).

We began with the title. In the language of the original, the title is *На Дрини ћуприја.*[219] It is followed by the thematic-rhematic title *На Дрини* (T) *ћуприја* (R). In the language of translation, there still remains

[219] *Ћуприја* in the Polish and the Macedonian language means bridge (*most, мост*).

the other thematic breakdown *Мостот* (T) *на Дрина* (R) – in the Macedonian translation and the respective translation in Polish – *Most* (T) *na Drinie* (R). In the language of the original the indicator of the actual breakdown is the word order comprised of elements of different examples of common, unindicated word order characteristic of the Serbian language, for example:

> Вишеградска ћуприја (Т) на Дрини (R) је задужбина великог везира Мехмед-паше Соколовића.
> (...) манифестација посвећена нобеловцу Иви Андрићу почела је полагањем цвијећа на камену крајпуташу подигнутом у част славном нобеловцу недалеко од **ћуприје (Т) на Дрини (R)**.

Here, varience exclusively applies to the language of the original – *ћуприја на Дрини* // *На Дрини ћуприја.* However, if we accept that the language of the original has an invariable character, this would mean that the Macedonian and the Polish translations are variants in comparison to the language of the original. In the Serbian language, word order inversion changes the thematic-rhematic structure of the title, hence, according to the author, *мост* (bridge) – *ћуприја* is rheme, as new information, and thus Andrić informs us of the topic he is to talk about; Drina (rheme) is known, but the bridge (*ћуприја*) that is to be built in the novel (in the future) is unknown.

The question here is whether such translated structures, containing different thematic-rhematic order in comparison to the original, are characteristic for Andric's complete text presented as his authoric strategy that should be implemented, presented, conveyed, used and accepted in translations. For this purpose we should compare examples of the original and the two translated text (Macedonian and Polish).The following examples illustrate this situation.

I

> **(OL)** Већим делом свога тока (Т1) река **Дрина протиче** кроз тесне гудуре између стрмих планина или кроз дубоке кањоне окомито одсечених обала (R1).
> **(LT1)** Со поголемиот дел од својот тек (Т1а) реката **Дрина тече** низ тесни грла меѓу стрмни планини или низ длабоки кањони на прудолно пресечени брегови (R1a).
> **(LT2)** Rzeka **Drina** (T1x) na znacznej przestrzeni swego biegu (R1b) **przedziera się** przez ciasne wąwozy pośród stromych gór lub głębokimi jarami wrzyna się w prostopadłe brzegi (T1y).

OL – T1 + R1
LT1 – T1a + R1a
LT2 – T1b (tx+ty) + R1b

II

(LO) Само на неколико места речног тока (T2) њене се **обале проширују** у отворене долине и стварају, било на једној било на обе стране реке, жупне, делимично равне, делимично таласасте пределе, подесне за обрађивање и насеља (R2).
(LT1) Само на неколку места од речниот тек (T2a) нејзините **брегови се прошируваат** во отворени долини и создаваат, на едната или на обете страни од реката, жупни, наместа рамни наместа брановити предели, погодни за обработување и за населби (R2a).
(LT2) Zaledwie w kilku miejscach (T2b) **rozwierają się one** w doliny tworzące po jednej lub po obu stronach skąpane w słońcu bądź równe, bądź faliste, dogodne pod uprawę i na osiedla obszary (R2b).

OL – T2 + R2
LT1 – T2a + R2a
LT2 – T2b + R2b

III

(OL) Такво једно **проширење** настаје (T3) и овде, код Вишеграда (R3), на месту где Дрина избија (T4) у наглом **завоју** (R4) из дубоког и уског теснаца (R4a) који стварају (T5) Бутковe стијене и Узавничке планине (R6).
(LT1) Така тие се **прошируваат** (T3a) и овдека, кај Вишеград (R3a), на местото каде што Дрина избликнува (T4a), правејќи наеднаш **завој** (R4a), од длабоката и тесна клисура (R5a) што ја прават (T5a) Бутковите Стени и Узавничките Планини (R6a).
(LT2) Takie **rozwarcie** powstaje (T3b) tu – koło Wyszegradu (R3b) – w miejscu, gdzie Drina wypada (T4b) zza ostrego **zakrętu** (R4b), z przepastnej, wąskiej gardzieli Butkowych Turni i Gór Uzawnickich (R5b).

OL – (T3 + R3) + (T4 +R4 + R5a) + (T5 + R6)
LT1 – (T3a + R3a) + (T4a + R4a + R5a) + (T5a + R6a)
LT2 – (T3b + R3b) + (T4b + R4b + R5b)

As evident from the second example 2, sintactic structure and actual sentence stratification are almost identical. Expressional differences can be seen in examples 1 and 3, especially when it comes to the Polish translated variant, including differences in word order, sintax and functional sentence perspective.

The description of the relationship between word order – syntax – sentence functional perspective includes just some of the observed trends of text variance (artistic work) and opens up space for thorough and comprehensive analysis that would confirm the conclusion regarding translation variance as constitutive property of translation.

D. FOLKLORE

I. Textual Categories of Time and Space in Folk Tales by Marko K. Cepenkov

Textual categories, unlike morphological and syntactical or lexical ones, perform at higher levels of expression and are related to the internal organization and pragmatic properties of text. In regards to grammatical characteristics of textual categories, Danuta Ostaszewska writes that this phenomenon hasn't been linguistically analyzed in detail, yet, primarily because there are not enough scientific texts belonging to different functional styles. Researchers of text structure and cohesion include the following in textual categories: informativeness, modality, delimitation, segmentation, coherence, completeness (integration, unification), completion, linear continuity (continuum), autosemantics, repetition, collection, thematisation. Here, A. Wilkoń[220] also includes the semantic category person, as well as the category author, narrator, reader (receiver), time and space. Therefore – as the author notes – text can be studied as a process, an action (linguistic action) or as a final product. The former being dynamic and the latter a static study. From communicational point of view, the former is considered to be more correct. Among other things, this was decisive for the more frequent research in whether texts perform from dynamic aspect, during their creation, or if they are linguistic products, in which case, those closest to communicational acting should undergo analysis. Folk tales belong to this type of texts.

Most characteristic trait of South Slavic folk tales collected by Marko K. Cepenkov is the marking of cohesion of narrative text through different linguistic means belonging to author's narration. This is related to the dominant role of the person who wrote the text down and its properties for creative transformation and secondary text editing expressed by the informer, and more often, fulfilled (expressed) from memory.[221]

---

220 A.Wilkoń, *Spójność i struktura tekstu...*, p. 39–68.

221 Marko K. Cepenkov as one of the Macedonian researchers, is considered to belong in the first generation of folk artists and writers, after Miladinov brothers. Cepenkov – a tailor

These include those expressions and linguistic means that primarily fulfill metatextual functions[222] in text merging and concern only the text that follows or proceeds them connecting its elements in cohesive and coherent whole. The following can be found among them:[223]

- арно ама (…арно ама Силјан беше фатил еден лош пат; 2/137).
- на тие зборови // на тие збораи (На тие збораи и друзи Силјанои… тие уште повеќе го насрчуале; 2/137).
- кога чул тие збораи (Кога чуло тие збораи момчето од змијата (2/24, 2/25) …од збор на збор; од збор на збор на царови уши (2/34)).

All these examples, as are *на тоа згора, арно ама, на тие збораи, од збор на збор* refer to the text in anaphoric and cataphoric manner taking the reader back to the line of text and announcing new information or connecting the characters with the narrative by interlinguistic relations. These units are part of the secondary system of internal (textual) behavior (the primary means referential behavior of textual events towards reality), which implements the mechanism of so-called internal deixis by means of which it determines the sequence of events and locations, however, not in their real world, but rather, in the linear flow of the expression. Their appearance in the text organizes and regulates its composition and structure and brings about the text to be merged and coherent. Thus, these expressions realize the textual category of time. This function can also be realized by expressions which reduplicate, which are completely doubled or just in the range of the basic lexeme or are completely repated as syntactic constructions and connections. For example:

> виде – невиде (видоа – невидоа, видов – невидов, видел – невидел (see); Виде-невиде сирота цареа ќерка го пушти и соколо… (The poor emperor's daughter released the hawk eventually…) (Ц3/216), Видела-невидела попадија… (2/19, 2/168)

> дран-недодран; Трештил прчко дран-недодран да бега од пустата болештина… (Flayed-unflayed, the swank blasted running away from the damn sickness…) (2/16)

---

by profession – in the years between 1856–1857, not only gathered folk tales, but, also, included his own words (often only some time after the recording) in the tales, which gives them a special stylistic coloration.

[222] M. Kawka, *Metatekst w tekście narracyjnym na przykładzie wybranych utworów literatury dla dzieci*, Kraków 1990.

[223] All examples come from the following sources: М.К. Цепенков, *Македонски народни умотворби*, ed. by К. Пенушлиски, Б. Ристовски, Т. Саздов, Скопје 1972, т. 1–10.

знајш, али не знајш?: Знајш, али не знајш? (Do you know or don't you?) (2/145)

страв – нестрав: страв – нестрав, на име божје, си рекол, ребрејќи, дојдовме на граница. (Fear – no fear, in the name of God, he said to himself, swaggering, we managed to the border.) (10/342)

тамоси – вамоси (вамо – тамо (here – there): тамоси, вамоси, го каптиса и сипаничар'лко. (You are here, you are there, you made quarrel with the scree business, too.)

пошто – зашто: ...да не работиш пошто – зашто. (...you should not work little money.) (5/45)

овде – онде: овде – онде шетајкум, сопрво ти нашол два брава... (Walking here and there, he rightfully found me two rams...) (2/22)

полека – лека: ...та полека – лека му се пикнала во пачајцата (2/35).

вур – тур (вурт – тут): вурт – тут, беше ујдисале за уште поскапо да му го продаи... (ЦЗ // 261)

турли – бе – турли: ...се мачеле со турли – турли мали неискажани (5/31).

Some of these constructions are in form of a true reproduction and repetition: *одил, одил* (*...одил, одил, одил неколку дена и излегол на врвот*, 2/118); *тамоси – вамоси, вамо – тамо, било – било, арно – арно* (92/51), *побегал – побегал малку и, за к'сметот от волкот еве ти ја кума лиса* (2/24); *Како било – било, тоа поминало* (10/329), *Арно, арно* (10/327) or multiple repetition of the whole word: *Одија, одија, одија, одија три дни и три ноќи...* (3/151) or only its fragment which have and onomatopoeic character: *чат – пат, вур – тур, таку – така, турли – бе – турли, молил – колил* (5/109), others, besides reduplication, use the mechanism of lexical (word) negation – *не* (no) (pol. *nie*) they can proceed the verb as well as the noun: *видел – невидел* (*Ај да се види и невиди*, 2/102; *виде – невиде сиромајио, се позамисли*, 5/17); *сме – несме, сакал нешел // сакаш – нешиш* (*...сакал – нешел, одил по цвеќињата*, 2/119; *...сакаш-нешиш треба да го поризаш*, 2/109), *страв – нестрав*; others are constructed based on sentence negation: *си било што не си било, ќе ти кажам – као не ќе ти кажам, је зборуват и не је зборуват // је зборуал и не је зборуал, што да можи и не можи* (2/50). The others are antonymic pairs: *дење – ноќе, делник – празник, пиши – избриши* (*збриши*), *малу – многу, тамо – вамо, зедовме – дадовме*; *зедоа, дадоа* (*Зедоа-дадоа зборои...*, 2/72), *дење – ноќе* (4/170). Very often, reduplications appear in similar contexts, synonymic contexts: *думавме – шеставме* (with variants: *мислев – шестав*), for example: *Думавме шеставме со Поп Спиркови и преесапивме да станеме ортаци...* (10/340, 2/5), *Ќути и молчи – Ќути и молчи, да оти мерак си имал за учение* (10/320); *одил и шетал – Вака викајќи, одил и шетал од град на град...* 2/120. Sometimes repetition are accompanied by a prefix that is added to the second part of the comparative *пре-* or *над-*: *Си било едно момче не толку јунак, ама многу итро и преитро* (4/134); – *Бидуат и надбидуат, честита царице, чунки тој не сака невеста* (5/267).

The following indicators of cohesion in authors narrations by M. Cepenkov are words literally repeated and partialy connected to the connector *што*, for example:

1. ...и паднал наземи како умрен. Лежал што лежал и едно време се испраи... (3/83)
   ...and he fell on the ground as if dead. He laid down as he laid and got up after a while...

2. Кога чуло тие зборои момчето од змијата, влегло во одајата и кога видел што да види: еден камен бесценет, светел како сонце! Си го зело и многу се израдуало (3/122).
   When the boy heard those words from the snake, he entered the chamber and he saw...: a precious stone, bright as the sun! He took it and was very happy about it.

3. ...тргнала да одат кај царот да му ја земат ќерка му. Одија што одија и отишле кај тој цар што имал најубаа ќерка... (3/106); Оделе што оделе по рамен пат... (5/105)
   ...they set off to take the king's daughter. They were advanced and advanced and they went to the king who had the most beautiful daughted... They were walking and walking along a straight road...

4. ...дај Боже да ви е к'сметлија! – му рекол. Седеле што седеле и, дошло време, си легнале сите да спијат... (3/191) // Седел што седел некоја година и пак си дошол дома со колку пари што беше спечалил (10/306).
   ...may the Lord give him good fortune! – he said. They set while sitting there and when the time came, they went to bed... He stayed while

staying there for a few years and went home again with the money he had earned.

5. Од тоа прекоруање што го прекоруале, беше му омрзнало... (3/199)
He got sick of the reproaching that he was reproached...

6. Играле што играле и на свршување и боднале коњите за в град на дизѓин (Ц10/307).
They were playing while playing and when they finished they rode the horses to town.

7. Спал што спал пијан попо и во зората се разбудил... (5/195)
The drunken prist slept while sleeping and woke up in the morning...

8. Бегале што бегале и пак арамите му беа излегле на стреќа (5/60).
They were running away while running away and then again, the thieves showed up in front of hime.

Textual category of time realized by constructions as are *седеле што седеле*, does not point to chronological relations of a given event relative to another one, which is constituent of the expression's content, neither to the moment of expression since atemporal constructions whose only property is to point to the time of the action in quantum sense are used for the text construction. *Седеле што седеле* only means that: 'they set for a long time' or 'they stayed somewhere for a long time' by intensifying the duration of the action without pointing out the actual details about chronology of an event relative to another event or about the moment of speaking about the said event and at the end, about how long the event itself lasted. *Седеле што седеле* points out only to as large a stretch of time (duration) as the narrator is allowed to move on to the next motive, to the next plot of the story at text level.

The events discussed in folk narrative occur in chronological and spatial order, i.e. earlier facts on the time axis are previous relative to the later ones. However, their order does not determine the chronology in regards to dates, months and years, neither the location in regards to real place names and space, but rather the time of the text and of the discourse in linear sense. Thus, events, places and space are allocated in accordance with the word order in the text and the discourse. However, here, as in the real world, the course of textual events is determined by language markers – textual categories of time and space. Exactly reduplications, doublings and repetitions of expressions, lexemes and free morphemes with undetermined meaning, which are irrelevant to temporal and spatial markers, are used to perform this function in the text. Therefore, dates and place determinations of events in folk tales do not even appear since their content is universal and extratemporal as a rule; chronology itself has got a textual (delimiting) character and refers only to elements of the composition and the narrative structure, which the reader requires in order to understand the text correctly.

All linguistic means listed above together with the components repeated within the frame of one syntactical structure – *лежал што лежал, седел што седел, играл што играл, видел што видел, одија што одија* – fulfill the function of the textual category of time, fill in the dialogical and narrative gaps, thus making it complete, both from the sender's and the recipient's point of view. In addition, as metatextual expressions, they do not introduce any new information about the event. Instead, they are creating the impression of the narration's continuity and guaranteeing the formal and substantial cohesion of text as well as helping the narrative flow.

Furthermore, reduplications temporally stretch the events (which the text deals with), and thus, they become more intensive, but above all else, their duration is textually determined, even though there are no temporal indicators. Textual categories thus chronologically realized do not determine events in relation to their real duration.

In the folk tales by M. Cepenkov, all mentioned textual categories – temporal and spatial – have a delimitating character – they determine places and order of narrative parts of the text, rather than chronology and localization of events in real time and real space, which are conditioned by the author's knowledge. These categories, in folk tales more than in other genres of expression, fulfill the function of text building and represent its typological mark and construction skeleton. Upon them rest events know to the author from the past or events taken over from the author's knowledge, which are not always coherent with the narrator's knowledge. In this regard, the mentioned reduplications and lexical repetitions are exactly determined by temporal and compositional order of language elements' appearance in a linear course of the text in folk tales.

II. *На тие зборои...* (*On those words...*) – Place and Function of Prepositions in Folk Tales by Marko K. Cepenkov

The preposition together with language elements accompanying it – the verb that substantively specifies the noun, which, in turn, dominates the preposition, in accordance with classical theory of word group, can, usually acting before the noun (only in some languages after it) fulfill grammatical or actual (spatial, etc.) function.

- In current researches of preposition's behavior in language, attention is paid to their semantic function, with acceptance or negation of Jerzy Kuryłowicz's[224] well-known thesis that the preposition is the main sub-morpheme of case.

Different semantic criteria primarily related to object localization or localization of events in place and time, are used for classification and determination of prepositions' actual (semantic) functions. In addition, different prepositions can express causative, purposeful meanings or can be just indicators of temporal and spatial relations.

By accepting, primarily, the semantic criteria, more or less correct or sometimes only approximate classifications of all possible semantic relations and meanings of prepositions (prepositional expression) are determined.

In addition, preposition functions are often considered exclusively in the range of their closest contextual connections, but never in broader sense than their function of connecting the verb with the preposition and the noun or just the preposition with the noun. Such manner of analysis is sometimes prone to formulating insufficiently motivated theses on the semantic independence of prepositions. Thereto, all possible semantic fillings used in poetic language are excluded.

---

224 J. Kuryłowicz, *O rozwoju kategorii gramatycznych*, Kraków 1968.

In elaborating the problem concerning prepositions, several criteria which serve to determine the said meanings of prepositions dominate. The type of prepositional construction meaning is decided by:

- Nominal context (type of connection with the noun);
- Verbal context (type of connection of the preposition with the verb);
- Both contexts together;
- Standpoint according to which, prepositions have semantic independence.

Most importantly, the preposition is placed in a sentence and together with independent (meaningful) expressions takes part in its construction. Accordingly, prepositions, similarly to case suffixes, take part in determination and establishment of the relations between expressions, parts of the sentence. However, majority of prepositions do not determine spatial and other relations existing in the real world totally unambiguously since a given relation can be built from several deferent prepositions or their combination. Also, majority of prepositions have multiple meanings, and the actual determination of prepositional construction meaning is based on nominal verbal or exterior context. However, the mentioned phenomena always show exclusively on sentence level, rather than in multiple sentence structures i.e. in the text.

Thus far, there hasn't been an opportunity to analyze prepositional constructions as if appearing at a wider (textual) level than their sentence and fulfilling a certain determined and non-spatial (semantic) functions in a wider multiple sentence text. Furthermore, to be analyzed as having been guaranteed, from functional (structural) and semantic perspective, a place beyond the sentence and taking part in text construction by any means and fulfilling some functions that could be decisive for its cohesion. So far, more attention was paid to morphological and semantic determinants of prepositional expressions' appearance in the sentence than it was paid to their role in multiple sentence structures (for example, in macrostructures by T. van Dijk[225]); or generally in text linguistics, this problem has never been considered from a wider perspective. Therefore, the preposition was integrally placed incide the sentence (within the expression) as an intratextual element, and its possible intertextual functions were less emphasizes and analyzed.

Folklore can be a suitable ground for observation of intratextual (inside the text) functions of prepositions, i.e. prepositional expressions. The word is about such narrative texts in which recorder's integration plays an obvious role in construction of the narration and the text. In this case, examples from folk tales collected in the work of

---

[225] T.A. van Dijk, *Textwissenschaft. Eine interdisziplinäre Einführung*, Tübingen 1960, p. 41–67.

Marko K. Cepenkov will be analyzed from this standpoint. The analysis will include prepositional constructions as are:

НА + ТИЕ ЗБОРОВИ...
AFTER + THOSE WORDS... + text (narration)

With variants

1. ОД // СО // ПРИ + ТИЕ ЗБОРОВИ // МУАБЕТИ...
(FROM // BY // ON + THOSE WORDS // CHATS...)

2. НА ТОА ЗГОРА...
(OVER AND ABOVE...)

3. НА ТОА ВИКАЊЕ...
(AFTER THAT SHOUTING...)

4. ОД ТОА СЛУШАЊЕ...
(HAVING HEARD THAT...)

5. НА ТОА РАЗМИСЛУАЊЕ...
(HAVING THOUGHT ABOUT IT...)

etc.

Here are the examples of such sentence structures:[226]

1. ...ако сакаш да те прстенуам за него и да си живеиме сите како цареи. *На тие зборои* што си и зборуваа, беше се задала силна циреа војска да иди кај нив да се бие... (Сер. 3, 21)
(...if you want me to, I will engage you to him and we could all live as emperors. *After* saying *those words* to each other, a strong imperial army headed towards them to fight...)

2. ...Колку момчиња сакале да ја видат и колку пари поарциле и пак не ја виделе, да ти сакаш да ја видиш за еден родан! *На тие зборои* од алајката што му и рекла, ич не се докачило момчето, ами се изнасмеало и ништо не је рекло... (Сер. 3, 42)
(...You know how many boys wanted to see it and how much money they had spent and still did not see it, but you want to see it for a single spinning

---

[226] All examples are taken from: М.К. Цепенков, *Македонски народни приказни...* (Numbers of specific volumes and pages are given in brackets.)

wheel! *After* hearing *those words* from the servent, the boy didn't try at all, just laughed and said nothing...)

3. ...чунки неќеше да 'а даит па царски синои приказани, без да е гаѓаат нишано, ја даде на еден сиромав. *На тие зборои* симициичето му се шукнал кај царот и, откоа му се поклонило, му рекло: (Сер. 3, 44)
...because he didn't want to give her to renowned princes without them shooting the target, he gave her to a poor guy. *After* hearing *those words* the baker went to the king and after bowing down he said:

4. Еве сум јунак над јунака, ако ја ватив со прво за опашката коњска, сега ќе ја ватам за коса, вака да знаиш! *Од тие зборои* многу мака му дојде на царцка ќерка, тики кога го удрила коњот како со камшикот по газ... (Сер. 3, 57)
Here, I am a hero above all heroes, if I rightfully grabbed it by its pony tail, now I will grab it by its hair, so that you know! *Those words* made the king's daughted very sad because when the horse was hit by the whip...

5. На четириесетте дни ако дојдам, баздруго ќе ти ја донесам Дуња Ѓузели, а пак ако не дојдам на четириесетте дни, да знаиш оти сум загубен од орело. *На тие зборои* од Патенталија, му дал изим царцки син и тргнал да оди на планината, да бара крај да ја земи Дуња Ѓузели (Сер. 3, 87).
If I come back in fourty days, I will nodoubtedly bring you Dunja Gjuzeli, and if I do not come back in fourty days, you should know that I have strayed off the path with the eagle. *After* hearing *those words* from Patentalija, the king's son gave him permission and went o the mountains to find a way to marry Dunja Gjuzeli.

6. – Не бој се момче! Стани и види ме убаво, оти како ти што имаш голем мерак на мене. така и јас на тебе, чунки така ни е наречено да се земиме двата. (...) *На тоа викање* од Дуња Ѓузели, ја чул еден змев од облаци и на часо беше се сторил еден голем орел, та беше се пуштил со голема сила на Дуња Ѓузели... и летнал... (Сер. 86 / 87)
– Do not be afraid, boy! Get up and look at me well because I like you as much as you like me since we were meant to be together. (...) *After* Dunja Gjuzeli *shouted that*, a dragon from the clouds heard her and suddenly turned into a big eagle fushing down towards Dunja Gjuzeli with great force... and it flew...

7. „Бре, јас сиромав – си велел само со себе – види колку алт'ни ми течеле од устата моја! Нема веќе јас да седам овде, за друг да печали

моето богатство". *На тоа размислуање* на детето, втасал вурнаџијата од дома и ватил да го утешуа детето... (Сер. 3, 153)
("Oh dear, poor me – he said to him self – see how how many gold coins flow from my mouth! I will no longer sit here for someone else to earn my treasure." Seeing the boy *thinking about it*, the baker came from home and started comforting the boy...)

8. Го гледате она момче што ја потпрело глаата на десната рака и се мислит? – му рекол еднио тргоец на двата (...) – У тоа момче има голем ум и разум и не је прао да биди телчар и гоедар, ами тргоец голем ум и дури за цар. *На тие зборои* го викнале момчето и го прашале од каде е и али има татко и мајка (Сер. 3, 165).
(Do you see that boy supporting his head with his right hand and contemplating? – said one of the merchants to the other two (...) – That boy has a great mind and intelligence and it is not right for him to be a shepherd of calves or cows but rather a merchant with a great mind and even a king. *After those words*, they called the boy and asked him where he was from and if he had a father and a mother.)

9. Мошне арно, девојко, си сторила и јас сум на твојио збор да бегаме далеку (...) *На тие зборои* беше кандисала цареа ќерка и беше ја испратил кај мајка си... (Сер. 3, 169)
(You have done very well, girl, I also think that we should get away from here (...) *After those words*, the kings daughter agreed to go and was sent to his mother's place...)

10. Јас пак велам: ај да го остаиме овде, али ќе си умри само, али ќе го изеит нешто, да белким толку грев ќе имаме. *На тие зборои* беше кандисал мажот (Сер. 3, 198).
(I, on the other hand, say: let's leave him here, he will either die on his own or will be eaten by something, so we will just as much sinful. *After those words*, the man was agreeable.)

11. Прости ми, брате, оти јас ми те отрув и младоста ти ја поцрнив! На *тие зборои* дотрчале царо, царицата и сите родеи и царцки големци... (Сер. 3, 218)
(Forgive me, brother, for poisoning you and blackenning your youth! *After* hearing *those words* the king, the queen and all family and royalman ran up to...)

12. Море, како ништо не јет бре? Ја дај го да го видам – му рекол бакало – оти страмен ќе бидиш. *На тие тешки зборои* од бакалот,

не можеше да се истаи од страм што му дошло, ами отворил раката и му ја покажал црешата (Сер. 3, 240).
(How do you mean, it's nothing? Let me see it here – said the shopkeeper – because you will be ashamed. *After those heavy words* spoken by the shopkeeper, he could not move because he was so ashamed but rather he opened his hand and showed him the cherry.)

13. Не оди в чаршија, мажу, да се продааш, ами појди кај брата ти и тамо работи наместо аргатин... *На тие женцки зборои,* беше склонил чоекот и беше ошол кај брата си... (Сер. 3, 270)
(Don't do go the marketplace, husband, to sell youself, but rather go to your brother's and work there as a day laborer... *After* hearing *those female words,* the man hid himself and went to his brother's...)

14. Шуќур, шуќур, што нема барем луѓе за да ме видат! Сега слегувањето мое ќе бидит за чудење, чунки ќе си паднеш озгора, а не да слезам. *На тие и друзи зборои,* што си и велело само со себе момчето, рипнало од смоква долу и ако и да се малку убило, ама барем си слезе (Сер. 3, 280).
(Thank God, thank God, for at least there are no people to see me! Now, my descend will be miraculous since I will fall from above instead of coming down. *After those and other words* that the boy said to himself, he jumped from the fig tree down and even if he hurt himself a little, at least he was down.)

15. Биди уверено, момче, оти за малку време ќе бидиш магаре и пак јас ќе те сторам чоек и ќе те благодарам со многу пари. *На тие зборои* неќело да стои магарето за да го тоара... (Сер. 3, 283)
(Be assured, boy, you will be a donkey briefly and I will turn you into a man again and thank you by giving you a lot of money. *After those words* the donkey did not want to stand still to be loaded...)

16. Ако ми поможит сега Господ да се вратам назад, знам јас како да је напраам на Дуња Ѓузели и честа на место да си ја донесам – си велело само со себе. *Со тие радосни и друзи зборои,* момчето беше се радуало... (Цеп 3, 283)
(If God helps me to come back now, I know what I need to do to Dunja Gjuzeli and bring my honor back to its place – he said to himself. *Those joyful and other words* made the boy happy...)

17. Му кажал и сите друзи маки што патил од Дуња Ѓузели и во адата, како се сторил магаре и како се отсторил. *На тие првите прикажуачки*

го разбрал царот оти о брат му и ја викнал сестра си, таа разбрала и се пуштиле... (Сер. 3, 285)
(He told him about all other pains he suffered form Dunja Gjuzeli on the island, too, how he was turned into a donkey and was unturned again. Hearing *those first recounts* the king understood that this was his brother and he called for their sister. She understood, too and they...)

18. Од уста в уста, на царо в уши – и царо беше разбрал оти филјан анџија од филијан село давал на патниците да јадат и да пијат бадијала. *Од тоа слушање* царот и веруал, и непара веруал (Сер. 3, 293).
(From mouth to mouth, in the kings ears – and the king found out that a certain pilgrim form a certain village gave passangers to eat and drink without charge. *Having heard that*, the king believed it but also didn't really believe it.)

19. Ајде ќе ти напраиме еден кат алишта, за по пат опинци шиени ќе ти купиме, кираџија ќе ти ватиме и некоја пара ќе ти даиме и за по пат, и за тамо. *На толку молење* што го молија, кандисал (Сер. 3, 311).
(We will give you some clotes; we will buy you sawn moccasins for the road; we will find a tenant and give you some money for the road and for when you get there. *Having been begged* so much, he agreed.)

20. Бог да чуа и да брани, чунки сакаш цар да си праиш и царски да живеиш, а не гледаш от ја истресов торбата од брашно... *При тие и друзи зборои* што беше му рекла жената му на аргатино, никако тој не ја слушал... (Сер. 3, 319)
(God forbid, since you want to become a king and marry a queen, but you can't see that I have shaken off the flour form the beg... *After* the woman *said those and other word* to the laborer, he did't want to hear a thing...)

21. Ако не знаиш, сине Алија, ќе научиш, гледај како прават сите, и ти така прави. *На тие зборои* од мајка му на аго Алија, кандиса и отиде на џамија... (Сер. 6, 30)
(If you don't know, my son Alija, you will learn; watch what everyone else is doing and you do the same thing. *Having* heard *those words* from squire Alija's mother, he agreed and went to the mosque...)

22. – Море старо, море – му рекла на мажа је што се праиш будала, кај је студи на невестата кога носит ново кожувче. *На тие зборои* од свекрвата беше ја пукнало пердето на невестата и беше го слекла кожувчето од себе... (Сер. 6, 39)

(– Hey you old man – she said to her husband, why do you play a fool, how can the bride be cold when she is wearing a fur. Hearing *those words* form her mother-in-law, the bride got mad and took of the fur...)

23. *Кога беше чул* тој одговор Влаот од Бугаринот, беше се сетил оти неќел да ѝ смешат бравите. *На тие муабети* беше дошле многу туѓари од Стамбол за да ѝ купуваат бравите (Сер. 6, 86).
(*When* the Vlach *heard* that answer from the Bulgarian, it occurred to him that he didn't want them to swith the locks. Hearing *those talks*, many merchants from Istanbul have come to buy locks.)

Prepositions are a characteristic mark of the structures listed here:

на (од, при, со, etc.) + тие зборои (those words)

and their appearance right after the characters have spoken. Their place in text structure is very important seen from several perspectives. As part of the narrative (i.e. author's narrative in third person) and in accordance with a wider thesis on metalinguistic function of every type of narration depending on the characters' speech, the mentioned structures can be considered as metastructures. They differ from other prepositional constructions because they primarily refer to the linguistic plane of characters' speech, and touch upon the relations existing between characters, objects or events to a lesser degree, or not at all, and they do not serve the external deixis. They start the narrative and they have a meta relation to dialogue. The mentioned constructions also function as prosthetic element in the text in order to facilitate the reader's, perhaps, from perspective of the content and the form, difficult transition from the plane of the character's speech to the narrative plane. Or if treated more widely, the transition from the plane of respective language towards the meta plane (metalanguage or metatext).

It is very difficult to say univocally, who the author of the constructions listed here is. For example:

на + тие зборови;
after + those words.

Whether it is an expression used by an authentic folk narrator (real author), or it is a person who recorded the spoken texts (collector of stories) or an implicit author – different from the real one. However, given that these constructions are primarily a proof of the narrator's or author's wider metalinguistic consciousness, they should, with greater certainty, be ascribed to the person who recorded the narrator's text, i.e. the collector. In our case, this was Marko K. Cepenkov. From this perspective, the narrative structure in folk literature can be a useful plane for observation of intratextual and intertextual functions of prepositional constructions, especially those in which there are traces left by the recorder in the text of the narrator.

It is considered that intertextuality is a mark of all texts, and especially of those in which relations towards other texts are expressed in different manners. The relation between text and intertext can be built in form of the Michael Riffaterre's[227] triangle who borrowed G. Frege's patten.

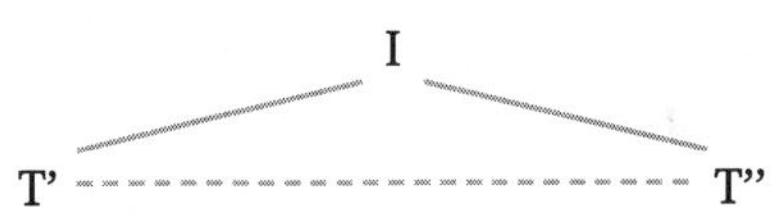

In the left corner, where Frege placed the sign, Riffaterre placed the text – "T". In the right corner, where Frege placed the meaning, Riffaterre placed the intertext – "T". Instead of sense, Riffaterre puts the interpretant – "I" – at the top of the triangle.

Intertextuality exists under the condition that the line from "T" to "T" passes through "I," and text interpretation in light of the intertext is the interpretant's function. The "T" – intertext can be read based on the "T" text, and considered to be an ideal text, for example, a median group of topics and motives. In our case, it is not only about a phenomenon that has a character of a simple allusion or is reminiscent of another text, but rather about borrowing of a certain text unit removed from its context and inserted into a new text. Relations between the narrator's text and these metastructures added by the author, would have an intertextual character. The same thing happens if there is a possibility to determine which genre a certain text can belong to.

Constructions as are *на* + *тие зборови* as in the case of Marko K. Cepenkov's texts, because of their connective, and even categorical repetitiveness, are evident indicators of the genre of the folk tale. Thus, the intertext can be a genre indicator. Undoubtedly, it could be said that this mark of Marko K. Cepenkov's folk narration is consistently present here – only the structure of those constructions can be altered.

---

227 M. Riffaterre, *Semiotyka intertekstualna: interpretant*, "Pamiętnik Literacki" 1988, LXXIX, z. 1, p. 303–304.

For example, instead of the nominal phrase: *на + тие зборои, од + тие зборои, со + тие зборови...* etc., a temporal sentence can be used: "Коа чул тие зборои младио филозоф од постарио...," "When the young philosopher heard those words from the older one...," "Кога чул Петко тој збор од жената си...," "When Petko heard those words from his wife" or, yet, another construction: "Слушајќи тие зборои...," "Heaving heard those words..."[228] Relations between these variant constructions are not made by their functions in the text and can be subject to a wider and more precise elaboration concerning the relationship between the author and narrator or characters in the stories. This pertains to more complete texts, their fragments and separate text elements. However, the intertextual element cannot be always noticed in a certain text as in Bachtin's "foreign speech,"[229] especially when this does not largely depend on the level and the manner of their structuralization. Therefore, intertextuality should be understood more widely – as it is done by J. Kristeva[230] (the author of the term). According to her, "...each text represents a complete embedding and transposition of another text." However, in order to completely elaborate the problem with intertextuality, its exponents should be semantically and formally found in the text. It can be said with greater certainty that here, prepositional constructions are one of the indicators of thus understood intertext.

Prepositional constructions as is *на + тие зборои* (after + those words) aside from their role as indicators of intertextuality (showing the other text in the text) function as expression organizers or metaorganizers of relations, between dialogue and narration with their basic metatextual function.

The third function of the analyzed construction, linked directly with the previous one, can be connected to textual anaphora and be considered within the frame of internal deixis. These constructions serve the so-called secondary system of referencing in the text.

The fourth function of prepositional constructions and their variants is related to expression pragmatics and to the discourse. This function can be said to be illocutive or, as a consequence of the first, perlocutive, since it is about what can be done by use of the previously expressed words, and the result that can be achieved only by expressing those words. This function can be found, amongst others, in the examples: 1, 6, 14, 22...

---

228 Semantically speaking, sentence formulation could even be the primary one, however, in narrative texts, its prepositional transformation was the one to make a career.

229 M. Bachtin, *Estetyka twórczości słownej...*

230 J. Kristeva, *Séméiotiké*, Paris 1969, p. 195.

Prepositions, i.e. prepositional expressions, treated intrertextually, not only exclusively as language indicators (markers), can fulfill the following functions in the text:

1) intertextual – as a signal of "foreign words,"
2) metatextual – as a genre indicator,
3) anaphoric – as a signal of text cohesion,
4) perlocutive – as indicator of words' creative strength over events and their result expressed by a construction of mimesis.

There functions are singled out based on the exmaples from folk tales gathered by Marko K. Cepenkov. However, it seems that similar constructions, as are: *на* + *зборои* or *на* + *тоа згора*, etc., can also fulfill the abovementioned functions, and thus have a universal character in any narrative text.

III. King Marko in the Folk Tales by Marko K. Cepenkov – A Cognitive Definition

The discussion on the issue of stereotypes and stereotypization in different kinds of text – primarily in folk but also in poetic and other types of texts – (in linguistic textology) has begun only recently.

The terms stereotypes, prototypes, profiling, linguistic picture of the world enter the field of linguistics as related to the development of text theory and cognitive semantics in the last 50 years. This issue is very wide and of interest to authors who represent the field of text grammar that make use of folk material and even touches upon cognitivism, primarily prototypes and idealized cognitive gestalts by G. Lakoff and M. Johnson[231] as well as the reconstruction of the linguistic picture of the world by Jerzy Bartmiński and Ryszard Tokarski.[232]

For a complete profile and a construction of the cognitive definition of Krale (King) Marko, the number of contexts (contextual meaning) in which this character appears, should be taken into consideration.

Only information contained in Cepenkov's folk stories have been used for a description of the linguistic picture of King Marko.

Reconstruction of the linguistic picture of Marko Krale in folk literature is very attractive and enticing. However, for our purposes, a limitation will be applied, to include only Cepenkov's folk stories.

According to Macedonian folklore researchers and some historians, *King Marko* (*Marko Krale, Krale Marko, Krali Marko, Marko Kraljević...*) is an authentic person for whom there is scant historical data.

He was born around 1334 // 1335 as a son of Vukashin. After Vukashin's death (1371), King Marko took ruled in Western Macedonia.

231 G. Lakoff, M. Johnson, *Metafory w naszym życiu*, transl. by T.P. Krzeszowski, Warszawa 1988.

232 J. Bartmiński, R. Tokarski, *Językowy obraz świata a spójność tekstu*, in: *Teoria tekstu*, ed. by T. Dobrzyńska, Wrocław 1986, p. 65–81.

As a vassal of Sultan Bayazid I, he died in the Battle of Rovine in 1395 while fighting for the Ottomans against Mircea the Elder. He is a historical figure who became a hero, and is described in the cycle about Marko Krale, one of the richest and most beautiful collections of folk epic stories of the Southern Slavic people. A large number of songs dedicated to him belong to Serbian folk literature, but Bulgarian folk epics also treat him as a folk hero.[233]

K. Penushliski in his book *Marko Krale – Legend and Reality* states:

> The most important good and bad sides of our men are incorporated in Marko's character. That is the reason why Marko Krale is so contradictory in our folklore and why, at the same time, he is so close and understandable even when some of his actions and deeds are normally unacceptable.[234]

Hence, it is obvious that the author builds the character of the hero according to the folk image, which has formed in the midst of a nation, according to the ambience of the common people, as can be met daily.

We can also ask if King Marko's character was really formed in the folk epics according to the models that can be seen in the everyday lives of Southern Slavic people or, maybe, he is an idealized image of a hero, constituted upon the ideal of the medieval western knight and, in the end, maybe, he is a character who is interpreted by every researcher and collector of folk tales according to their own intuition and will.

A more objective answer to this question might be provided by a profile of the legendary character and a reconstruction of the linguistic picture of King Marko based on the folk tales collected and written down by Cepenkov. Hence, in accordance with the methodological principals of cognitive semantics, that would be the linguistic stereotype of King Marko built exclusively on the basis of folk tales, and therefore with less likely, if any, claim to historical credibility.

The basic notion in research dealing with a reconstruction of the linguistic picture of the world emerging in a given text is the **point of view**.[235] The notion of point of view contains (according to M. Bakhtin[236])

---

233 W. Kopaliński, *Słownik mitów i tradycji kultury*, Warszawa 1985.

234 *Марко Крале легенда и стварност*, ed. by К. Пенушлиски, Скопје 1983, p. 14.

235 M. Kawka, *Literacki i dziennikarski punkt widzenia*, in: *Dziennikarstwo a literatura w XX i XXI wieku*, ed. by K. Wolny-Zmorzyński, W. Furman, J. Snopek, Warszawa 2011, p. 71–80.

236 M. Bachtin, *Estetyka twórczości słownej...*; idem, *Problemy poetyki Dostojewskiego*, transl. by N. Modzelewska, Warszawa 1970.

the possibility for stylistic identification of linguistic varieties and genres of expressions. According to the author, style presupposes the presence of an authoritative point of view. The point of view establishes the initial manner of categorization of reality, seen from the perspective of an ordinary person – an anthropocentric categorization in which predispositions and man's basic needs play the most important role in molding of the linguistic picture of the world. Thus, the subject of the analysis aiming at a construction of a suitable (cognitive) definition – man, animal, plant, object, etc. – is subjected to a multi-aspect observation. The composition of those aspects is not accidental and it is formed in certain configurations that create an objective (societal), permanent, internally integrated structure of the notion. In this case, we are also talking about the construction of the linguistic picture of the world based on the definition of notions and defense of scientific definitions (scientific and encyclopedic) by means of definitions supported by the common knowledge best grounded in folklore texts.

For example, according to J. Bartmiński, "when defining a star, the definition should comprise such aspects as: appearance and number, place and time of occurrence." The following should be an adequate definition (I call it "cognitive definition") in the ordinary linguistic picture: *the stars* are one of the many small lights on the sky that can be seen at night, that are grouped in constellations and of which it is said that they *shine, blink, glow, kindle, twinkle, fall*... The folk encyclopedia should also be added: ...and are believed to be man's companions from birth to death, and their groupings and attitude can tell people's futures.[237]

One well-built cognitive definition should comprise information of the matter, function, structure and action of the subject. Obviously, that depends on the type of the defined term. The following should be taken into consideration when defining people: name or names, character of their language, events in which they personally took part, and special traits. The name is very important for demonic, legendary or mythological characters[238] (here we should include all varieties of the name – Marko Krale, Krale Marko, Krali Marko, Kraljević Marko, King

---

[237] See: J. Bartmiński, *Punkt widzenia, perspektywa, językowy obraz świata*, in: *Profilowanie pojęć. Wybór prac*, Lublin 1993, p. 99–100.

[238] In this regard, see J. Bartmiński's definition of a stereotype, whose subjects the sterotype below the term (name). According to him, stereotypes are: "ustabilizowane kulturowo i językowo charakterystyki przedmiotów podporządkowanych nazwie" (culturally and linguistically stabilized characteristics of the objects subject to the name (name or notion)). J. Bartmiński, *Czym zajmuje się etnolingwistyka?*, "Akcent" 1986, 4 (26), p. 20–22.

Marko) as are the appearance, origin, transformations, places of living, time of occurrence, and action.

Here are some examples of explications for cats according to the concept of facets by A. Wierzbicka:[239]

// CATEGORY //	kind of animal
// HABITAT //	lives with people, in or near people's houses
// SIZE //	small enough for a person to pick them up with both hands
// APPEARANCE //	have soft fur, round head, pointed ears
// BEHAVIOR //	they like to be clean and lick their body
// RELATION WITH PEOPLE //	they are useful to man because they catch and kill certain kinds of pests

All those categories should find suitable linguistic indicators in a certain text and should be in relation to the described term. However, the main goal in forming of cognitive definition is building of such an explication of the term that could allow the reconstruction of a typical object, and have its properties grouped in compositions of categorical traits (facets) – for people these would be such facet categories as: /NAME/, /APPEARANCE/, /SIZE/, /BEHAVIOR/, /RELATION WITH OTHER PEOPLE/, /AXIOLOGICAL TRAITS – VALUE/, /ORIGIN/, /TIME AND PLACE OF ACTION/, /MEANS OF MOVEMENT/, etc. All those facet categories would also be important for a reconstruction of the notion and the definition of King Marko. In constructing such a definition, we usually depose large number of linguistic utterances (texts). From all those texts (utterances), in order for us to define the object or the notion, we should choose those that contain typical traits. The definition will, primarily, comprise stereotypical traits, and their stereotypes will be decided by the reoccurrence of the given trait. In addition, the stereotypical trait is most often the presupposition of the sentence. This is the type of definition we are talking about in the case of the legendary character King Marko.

In Cepenkov's texts, the character of King Marko appears in approximately fifteen folktales and these will be further analyzed for the purpose of forming a cognitive definition for the character of King Marko. They include:

---

239 A. Wierzbicka, *Lexicography and conceptual analysis*, Ann Arbor 1985. See also the explication of sentence unit *kot /мачка/* in: J. Anusiewicz, *Lingwistyka kulturowa*, Wrocław 1994, p. 117–139.

1. Предание за Марко Кралевиќ и Секула Детенце кога си делеле царството (590);
   Folktale on Marko Kralević and Sekula Child When They Were Dividing the Empire (590);
2. Крале Маркови камења (591);
   King Marko's Stones (591);
3. Дупен камен (592);
   Drilled Stone (592);
4. Марков камен во с. Љуботен (593);
   Marko's Stone in the village Ljuboten (593);
5. Трите камења од Марка Кралета (594);
   King Marko's Three Stones (594);
6. Станков камен во с. Бугарска Влаца и спомен за Марка Кралета (595);
   Stanko's Stone in the village Bulgarian Vlaca and King Marko's Monument (595);
7. Црквата Свети Спас и Марко Крале во Софија (596);
   The Church St. Spas and King Marko in Sofia (596);
8. Предание за Охридското и Пелистерското Езеро и Марковата стерна (597);
   Folktale on Ohrid and the Pelister Lakes and Marko's Dam (597);
9. Предание за Прилеп, Варош и околината и за бегањето на Марка Кралета од Варош (600);
   Folktale on Prilep, Varosh and their Surroundings and King Marko's Escape from Varosh (600);
10. Предание за Калето Исар над град Тетово (604);
    Folktale on Isar Kale over the City of Tetovo (604);
11. Град Кичаа и Китино Кале (605);
    City of Kichaa (Kichevo) and Kita's Kale (605);
12. Маркои Кули и Кукул (607);
    Marko's Towers and Mount Kukul (607);
13. Марковото Кале на Исарот во Штип (608);
    Marko Kale of the Isar in Shtip (608);
14. Село Никодим (Прекуричко), Тиквешко (613);
    Nikodim Village (Prekurich), Tikvesh (613);
15. Крк Кардаш (657);
    Krk Kardash (657).

The character of King Marko, appearing in all listed folktales, has specific traits and appearance, he acts, moves and is subject to the judgment of others. A very important element in the description of the character's action is the consequence of such an action that causes a permanent change in nature, and in the given case, the action itself is magical. All those element comprise the linguistic picture of the world as: "A sum of views more or less instituted in the language, situated in the meanings of the expressions, or they are implicit forms of those meanings."[240]

Only information contained in Cepenkov's folktales will be used in the description of the linguistic picture of King Marko's character. That will be the linguistic picture of the character, as handed down by Cepenkov, that does not assume a complete interpretation, and can only be completed after an analysis of all the South Slavic texts on King Marko – folklore, historical, literary and other texts. Cepenkov's most typical and most important trait in building of the stereotype of King Marko's character, is his relation with and action on, huge stones (traits that are undoubtedly mythological, only to mention the myth of Sisyphus here): lifting, transporting, throwing, cutting (with a saber), drilling, implanting in the ground, etc.:

> Зел Марко едно камчиште, та ти го фрлил од кулите за кај с. Коњари (591).
> (Marko took a big rock and threw it from the towers to the village of Konjari) (591).[241]

> Некое време дошол Марко Крале на Витош горе и отаде беше го фрлил камено воденички... (596)
> (At one time, King Marko came to Vitosha and from up there, he threw the mill stone across...) (596)

> Врлајќи Марко каменот, одошто ѓо фрлил силно (...) паднал (...) колку пол сат далеку од калето (608).
> (When Marko threw the rock across, because he threw it so forcefully (...) it fell (...) just half an hour from the Kale) (608).

---

240 J. Bartmiński, *Punkt widzenia, perspektywa, językowy obraz świata...*, p. 91. See the definition of J. Anusiewicz: „Określony sposób ujmowania języka rzeczywistości (zarówno pozajęzykowej, jak i językowej), istniejący w semantycznych, gramatycznych, syntaktycznych i pragmatycznych kategoriach danego języka naturalnego, innymi słowy – jest to określony sposób odwzorowywania świata dany w pojęciowym rozczłonkowaniu zawartym w języku ujmującym ten świat". ("The specified manner of encapsulating a language of reality (both extralinguistically as well as linguistically) existing in the semantic, gramatical, syntactic and pragmatic categories of a given natural language, in other words – it is a specific manner of transferring data in a conceptual segmentation contained in a language which is formalized in the world.") J. Anusiewicz, *Lingwistyka kulturowa*, p. 113.

241 All examples are from: М.К. Цепенков, *Македонски народни умотворби...*, Vol. 7. (Page numbers are given in brackets.)

(...) грабнал една спила (...) ја кренал на десната рака и потскочил неколку носе и ја врлил спилата (593).
(...) grabbed one crag (...) lifted it up with his right hand and jumped forward few steps and threw the crag away (593).

In texts relating to the hero's superhuman strength, the stone, rather than the man, becomes the main object of King Marko's action. This is what King Marko can do with this object:

Уште не беше ги дорекол тие зборови, изваил сабјата од ножница и мавнал на еден камеп неколкупати, та отсекол едно парче колку иљада ока и го дигнал па колено, та го кренал на една рака и го врлил на сестра си за да ја отепа.
He still hadn't finished those words when he drew out his saber from its sheath and struck a stone several times, and lifted it up on his knee, then took it in one hand, and threw it at his sister to slaughter her (608).

However, if the hero does not manage to throw the stone as far as he wanted, he can always cut it in half with a saber and name it after himself – Marko's Stone. This is how the folklore etymology of some Macedonian toponyms is created.[242]

Сакав в селото да го фрлам каменот, арно ама преесапив да не истепам селаните (...) Чекај да му појдам да го пресечам со сабјава за да се паметуа и да се вика Марков Камен (593).
(I wanted to throw the stone in the village, howbeit, I changed my mind so as not to smash the villagers (...) Let me go and cut it with this saber, for it to be remembered and to be called Marko's Stone) (593).

The stones bear the marks of Marko's hands (fingers) or of his horse:

На тие два камења имало нишан од рацете на Марка кај го фатил со рака да го фрли... (591)
(Those two stones bore the marks of Marko's hands, left there when he grabbed it with his hand and threw it away...) (591)

---

242 This is an attempt to explain the unusual forms and sizes of stones, crags and rocks that are present in a large number of legends and folktales, from all corners of the world. In India, the rock that the evil goddess Darwa threw at the mountain goddess Parvata, and the rock that Dera threw at Buddha, may be seen. See: W. Kopaliński, *Słownik mitów i tradycji kultury...*, p. 456. Folktales about stones brought down by the devil, are very frequent in Poland – *Devil's Stones*.

> Во камено воденички има нишан од прстите на раката Маркова коа го фатил и го фрлил. Тие нишани од прстите Марко ги нема од згорното лице, чунки биле здолното лице (596).
> The mill stone bears the marks of Marko's hand (fingers) left there when he grabbed it and threw it away. Those marks of Marko's fingers, were not left on the upper side but on the lower side of the stone (596).

> На тие камења има стапалки од коњо на Марка и кај што слегол од коњо Марко, и кај шшо стапил (591).
> The hoof prints of Marko's horse are on the stone, as well as the place where he got off the horse and stepped down (591).

The opinion on King Marko's heroism is connected to his relation to the stones, on which he left permanent marks (sign marks), handed down directly or by use of a presupposed meaning.

> Тоа нешто Марко го напраил, едно за да се прикажуат и, друго, да му докажи на Шарца пеливана да јет Марко појунак од Шарца...
> What Marko did was, on one hand, to spin a yarn, and on the other, to prove to his horse Sharec that Marko was more of a hero that Sharec was... (593) – presupposition – Marko is a hero.

From the other traits of King Marko, which certainly place him in the category of human beings, the following should be emphasized:

1. A presupposition that he is a king – *...among all king was also Marko of Prilep* (593) – a presupposition – Marko is a king.
2. A presupposition that he is a hero – *Sekula is more of a hero than Marko* (590) – a presupposition – Marko is a hero.

He has two sisters – Kita and Angelina. He does bad things – less often amusements (oppression, slaughter, wishes evil to someone, curses, envy, lying, seeks a way to kill someone) – *Stories of those ruined towers today are handed down by old folks since they were made with horrible oppression (...) by King Marko* (607); *...when Marko saw that the old woman and the little children turned to stone, he felt no remorse and did not release the women, but still made them become stones* (607); *...(King Marko) sought a way to kill him* (590); *Marko envied his bravery* (590); *Marko wished for Sekula's doom* (590).

3. He is hiding in a cave – *...he hid in one cave* (600); but everywhere there are marks he had made – *...King Marko's marks are everywhere, so there are also some of them in the city of Sofia* (596).

4. He builds churches, monasteries (but he does not enter there) – *...and King Marko had built most of the churches and monasteries (...) but he didn't enter any of them on Sundays or holidays* (600).

In defining King Marko's character based on the traits contained in Cepenkov's folk tales, one can say that his basic, typical and hence constitutive trait, which, usually, also reflects on the human opinion regarding his character, is his unlimited, magical, mythical power over objects – stones, crags, rocks.

A cognitive definition for King Marko would be ***King Marko*** – *a person with partially superhuman traits – a king from Prilep; he has two sisters – Kita (he wants to kill her with a huge stone) and Angelina // he has a nephew Sekula // he is very strong – he can cut, throw, drill huge stones, steps, rocks and crags // he rides a horse – Sharec or a mule // he hides in a cave // builds churches, monasteries and towers, but he does not enter there on Sundays and holidays; does bad things – oppresses, lies, curses others; he has fun and games less often.*

King Marko is the character who, although mythically built, is highly anthropomorphized, has superhuman strength, but is also created as a legendary family hero. His most important prototypical trait is his unlimited, mythical power, that helps him rule over huge objects – stones, rocks, cliffs and crags, which he throws, twists, breaks and cuts.

IV. Linguistic Stereotypes in Polish and Macedonian Folk Texts by Oskar Kolberg and Marko K. Cepenkov

The emergence of stereotypes and stereotypization in different types of texts (primarily in folklore, but also in poetic and other types of texts) has been discussed in linguistics in our times.[243]

The terms STEREOTYPE, PROTOTYPE, PROFILING entered linguistics when related to the development of grammar, text and cognitive semantics[244] – over the course of the last 20–30 years.

The problem is very wide and of interest to authors who represent the theory of text using folklore material and achievements of cognitivism, primarily the concept of prototype by Eleonora Rosh[245] and the reconstruction of the linguistic world view.[246]

The functioning of stereotypes and stereotypisation in natural languages is not new since it is very frequently discussed in everyday communication. Thus, most often we speak about stereotypes of peoples, nations, ethnical groups, citizens of certain regions, cities and the like. For example, Warszawianin (Varsovian) – is a man who doesn't work much,

243 The term stereotype is introduced by the American publicist Walter Lippmann in his book Public Opinion (New York 1922). After that the term appeared in literary science (Z. Mitosek, *Literatura a stereotyp*, Wrocław 1974), philosophy (H. Putnam, *Mind, Language and Reality*, "Philosophical Papers" 1975, 2, Cambridge 1975; A. Schaff, *Stereotypy a działanie ludzkie*, Warszawa 1981) and linguistics (J. Bartmiński, *Stereotyp jako przedmiot lingwistyki*, in: *Z problemów frazeologii słowiańskiej*, ed. by M. Basaj, D. Rytel, Vol. 3, Wrocław 1985).

244 See: G. Lakoff, M. Johnson, *Metafory w naszym życiu*; H. Kardela, *Gramatyka kognitywna jako globalna teoria języka*, in: *Język a kultura*, Vol. 8, *Podstawy metodologiczne semantyki współczesnej*, ed. by I. Nowakowska-Kempna, Wrocław 1992, p. 9–22.

245 E. Rosch, *Principles of Categorization*, in: *Cognition and Categorization*, ed. by E. Rosch, B.B. Lloyd, New Jersey 1978, p. 27–48.

246 J. Bartmiński, *Językowe podstawy obrazu świata*, Lublin 2006.

but who will always manage, be a braggart and a capable man..., Krakowianin (– from Cracov) – is a brave, merry, stingy, conservative and prideful man. In the stereotype of a Polish man there are three basic features: patriotism, bravery and hospitality. A French man is elegant and delicate for the Polish people. A Polish man is pathetic for the Czechs, and a nationalist for the German people. The German is a foreigner with whom the Polish cannot communicate – a mute man (pol. Niemiec).[247]

In general, given the language of human behaviuor, as a means of communication, stereotypes are negatively valuated as dangerous for normal understanding between people. However, it is clear for linguists that stereotypes are consistant elements of the language related to its essence. Therefore, stereotypisation does not only concern people and nations but also includes societal situations, human behavior, elements of the closest human surroundings, objects of nature, animals and plants, and elements of space, related to the categorisation of reality (scientific and common). The effect of the first is produced by the notions, and stereotypes are a result of the second. Another important mark of this distinction is the fact that notions are dominated by an intellectual element, and stereotypes are dominated by an emotional element. The notions are open to change, but stereotypes are very hard to change. It could even be said the there is some natural tendency within a language to create stereotypes for those people, animals, and plants derived from the fact that everything affected by stereotypes stops being dangerous and becomes positive. People stereotype themselves in every possible way, verbal and nonverbal, and yet, the stereotype is very strongly connected to language. It is even considered that the meaning and the stereotype are one and the same, as does Anna Wierzbicka,[248] and according to Roland Barthes,[249] in every sign sleeps this monster – the stereotype.

Linguistic indicators (semantic and structural) are the most important grounds for the identification of stereotypes. In language, marks that are typical, repetitive, durable and most common in certain stylistic language units, are most amenable to stereotypization. Linguistic tools used for the identification of stereotypes may include the following:

1. The manner of naming a person, object, animal, plant. For example, in the Polish language, the word Niemiec (German) means one who is mute (as is the case in folk ethymology).

---

247 See: J. Bartmiński, *Jak zmienia się stereotyp Niemca w Polsce?*, "Przegląd Humanistyczny" 1995, XXXVIII, 5 (326), p. 81–101.

248 A. Wierzbicka, *Lericography and conceptual Analysis,* Ann Arbor 1985.

249 R. Barthes, *Mit i znak,* transl. by W. Błońska, Warszawa 1970.

2. The metaphoric meaning of words. The Polish word *Cygan* (Roma) is used to mean a man of Roma nationality and a liar. *Małpa* (monkey) is an animal and a man who does monkey business, who gloats over others.
3. The qualitative meaning of derivative words. Madness – going mad.
4. Phraseologisms. *Mało* (*малку*) – *tyle, co kot napłakał* – *Колку за нокте.* (As much as a finger nail.)
5. Proverbs. *Kot zawsze spada na cztery łapy. Мачката секогаш паѓа на нозе.* (A cat always lands on its feet.)

The structure of the semantics in the titles of folk stories. In Polish texts, this phenomenon is less obvious – titles of one or two words prevail, however, in the titles of Cepenkov's stories they are almost mature stereotypes (thereto, we approache them with some reserve in regards to whether the titles are written by Cepenkov or are from a later date), for example:

A LAZY WOMAN (383)[250]
THE WOMAN WHO WANTED TO MAKE BREAD WITHOUT FLOUR AND WITHOUT BUTTER (384)
A LAZY WOMAN WITH A BROOM (390)
THE WOMAN WHO MARRIED TWO MEN, ONE A COLLECTOR, AND THE OTHER AN EATER (392)
PROTECT ME GOD FROM THE FEMALE MESS (395)
THE HONEST WOMAN WITH A WATERMELON (398)
CUNNING – A FOOLISH WOMAN WHO WAS THE LAZIEST OF THEM ALL (402)
FEMALE CUNNING (409)
A WIFE OF TWO LYING THIEVES (422)

The stereotype includes a speaker's misplaced world view. For example, in the Polish language, MOTHER is defined as the person who gives birth, a parent with the following traits: she loves, she cares, she is good and understanding. A **mother's** main functions are:
The preparation of food, bringing supplies and washing clothes. The following objects are associative with a mother: plate, roll, towel, market bag, washing machine, detergent and diapers. However, other stereotypes of a mother function in Polish language texts, and the basic content of the notion is proliferated in a different manner. For example, in Polish folk

[250] All examples according to М.К. Цепенков, *Македонски народни приказни во десет книги*, Скопје 1972, т. 2 (the number of the story is in brackets).

songs, the basic content of the notion **mother**, is proliferated as a sum of biological, societal and religious traits. The image of the mother as a parent, a housekeeper and a deceased mother prevails. In accordance with the model of a mother – a parent, we can single out a caring mother who swings a cradle, and feeds and clothes her children. Her place of action is the home, and the objects she uses are the cradle and the shirt. She is characterized by love and fear. Further on, in folk texts, we come across a mother – tutor, a mother – manager and a mother – advisor.

It is completely obvious that in Macedonian folk texts (stories, legends, etc.) a certain world view is expressed. The analysis of the linguistic world view, which means an analysis of grammatical and semantic categories related to elements from the reality and concrete characteristics of objects, as well as to the primary human behaviour, may allow the formulation of a complete world view in both national folklores, the Polish and the Macedonian.

The object of comparison in the respective language stereotypes would be, above all, folk text gathered by O. Kolberg[251] in the second half of the 19th century, and the text gathered by M. Cepenkov at aproximatelly at the same time. As is well known, Marko K. Cepenkov gathered his materials in the period between 1899–1900, and Oskar Kolberg completed his collection in 1890, after 25 years of active work.

After analyzing a group of texts by Cepenkov (magical stories) and by Kolberg (folk stories) it becomes apparent that in this group, the most often represented stereotypes match the sterotypes representing the elements of the linguistic world view are:

1. Images from cosmic elements, the sun, moon, earth, fire, water (healing), air, and stars.
2. Images of animals, *birds, plants, a horse, ox, pig, dog, cat, cow, wolf, lion, eagle, crow, raven, heron, hawk, oak, birch, weeping willow, poplar, or aspen.*
3. Images of nations: in Cepenkov's texts, there are stereotypes of the cunning Bulgarian, the witless Greek, the lying Egyption, and the savant Macedonian.
4. Images of people: *impious man, poor man, pious man, hermit, simple man and, rich man.*
5. Images of the inhabitants of some regions and municipalities, the *Turkish tsar.*
6. Images of occupations: *a peasant, priest, shepherd* (*lazy*), *a matchmaker, a monk, a fisherman, healer, robber, and stonemason.*

---

251 All examples according to O. Kolberg, *Dzieła wszystkie*, Wrocław–Poznań 1966.

7. Images of family members: *a mother, father, brother, sister, grandfather, grandmother, wife (lazy, honest), husband, child, daughter (lazy), a young bride, priest's wife.*
8. Images of mythological, ideological and religious phenomena: *devil, vampire, fairies, Tsars, kings' daughters and sons, a king's daughter-in-law, a grieved king, winged horses, also (hell, an abyss, eternity), Satan, heaven, God, magician, angels, saints, Christ, the Apostles, Moses, Adam and Eve.*
9. Images of the left and the right side: the child who dreamt of the sun on his right shoulder and the moon on his left.

These are only part of the stereotypes found in the folk texts of Kolberg and Cepenkov, which should be still subjected to further intensive research. This material provides many opportunities for a detailed study, primarily of two national folklores (in this case, the Macedonian and the Polish folklores), but it also allows for the inclusion of other Slavic folklores.

Annex

Stereotypes for *diabeł* – the devil (lat. *Diabolus* – ethymological it means gossiper).

The devils in Oskar Kolberg	**The devils in Marko K. Cepenkov**
diabeł, czart	ѓавол, едноноѓиот (devil, the evil one)
wszechmocny, zły	од жал си крши нога (he breaks his leg out of grief)
ma racice	преправен е како човек (masked as a man)
robi coś za kogoś	е во човекот (as a man)
stoi na straży wieży Babilońskiej	изгледа како луѓе црни, со очите побелени, забите оклештени, роѓои за стаори (they look like black people with whitened eyes, grinning smile, rusty teeth as if rats)
lata	може да пукне, може да се сториневиден (he may pop off, may disapear)
jeździ w karecie sześcioma karymi końmi	принесува лоши мисли на човек за да го согреши во нешто (conveys bad thoughts to a man so as to make him do something wrong)

V. On the Development and Needs Of Textology, That Is, On Scientific Editing in Macedonia Related to The Phototypic Edition of the Anthology of the Miladinov Brothers

In Polish linguistics, the word textology has two meanings. The first refers to text theory and includes all the mechanisms related to the creation of multi-clause expressions and analysis of a text's structure and its diverse description, including its variations and intertextual relations and stylistic derivations. This implies linguistic textology.

The second meaning of textology refers to the complete action of the text and with the text in the field of text pragmatics, which leads to the publication of an authentic, correct text that is in accordance with the intention, that is, the will of the author. In scientific editing (for example the art of scientific editing, Fr. *science d'édition*, Germ. *wissenschaftliches edieren*), it is the most important editing criterion, but it primarily concerns the editing of literary works. And this is textology without an attribute, and the word itself is used in its original meaning as literature or literary textology, at the same time denoting a scientific editing.

On this occasion we will discuss only the second meaning of the term textology. A scientific editing or literary textology has at its disposal its own typical terminology and rules primarily related to text processing prepared for printing. It is mainly about critical text analysis and critical apparatus that must contain all the textual variations of the preceding literary work as well as the explanations, conjectures and emendations (all corrections and recensions) that need to be placed in the thus constructed critical edition and to be in accordance with the author's will. All this should be provided by one procedure of comparison and introduction of necessary alterations and thus, to achieve the determination of the grounds for editing.

The scientific editor or textologist primarily needs to deal with the author's original text, the authorized text, the text published at the time when the author was still alive, the first edition (editio princeps) or, at the end of the day, with the phototypic edition if the original text does not exist. Therefore, it is very important for all literary and linguistic operations that the text undergoes to be performed on the original texts, for example manuscripts, primarily those in accordance with or closest to the author's intention (edition authentica or edition verietur).

Only editions of Macedonian playwrights from the period between the two World Wars, especially Risto Krle, Anton Panov, Vasil Iljoski – the founders of Macedonian theatrical literature – will be mentioned here. Their original texts (in textological sense) are not available, partially because they are private property. Even in the later editorial adaptations (rather *modifications*, which, however, are scientifically impermissible although are considered to be more available and understandable for the readers) they become available for studies of various characters including scientific descriptions, university didactics, etc.

In this context, the phototypic editions are not as important for the Macedonian textology as are the sporadic editions by Pejchinovich, Prlichev, Racin or the complete works of Miladinov brothers which have a documentary value, but there is also a necessity for critical editions equipped with an integral critical apparatus. Not ignoring the value of the Miladinov brothers' phototypic edition, folklore textology should also be pointed out and critical editions of Cepenkov's and Shapkarev's works should be expected to undergo a procedure by the same apparatus, whereupon, text editions with full critical apparatus are suggested so that they could be compared to the previous editions word by word – a text collation (lat. *collation*; eng. collation of the text) should be performed.

It is necessary, for the complete scientific editorial approach to be realized, the Anthology by the Miladinov brothers to be compared to its previous editions. These include the editions by H. Polenakovik', T. Dimitrovski and D. Mitrev, and the phototypic edition by M. Kitevski. Differences can be noticed at first glance, and these are not only in the graphics. Not going any further and leaving this topic for another occasion, I would like to emphasis here that before Macedonian philology stands an imperative need for taking into consideration the Anthology's previous editions, theatrical literature, poetry and prose written before the language codification, and for introduction of precise editorial standards which will unify the approach towards these texts, thereby respecting the primary will of the authors as well as the prevalent language and culturological context.

Conclusion

Today, the Macedonian language is developing spontaneously. It is changing in accordance with the habits of interpersonal communication, and the number of authors and poets who write original works is increasing. However, it should be emphasized that this hastened development, is under constant linguistic and ethnic pressure, imposed by the Albanians. After the proclamation of independence in September 1991, the majority of the population was Macedonian, and spoke the Macedonian language, however, they represented just over 64% of the population in the Republic. Moreover, the Macedonian language is the main (official) language in the country, liberating itself, at least legally, from former Serbian domination, and today, it strives not to be subjected by anything.

Bibliography

Anusiewicz J., *Lingwistyka kulturowa*, Wrocław 1994.

Austin J., *How to Do Things with Words*, London 1971.

Bachtin M., *Estetyka twórczości słownej*, transl. by D. Ulicka, Warszawa 1986.

Bachtin M., *Problemy poetyki Dostojewskiego*, transl. by N. Modzelewska, Warszawa 1970.

Barthes R., *Mit i znak*, transl. by W. Błońska, Warszawa 1970.

Bartmiński J., *Folklor – język – poetyka*, Wrocław 1990.

Bartmiński J., *Jak zmienia się stereotyp Niemca w Polsce*, "Przegląd Humanistyczny" 1995, XXXVIII, 5 (326), p. 81–101.

Bartmiński J., *Językowe podstawy obrazu świata*, Lublin 2006.

Bartmiński J., *Punkt widzenia, perspektywa, językowy obraz świata*, in: *Profilowanie pojęć. Wybór prac*, Lublin 1993.

Bartmiński J., *Stereotyp jako przedmiot lingwistyki*, in: *Z problemów frazeologii słowiańskiej*, ed. by M. Basaj, D. Rytel, Vol. 3, Wrocław 1985.

Bartmiński J., Niebrzegowska S., *Profile a podmiotowa interpretacja świata*, in: *Profilowanie w języku i w tekście*, ed. by J. Bartmiński, R. Tokarski, Lublin 1998.

Bartmiński J., Niebrzegowska-Bartmińska S., *Tekstologia*, Warszawa 2014.

Bartmiński J., Tokarski R., *Językowy obraz świata a spójność tekstu*, in: *Teoria tekstu*, ed. by T. Dobrzyńska, Wrocław 1986.

Bellert I., Saloni Z., *O opisie semantycznym haseł czasownikowych*, in: *Semantyka i słownik, Wrocław 1972.*

Bobrowski I., *Czy Joanna Mucha gwałci język*, "Język Polski" 2012, XCII.

Bogusławski A., *Preliminaries for Semantic-Syntactic Description of Basic Predicative Expressions with Special Reference to Polish Verbs, in: O predykacji, Wrocław 1974.*

Bojar B., Korytkowska M., *Problemy modelowania kategorii modalności a wykładniki leksykalne tej kategorii*, in: *Studia gramatyczne bułgarsko-polskie*, Vol. 4, *Modalność a inne kategorie językowe*, Warszawa 1991.

Brunnbauer U., *Drevna nacionalnost i vjekovna borba za državnost: historiografski mitowi u Republici Makedoniji (BJRM), in: Historijski mitowi na Balkanu, Sarajevo 2003.*

Buttler D., *Innowacje składniowe współczesnej polszczyzny*, Warszawa 1977.

Bühler K., *Teoria języka*, transl. by J. Koźbiał, Kraków 2004.

Census of population, households and apartments in Republic of Macedonia, 2002, Skopje, May 2004.

Chafe W.L., *The Meaning and Structure of Language*, Chicago, London 1971.

Chomsky N., *Aspects of the Theory of Syntax*, Cambridge 1965.

Chomsky N., *Syntactic Structures*, The Hague 1957.

Comrie B., *Causative Verb Formation and Other Verb-deriving Morphology. Language Typology and Syntactic Description, Vol. 3, ed. by T. Shopen, Cambridge 1985.*

de Beaugrande R., Dressler W.U., *Wstęp do lingwistyki tekstu*, transl. by A. Szwedek, Warszawa 1990.

Derrida J., *Pismo i telekomunikacja*, "Teksty" 1975, 3.

Draganov P., *Novie glasnie zvuki v sovremenih makedonsko-slavjanskih i bulgarskih govorah*, "Ruskii filologiceskii vestnik," XIX, g. 10, Varsava 1888.

Dubisz S., Porayski-Pomsta J., Sękowska E., *Leksykalny kod polityczny we współczesnej komunikacji językowej*, in: *Polska polityka komunikacyjnojęzykowa wobec wyzwań XXI wieku*, ed. by S. Gajda, A. Markowski, J. Porayski-Pomsta, Warszawa 2005.

Duszak A., *Tekst, dyskurs, komunikacja międzykulturowa*, Warszawa 1998.

Eco U., *Experiences in Translation*, Toronto 2001.

Encyklopedia językoznawstwa ogólnego, ed. by E. Polański, Wrocław 2003.

Fillmore Ch., *The Case, for Case*, in: *Universals in Linguistic Theory*, ed. by E. Bach, R.T. Harms, *New York 1968, p. 1–88.*

Fillmore Ch., *Verbs of Judging: an Exercise in Semantic Description*, in: *Studies in Linguistic Semantics, ed. by Ch.J. Fillmore, T.D. Langendoen, New York 1971.*

Friedman V.A., *Charakterystyka socjologiczna współczesnego języka macedońskiego*, "Socjolingwistyka" 1993, XII–XIII.

Gjurkova A., *Sociolingvistička situacija u Makedoniji od 1991. do danas*, in: *Jezik između lingvistike i politike, ed. by V. Požgaj Hadži, Beograd 2013.*

Głowiński M., *Nowomowa po polsku*, Warszawa 1991.

Gołąb Z., *Próba klasyfikacji syntaktycznej czasowników polskich (na zasadzie konotacji)*, BPTJ XXV, 1967, p. 1–43.

Gołąb Z., *The Grammar of Slavic Causatives*, in: *American Contributions to the Sixth International Congress of Slavists*, Prague 1968.

Grice H.P., *Logika i konwersacja*, transl. by J. Wajszczuk, "Przegląd Humanistyczny" 1977, 6 (also: *Logika a konwersacja*, transl. by B. Stanosz, in: *Język w świetle nauki*, ed. by B. Stanosz, Warszawa 1980).

Grochowski M., *Środek czynności w strukturze zdania. Narzędzie, substancja, materiał*, Warszawa 1975.

Grzegorczykowa R., *Pojęcie językowego obrazu świata*, in: *Językowy obraz świata*, ed. by J. Bartmiński, Lublin 1999, p. 41.

Grzegorczykowa R., *Wstęp do semantyki językoznawczej*, Warszawa 1990.

Helbig G., Schenkel W., *Worterbuch zur Valenz und Distribution deutscher Verben*, Leipzig 1969.

Jakobson R., *O językoznawczych aspektach przekładu*, in: idem, *W poszukiwaniu istoty języka*. Wybór pism, Vol. 2, ed. by R.M. Mayenowa, Warszawa 1989.

Jakobson R., *Szyftery, kategorie czasownikowe i czasownik rosyjski*, in: *W poszukiwaniu istoty języka. Wybór pism*, Vol. 2, ed. by M.R. Mayenowa, Warszawa 1989.

Kardela H., *Gramatyka kognitywna jako globalna teoria języka*, in: *Język a kultura*, Vol. 8, *Podstawy metodologiczne semantyki współczesnej*, ed. by I .Nowakowska-Kempna, Wrocław 1992.

Katz J.J., *Semantic Theory*, New York 1972.

Kawka M., *Czasowniki typu „pozrabiać, naponapisywać" w polskich gwarach*, "Zeszyty Naukowe UJ. Prace Językoznawcze" 1974, 14.

Kawka M., *Dyskurs szkolny. Zagadnienia języka*, Kraków 1999.

Kawka M., *Intensiva prefiksalne (na materiale gwarowym)*, "Poradnik Językowy" 1973, 3.

Kawka M., *Literacki i dziennikarski punkt widzenia*, in: *Dziennikarstwo a literatura w XX i XXI wieku*, ed. by K. Wolny-Zmorzyński, W. Furman, J. Snopek, Warszawa 2011.

Kawka M., *Macedończycy*, in: *Jak zwracają się do siebie Europejczycy?*, ed. by M. Marcjanik, Warszawa 2013; http: // wydawnictwo.wdinp.uw.edu.pl // zasoby // pliki // abstrakty // jak%20sie%20zwracaja.pdf (accessed on: 15 May 2015).

Kawka M., *Metatekst w tekście narracyjnym na przykładzie wybranych utworów literatury dla dzieci*, Kraków 1990.

Kawka M., *O kodyfikacji normy współczesnego języka macedońskiego*, in: *Język w przestrzeni społecznej. Profesorowi Władysławowi Lubasiowi na siedemdziesiąte urodziny*, ed. by S. Gajda, K. Rymut, U. Żydek-Bednarczuk, Opole 2002.

Kawka M., *O pomnikach i statuach w macedońskim dyskursie parlamentarnym*, in: *Macedoński dyskurs niepodległościowy*, ed. by I. Stawowy-Kawka, Kraków 2011.

Kawka M., *Sześć dyskursów o języku*, Skopje 2012.

Kawka M., *Współczesny dyskurs polityczny na temat pomników (na przykładzie Macedonii)*, in: *Międzycywilizacyjny dialog w świecie słowiańskim w XX i XXI wieku. Historia – religia – kultura – polityka*, ed. by I. Stawowy-Kawka, Kraków 2012.

Kawka M., Płaneta P., *Dyskursy o Macedonii*, Kraków 2013.

Klemensiewicz Z., Urbańczyk S., Lehr-Spławiński T., *Gramatyka historyczna języka polskiego*, Warszawa 1964.

Kolberg O., *Dzieła wszystkie*, Wrocław 1966.

Kopaliński W., *Słownik mitów i tradycji kultury*, Warszawa 1985.

Kristeva J., *Séméiotiké*, Paris 1969.

Kucała M., *Rozwój iteratiwów dokonanych w języku polskim*, Wrocław 1966.

Kurkowska H., *Polityka językowa a zróżnicowanie społeczne współczesnej polszczyzny*, "Socjolingwistyka" 1977, 1.

Kuryłowicz J., *O rozwoju kategorii gramatycznych*, Kraków 1968.

Kuryłowicz J., *The Inflectional Categories of Indo-European*, Heidelberg 1964.

Labocha J., *Tekst, wypowiedź, dyskurs w procesie komunikacji językowej*, Kraków 2008.

Lakoff G., *Irregularity in Syntax*, New York 1970.

Lakoff G., Johnson M., *Metafory w naszym życiu*, transl. by T.P. Krzeszowski, Warszawa 1988.

Landwehr J., *Poststrukturalistyczne wyzwanie. Próba dekonstrukcji*, transl. by M. Łukasiewicz, "Teksty Drugie" 1990, 2.

Langacker P., *Wykłady z gramatyki kognitywnej*, ed. by H. Kardela, Lublin 1995.

Laskowska E., *Dyskurs parlamentarny w ujęciu komunikacyjnym*, Bygdoszcz 2004.
Lawn R., *Tu and Twitter: Is it the end for 'vous' in French?*, "BBC News Magazine" 2012, 7 September.
Lewaszkiewicz T., *Prasłowiańskie dziedzictwo leksykalne w języku macedońskim (rekonesans badawczy), in: XL Научна конференција на Мегународниот семинар за македонски јазик, литература и култура (Охрид, 29–30 јуни 2013 година), Скопје.*
Lippmann W., *Public Opinion*, New York 1922.
Lord A.B., *The Singer of Tales*, Cambridge 1960.
Lory B., *Approches de l'identité macédonienne*, in: *La République de Macédoine: Nouvelle venue dans le concert européen*, C. Chiclet // B. Lory (Auteur), Paris 1998.
Lubaś W., *Polska polityka językowa*, Opole 2009.
Lubaś W., *Polskie gadanie. Podstawowe cechy i funkcje potocznej odmiany polszczyzny*, Opole 2003.
Lunt H.G., *Old Church Slavonic Grammar*, 7th ed., Berlin–New York 2001 (1st ed. Mouton 1955).
Lyons J., *Semantyka*, transl. by A. Weinsberg, Vol. 1, Warszawa 1984, Vol. 2, Warszawa 1998.
Małecki M., *Dwie gwary macedońskie (Suche i Wysoka w soluńskiem)*, Kraków 1934.
Mańczak W., *Język staro-cerkiewno-słowiański – kompromis między dialektem macedońsko-bułgarskim a morawsko-panońskim, in: Językoznawstwo. Prace na XIV Międzynarodowy Kongres Slawistów w Ochrydzie 2008, Warszawa 2007.*
Marcjanik M., *Grzeczność w komunikacji językowej*, Warszawa 2007.
Mareš F.V., *Makedonská gramatika*, Skopje 1994.
Markowski A., *Kultura języka polskiego. Teoria. Zagadnienia leksykalne*, Warszawa 2005.
Martin Rojo L., van Dijk T.A., *There Was a Problem, and It Was Solved: Legitimating the Expulsion of Illegal Migrants in Spanish Parliamentary Discourse*, "Discourse & Society" 1997, 8 (4), p. 523–566.
Martin Rojo L., van Dijk T.A., *Habia un problema y se ha solucionado. La legitimacion de la explusion de inmigrantes „ilegales" en el discurso parlamentario espanol*, in: Poder decir o El poder de los discursos, ed. by L. Martin Rojo, R. Whittaker, Madrid 1998.
Mayenowa M.R., *Poetyka teoretyczna. Zagadnienia języka*, Wrocław 1974.
Mayenowa M.R., *Posłowie: inwentarz pytań z teorii tekstu*, in: *Semantyka tekstu i języka*, ed. by M.R. Mayenowa, Wrocław 1976.
Mayenowa M.R., *Spójność tekstu a postawa odbiorcy*, in: *O spójności tekstu*, ed. by M.R. Mayenowa, Wrocław 1971.
Michałowski P., *Moje, cudze, wspólne, niczyje*, in: *Ja, autor. Sytuacja podmiotu w polskiej literaturze współczesnej*, ed. by D. Śnieżka, Warszawa 1996.
Mitosek Z., *Literatura a stereotyp*, Wrocław 1974.
Moroz-Grzelak L., *Macedońska pamięć historyczna. Imaginarium pomnikowe*, in: *Bałkany Zachodnie*, ed. by P. Chmielewski, S. Szczesio, Łódź 2013.
Neshkovska C., Lazarevska-Stenchevska J., *Verbal Irony in Political Discourse*, in: Proceedings of the International Applied Linguistics Conference: Practice in Language,

Language in Practice (PLLP), 7–8 June 2013, Skopje, Republic of Macedonia; http://www.fon.edu.mk/files/ZBORNIK_lingvistika.pdf (accessed on: 15 May 2015).

Němec J., *O slovenské předponě po-slovesné*, Slavia XXIII, Praha 1954.

Nida E., *Zasady odpowiedniości*, transl. by A. Skucińska, in: *Współczesne teorie przekładu: Antologia*, ed. by P. Bukowski, M. Heydel, Kraków 2009.

Nitsch K., *Wybór pism polonistycznych*, Vol. 3, *Pisma pomorzoznawcze*, Wrocław 1954.

Ohmann R., *Literatura jako akt*, in: *Studia z teorii literatury. Archiwum "Pamiętnika Literackiego"*, Wrocław 1988.

Orwell G., Rok 1984, Warszawa 2001.

C. E. Osgood, *Semantic differential technique in the comparative study of cultures*, "American Anthtropologist" 1964, 66(3), p. 171-200, http://dx.doi.org/10.1525/aa.1964.66.3.02a00880.

Ożóg K., *Język w służbie polityki*, Rzeszów 2004.

Parry A., *The Making of Homeric Verse: The Collected Papers of Milman Parry*, ed. by A. Parry, Oxford 1971.

Pauliny E., *Štruktúra slovenského slovesa; štúdia lexikálno-syntaktická*, Bratislava 1943.

Piernikarski C., *Czasowniki z prefiksem po- w języku polskim i czeskim*, Warszawa 1975.

Platt J.T., *Grammatical Form and Grammatical Meaning. A tagmemic view of Fillmore's Deep Structure Case Concepts, ed. by S.C. Dik, J.G. Kooij, Amsterdam–London.*

Płaneta P., *Dyskurs o Macedonii na łamach polskiej prasy w latach 2000–2007*, in: *Tożsamość narodowa w społeczeństwie multietnicznym Macedonii*, ed. by M. Kawka, I. *Stawowy-Kawka, Kraków 2008.*

Polański K., *Z prac nad słownikiem syntaktyczno-generatywnym czasowników polskich*, in: Prace Językoznawcze UŚ, Vol. II, 1973.

Pulevski G., *Slavjansko-naseleniski-makedonska slognica rečovska*, Sofia 1880.

Putnam H., *Mind, Language and Reality*, "Philosophical Papers" 1975, 2.

Riffaterre M., *Semiotyka intertekstualna: interpretant*, "Pamiętnik Literacki" 1988, LXXIX, 1.

Rojzenzon L.I., *Slawjanskaja glagolnaja poliprefiksacija*, Minsk 1970.

Rosch E., *Principles of Categorization*, in: *Cognition and Categorization*, ed. by E. Rosch, B.B. Lloyd, New Jersey 1978.

Saloni Z., *Cechy składniowe czasownika polskiego*, Wrocław 1976.

Sandauer A., *Samobójstwo Mitrydatesa*, in: idem, *Eseje*, Warszawa 1968.

Schaff A., *Stereotypy a działanie ludzkie*, Warszawa 1981.

Schopenhauer A., *Die eristische Dialektik: Die Kunst, Recht zu behalten*, 1864 (Polish edition: *Erystyka, czyli sztuka prowadzenia sporów*, Warszawa 2002).

Searle J., *Speech Acts. An Essay of the Philosophy of Language*, Cambridge 1969.

Słownik języka polskiego, red. W. Doroszewski, Vol. 1–11, Warszawa 1958–1969.

Słownik syntaktyczno-generatywny czasowników polskich, ed. by K. Polański, Vol. 1–5, Wrocław 1980.

Słownik terminologii językoznawczej, ed. by Z. Gołąb, A. Heinz, K. Polański, Warszawa 1970.

Stawowy-Kawka I., *Albańczycy w Macedonii (1994–2001)*, Kraków 2014.

Stawowy-Kawka I., *Historia Macedonii*, Warszawa 2000.

Stockwell P., *Poetyka kognitywna. Wprowadzenie*, ed. by E. Tabakowska, Kraków 2006.
Tesniére L., *Elements de syntaxe structurale*, Paris 1959.
Thelin Nils B., *Towards a Theory of Aspect, Tense and Actionality in Slavic*, "Acta Universitatis Upsaliensis, Studia Slavica Upsaliensia" 1978, 18.
Tokarski P., *Kulturowe i językowe aspekty profilowania*, in: *Profilowanie w języku i w tekście*, ed. by J. Bartmiński, R. Tokarski, Lublin 1998.
Tomiczek E., *System adresatywny współczesnego języka polskiego i niemieckiego. Socjolingwistyczne studium konfrontatywne*, Wrocław 1983.
van Dijk T.A., *Badania nad dyskursem*, in: *Dyskurs jako struktura i proces. Praca zbiorowa*, ed. by T.A. van Dijk, transl. by G. Grochowski, Warszawa 2001.
van Dijk T.A., *Textwissenschaft. Eine interdisziplinäre Einführung*, Tübingen 1960.
von Humboldt W., *On Language, On the Diversity of Human Language Construction and Its Influence on the Mental Development of the Human Species, ed. by M. Losonsky, Cambridge 1999.*
Voss Ch., *Great Macedonia as a „Mental Map" in the 20th and 21st Century*, "Sprawy Narodowościowe" 2007, 31.
Wierzbicka A., *Dociekania semantyczne*, Warszawa 1969.
Wierzbicka A., *Lericography and Conceptual Analysis*, Ann Arbor 1985.
Wierzbicka A., *Semantyka. Jednostki elementarne i uniwersalne*, Lublin 2006.
Wilkoń A., *Spójność i struktura tekstu. Wstęp do lingwistyki tekstu*, Kraków 2002.
Witosz B., *Dyskurs i stylistyka*, Katowice 2009.
Wojtak M., *Głosy z teraźniejszości. O języku współczesnej polskiej prasy*, Lublin 2010.
Wołoszynow W.N., *Z historii form wypowiedzi w konstrukcjach języka*, in: *Rosyjska szkoła stylistyki*, chosen and ed. by M.R. Mayenowa, Z. Saloni, Warszawa 1970.
Zawadowski L., *Lingwistyczna teoria języka*, Warszawa 1996.
Żółkiewski S., *Teksty kultury. Studia*, Warszawa 1988.
Żydek-Bednarczuk U., *Wprowadzenie do lingwistycznej analizy tekstu*, Kraków 2005.

Бондарко А.В., *Модальность. Вступительные замечания. in: Теория функциональной грамматики: Темпоральность. Модальность*, ed. by А.В. Бондарко, vol. 2. Ленинград, 1990.
Велевска М., *Преводни еквиваленти на некои конструкции со нелични глаголски форми од француски јазик на македонски*, XXXIII Научна конференција на XXX–IX Меѓународен семинар за македонски јазик, литература и култура. Охрид 28–29 VIII 2006. Лингвистика, Скопје 2007.
Веновска-Антевска С., *Критичка анализа на дискурсот (КАД) на претседателските и локалните избори во март 2009 година во Република Македонија*, in: *Macedoński dyskurs niepodległościowy*, ed. by I. Stawowy-Kawka, Kraków 2011.
Веновска-Антевска С., *Сврзникот но во македонскиот јазик: дијахронија, синхронија, перспективи*, Скопје 2003.

Веновска-Антевска С., *Структурата и врзаноста на текстот во „Дениција" од Петре М. Андреевски*, in: Зборник во чест на Проф. д-р Лилјана Минова-Ѓуркова по повод 70 години од раѓањето, Скопје 2009.

Верковић С.И., *Народне песме македонски Бугара*, Белград 1860.

Гочкова Т., *Именското обраќање во македонскиот јазик*. Магистерска работа. Универзитет „Св. Кирил и Методиј," Филошки факултет, Скопје 1993 (необјавен труд).

Димитровски Т., *Белешки за транскрипцијата на текстовите во Зборникот на Миладиновци*, in: Д. и К. Миладиновци, *Зборник на народни песни.* Под редакција на Харалампие Поленаковиќ и Тодор Димитровски, Скопје 1983.

Дрвошанов В., *Турски лексеми од роднинската терминологија во горанскиот говор*, Македонски јазик LXI, Скопје 2010.

Дучевска А., Танушевска Л., *Тематската прогресија и лексичката реализација во еден расказ на Бруно Шулц*, Годишен зборник 32 // 1, Скопје 2006.

Интенцијално-синтаксички речник на македонските глаголи, Vol. 1–6, *Институт за македонски јазик „Крсте Мисирков"*, ed. by Б. Корубин и С. Велковска (група автори), Скопје 1992–2001.

Искушенијата на Давидовата ѕвезда, ed. by М. Томовски, Е. Клетников, Скопје 2002.

Историја на македонскиот народ, кн. 1–3, ИНИ, Скопје 1969.

Историја на македонскиот народ, кн. 1–3, ред. К. Битовски, Н. Велјановски, И. Катарџиев, Б. Панов, А. Стојановски, ИНИ, Скопје 2000.

Јакимовска-Тошиќ М., *Ораторско-прознитe книжевни состави на Св. Климент Охридски*, in: *Книжевни и културни модели во македонската средновековна литература*, http: // www.akademik.mk/oratorsko-proznite-knizhevni-sostavi-na-sv-kliment-ohridski-prof-d-r-maja-jakimovska-toshik (accessed on: 20 May 2015).

Каранфиловски М., *Ениџевардарскиот говор*, Скопје 2013.

Киселиновски С., *Македонија низ вековите*, Скопје 1998.

Китевски М., *Денеска се Свети седум маченици Макавејски, Богородични поклади*, http: // sitel.com.mk/deneska-se-sveti-sedum-machenici-makavejski-bogorodichni-pokladi (accessed on: 7 April 2015).

Конески Б., *Граматика на македонскиот литературен јазик*, Дел I и II, Скопје 1976.

Конески Б., *Македонскиот XIX век. Јазични и книжевно-историски прилози*, Скопје 1986.

Конески К., *Зборообразувањето во современиот македонски јазик*, Скопје 1995.

Корубин Б., *За дезаргументизацијата на транзитивните и аргументизацијата на интразитивните глаголи*, "Studia Gramatyczne" 1982, V.

Коцевски Д., *Критиката како заблуда. Прдизвиците на текстуалноста*, Скопје 1988.

Марко Крале легенда и стварност, приредил К. Пенушлиски, Скопје 1983.

Миладиновци Д. и К., *Зборник на народни песни*, Скопје 1983.

Минова-Ѓуркова Л., *Обраќањето во македонскиот јазик*, Предавања на XXII Меѓународен семинар за македонски јазик, литература и култура, Скопје 1990.

Минова-Ѓуркова Л., *Синтакса на македонскиот стандарден јазик*, Скопје 1994.

Мисирков К.П., *Библиографија*, Скопје 2009.

Мисирков К.П., *За македонцките работи*, II – издание. Предгор кон II-то издание Д. Џамбаз, Скопје 1946.

Мисирков К.П., *За македонцките работи*, јубилејно издание, Скопје 2003.

Мисирков К.П., *За македонцките работи*, Јубилејното издание по повод на стогодишнината од раѓањето на авторот, Скопје 1974.

Мисирков К.П., *Неколку збории за македонцкијот литературен јазик*, Скопје 1948.

Мојсова-Чепишевска В., *Современа македонска проза*, in: *Современа македонска литература*, I и II дел, Скопје 2004.

Огњанов Т., *Трпелива одбивност владее во културата*, "Dnevnik" 2009, 9 October, http: // www.dnevnik.com.mk/default.asp?ItemID=9D3E42AB6F5E0444AEB33639C-8C12AEB (accessed on: 12 September 2012).

Пандев Д., *Општа реторика (дискурсна лингвистика)*, Скопје 2013.

Пенушлиски К., *Одразот на фолклорната традиција врз македонската уметничка проза*, in: *Битовото и историското во македонската уметничка проза*, Скопје 1986.

Прличев Г., *Кратка словенска граматика*, ed. by Д. Пандев и Д. Стефанија, заедно со македонски превод и коментар, Охрид 1994.

Пулевски Ѓ., *Славјанско-населениски-македонски Слогница Речовска*, Софија 1880.

Речник на македонскиот јазик: со српскохрватски толкувања, ed. by Б. Конески, т. I–III, Скопје 1961–1966.

Ристески С., *Создавањето на современиот македонски литературен јазик*, Скопје 1988.

Ристовски Б., *Бугаринот Петар Драганов за посебноста на македонската нација, историја, јазик, и култура*, in: *Сознајби за јазикот, литературата и нацијата*, Скопје 2001.

Спасов А., *Развојниот пат на Рацина*, in: *Кочо Рацин. Стихови и проза*, Скопје 1966.

Старова Л., *Балканвавилонци*, Скопје 2014.

Стоевска-Денчова Е., *Именување на роднинските односи во македонските дијалекти од словенски и балканистички аспект*, Скопје 2009.

Стојановски А., Катарџиев И., Зографски Д., Апостолски М., *Историја на македонскиот народ*, Скопје 1988.

Тунтев А., *Република Македонија. Прва декада (1990–1999)*, Скопје 2005.

Цветковски Ж., *Уште нешто за конгруенцијата*, in: *Стандарднојазичната норма и македонскиот јазик. Јазикот и идентитет*. Зборник на трудови од Научниот собир одржан на 15 април 2010, Скопје 2011.

Цепенков М., *Македонски народни приказни во десет книги*, Скопје 1972.

Цепенков М., *Пословици, поговорки, гатанки, клетви и благослови*, Скопје 1972; *Македонско народно творештво. Пословлци и гатанки*, Скопје 1969.

Цепенков М.К., *Македонски народни умотворби*, ed. by К. Пенушлиски, Б. Ристовски, Т. Саздов, Скопје 1972, Vol. 1–10.

Чашуле И., *Модалните глаголи во македонскиот јаик*, Прилози на МАНУ, X1V // 2, Скопје 1989.

Чинго Ж., *Големата вода, Сребрените снегови, Ал*, Скопје 1992.

Шапкарев К., *Sbornik ot byłgarski narodni umotworenija*, Софија 1891–1894.

Documents

http: // feduta.livejournal.com/229520.html (accessed on: 12 October 2012).

http: // www.mkd.mk/makedonija/skopje/uchenicite-albanci-vo-srednoto-hemisko-uchilishte- baraat-profesori-albanci (accessed on: 7 February 2015).

http: // www.tvn24.pl/wiadomosci-ze-swiata,2/wiecej-ich-u-sasiadow-niz-we-wlasnym-kraju-albanczycy-problem-balkanow,488822.html (accessed on: 12 February 2015).

Interim Accord between the Hellenic Republic and the FYROM, New York (accessed on: 12 March 2015), 13 September 1995 (http: // www.hri.org/docs/fyrom/95-27866.html).

АСНОМ. Документи од Првото и Второто заседание на АСНОМ, Скопје 1984, т. I, кн. I.

Македонски историски речник, ed. by С. Киселиновски, Скопје 2000.

Македонски правопис изработен од Комисијата за јазик и правопис при Министерството на народната просвета, Skopje 1945.

Попис на населението, домаќинствата и становите во Република Македонија, 2002, Скопје, мај 2004.

Рамковен договор, http: // mls.gov.mk/images/laws/Ramkoven_dogovor.pdf (accessed on: 12 February 2015); http: // www.ucd.ie/ibis/filestore/Ohrid%20Framework%20Agreement.pdf (accessed on: 12 February 2016).

Ристески С., *Стенографски белешки од првата јазична комисија. Факсимил*, Скопје 2000.

Стенографски белешки од Педесет и третата седница на Собранието на Република Македонија, одржана на 4 мај 2009 година Седницата се одржа во Собранието на Република Македонија, сала 1, со почеток vo 11,31 ~asot. Документ 328 КВ – 05 May 2009, http: // www.sobranie.mk/ext/sessions1.aspx?Id=47F95433-B52C-465A-AA84- 43187C262B4C (accessed on: 15 February 2015).

Устав на Република Македонија, http: // www.sobranie.mk/ustav-na-rm.nspx (accessed on: 15 February 2015).

Constitution of Republic of Macedonia, http: // www.sobranie.mk/ustav-na-rm.nspx (accessed on: 15 February 2015).

Literature

Абаџиев Ѓ., *Пустина*, Скопје 1980.

Андреевски П.М., *Огнот не знае, пепелта не знае*, in: *Тоа тогаш*, ед. А. Драговиќ, Скопје 2007, p. 155-157.

Андрић И., *На Дрини ћуприја*, Нови Сад 1971, превод: (пол.) *Most na Drinie*, превод: H. Kalita, Warszawa 2007; (мак.) *Мостот на Дрина*, превод: Б. Корубин, Скопје 1977; (анг.) *The Bridge on the Drina*, превод: L.F. Edwards, Chicago 1977.

Георгиески Т., *Црно семе*, Скопје 1980.

Ѓузел Б., *Куќа цел свет*, Скопје 1974.

Дракул С., *Белата долина*, Скопје 1980.

Јаневски С., *Стебла*, Скопје 1976; *Шеќерна приказна*, Скопје 1980.

Костов В., *Нов ум*, Скопје 1980.

Малески В., *Разбој*, Скопје 1980.

Стрезовски Ј., *Свето проклето*, Скопје 1980.

Урошевиќ В., *Расказ за тоа како се пишуваат раскази*, in: *Ноќниот пајтон*, Скопје 1972.

Фотев М., *Потомците на Кат*, Скопје 1980.

Чашуле К., *Простум*, Скопје 1980.

Чинго Ж., *Големата вода*, Скопје 1980; *Wielka woda*, transl. by D. Cirlić-Straszyńska, Warszawa 1984.

Чинго Ж., *Пасквелија*, Скопје 1968.

Ширилов П., *Земја во дулбија*, Скопје 1977.

Шопов А., *Црно сонце*, in: *Одбрани дела. Поезија*, Книга втора, Скопје 1976.

Index

Technical editor
Anna Poinc-Chrabąszcz

Proofreading
Halina Hoffman

Typesetting
Marta Jaszczuk

Jagiellonian University Press
Editorial Offices: Michałowskiego 9/2, 31-126 Kraków
Phone: +48 12 663 23 81, +48 12 663 23 82, Fax: +48 12 663 23 83